D1553166

WOMEN AND RACE IN CONTEMPORARY U.S. WRITING

AMERICAN LITERATURE READINGS IN THE 21ST CENTURY

Series Editor: Linda Wagner-Martin

American Literature Readings in the 21st Century publishes works by contemporary critics that help shape critical opinion regarding literature of the nineteenth and twentieth centuries in the United States.

Published by Palgrave Macmillan

Freak Shows in Modern American Imagination: Constructing the Damaged Body from Willa Cather to Truman Capote
   By Thomas Fahy

Arab American Literary Fictions, Cultures, and Politics
   By Steven Salaita

Women and Race in Contemporary U.S. Writing: From Faulkner to Morrison
   By Kelly Lynch Reames

WOMEN AND RACE IN CONTEMPORARY U.S. WRITING

From Faulkner to Morrison

Kelly Lynch Reames

palgrave
macmillan

NORTHWEST MISSOURI STATE
UNIVERSITY LIBRARY
MARYVILLE, MO 64468

WOMEN AND RACE IN CONTEMPORARY U.S. WRITING
© Kelly Lynch Reames, 2007.

A version of chapter 2 appeared in *The Faulkner Journal*, 14:1 (Fall 1998). Copyright © 1998 by the University of Central Florida. Reprinted with the permission of *The Faulkner Journal* at The University of Central Florida.

All rights reserved. No part of this book may be used or reproduced in any manner whatsoever without written permission except in the case of brief quotations embodied in critical articles or reviews.

First published in 2007 by
PALGRAVE MACMILLAN™
175 Fifth Avenue, New York, N.Y. 10010 and
Houndmills, Basingstoke, Hampshire, England RG21 6XS
Companies and representatives throughout the world.

PALGRAVE MACMILLAN is the global academic imprint of the Palgrave Macmillan division of St. Martin's Press, LLC and of Palgrave Macmillan Ltd. Macmillan® is a registered trademark in the United States, United Kingdom and other countries. Palgrave is a registered trademark in the European Union and other countries.

ISBN-13: 978–1–4039–7238–5
ISBN-10: 1–4039–7238–9

Library of Congress Cataloging-in-Publication Data is available from the Library of Congress.

A catalogue record for this book is available from the British Library.

Design by Newgen Imaging Systems (P) Ltd., Chennai, India.

First edition: January 2007

10 9 8 7 6 5 4 3 2 1

Printed in the United States of America.

810.9
R288w

For my parents,
Sam and Patty Reames

CONTENTS

ACKNOWLEDGMENTS

Over the years, many people have read parts of this work and helped clarify my thinking. I want to thank Kate Drowne, Leslie Frost, Jennifer Haytock, Tim Spaulding, Scott Walker, Neil Watson, and Shannon Wooden for generously sharing their criticisms, questions, ideas, and encouragement; and Elizabeth Cox for her willingness to discuss her work. I also want to thank the Center for the Study of the American South and the English Department at the University of Chapel Hill for awards that allowed me to visit the Lillian Hellman Collection at the Harry Ransom Humanities Research Center, University of Texas at Austin; Pat Fox and the other librarians at the Ransom Center for their help; and Western Kentucky University for course releases that provided me with time to work on this book. Farideh Koohi-Kamali, Julia Cohen, and Elizabeth Sabo of Palgrave have been very helpful in seeing this book through the production process, and I am grateful to Maran Elancheran for his careful copyediting of the manuscript. Finally, thanks go to my parents for their ongoing support; this book is dedicated to them.

That we not hide behind the mockeries of separations that have been imposed upon us and which so often we accept as our own. . . . And all the other endless ways in which we rob ourselves of ourselves and each other.

Audre Lorde, *"The Transformation of Silence into Language and Action"*

CHAPTER 1

Introduction

When Sadie, a desperate and destitute character in Gloria Naylor's 1992 novel *Bailey's Cafe*, recognizes a wealthy white woman as the woman she worked with years earlier in a brothel, she fleetingly hopes that she has found the help she needs to keep from losing her home. She tries to force the woman to acknowledge her and their former relationship but is quickly disappointed:

> It took less than a second: the recognition, the mouth arching up in a smile, the eyes demanding applause for the lighted windows of the mansion, the Vassar-bound daughter beside her, the smooth idling of the black sedan, the husband behind the wheel. On the heels of that second, the daughter was speaking, Mother, who . . . ? Nobody, the blonde said as she shook off Sadie's hand and herded the girl toward the car.
>
> —I need work, Sadie called behind her.
>
> Without turning her head she answered, I'm sorry; my staff is full. The heavy door opened and those long legs swung in. Sadie took a step forward, her voice louder, her meaning clear:
>
> —I'll still come tomorrow. I need the work.
>
> But her last glimpse of those green eyes as the car pulled off told her there was no danger in her threat. He was a john, Sadie, the eyes said. A smart john who knew we make the best wives. (59)

In the brothel, Sadie, a black woman who has also worked as a prostitute, was the personal maid to "the blonde," who is never given a name. Sadie tended to the white woman's hair and body between customers. After the brothel shut down, both women married, and their different fates are an embittered criticism of marriage as an institution that discriminates according to race and class but commodifies women's work and bodies regardless. Sadie ends up living in poverty with an abusive husband. The blonde, in contrast, acquires all the trappings of wealth.

Naylor's storyline crystallizes many of the tensions that infuse relationships between African American women and white women in the United States. That the characters' connection stems from their former employment in a brothel suggests, as does much imaginative literature depicting such relationships, that significant interracial interactions between women occur at the margins of society. Sadie's job as the blonde's personal maid simultaneously represents a more common arrangement: the white woman employs the black woman. Furthermore, Sadie's job requires that she maintain the blonde's body. The blonde "insisted on Sadie changing her entire hairdo between each customer," and Sadie daydreamed her time away as "she'd powder over freckles on the bare cleavage and shoulders" (48, 49). These tasks replicate two important historical patterns: first, that black women are employed (or in the antebellum period, enslaved) to tend to white people's physical needs in general and white women's bodies and dress in particular and, second, that black women are assumed to be more physical and therefore fit for such work, whereas white women are assumed to be dissociated from their bodies. The contemporary setting of Naylor's novel shows that even late in the twentieth century, assumptions about African American women and white women and the patterns of their relating remained largely determined by stereotypes and patterns established in the antebellum United States.

When the blonde not only rejects Sadie's request for work but also calls her "Nobody," she fulfills the role that Minrose Gwin calls "White Woman as the Breaker of Promises" ("A Theory of Black Women's Texts and White Women's Readings" 25). As Gwin and others argue, when white women betray black women, often they do so because of their reliance upon the economic and social power of white men. In the case of Naylor's novel, the blonde's marriage mandates her dismissal of Sadie, or, rather, the white woman's indifference to the black woman's plight. Through her wealthy white husband she has gained social status, prosperity, and security, and her role now is to serve his needs and protect the public image of her family. Sadie's marriage, in contrast, did not forestall her economic downward spiral. Whiteness has allowed the blonde social mobility, despite the prostitution in her past—even, Naylor suggests, in part because of it; such mobility is denied Sadie because she is black. Not only does membership in the culturally dominant race quite simply ensure more possibilities, the social prescriptions that prohibit the blonde's acknowledging her relationship with Sadie presume the coexistence of whiteness with wealth, blackness with poverty.

Women and Race in Contemporary U.S. Writing examines how some writers in the latter half of the twentieth century confronted racial stereotypes and cultural patterns to imagine new possibilities for relationships between African American women and white women. The racial dynamics within the texts I discuss interrogate racialized and gendered notions of American identity and suggest that African American women and white women will remain unable to establish meaningful relationships until white women recognize and reject the privileges of whiteness. Furthermore, white women's development of their own identities will remain bound by the restrictive definitions of white femininity until they do so.

LITERARY CRITICISM ON WOMEN'S RELATIONSHIPS

Until recently, few critics had addressed relationships between black and white women in literature. In a 1985 article, Elizabeth Schultz surveys a number of novels that attempt nonstereotypical portrayals of interracial friendships between women and finds that white women novelists depict these relationships in much the same way that white male novelists depict equivalent relationships between men: these writers use the interracial friendship to confront racism, but once the relationship has encouraged the white character's growth, the black character disappears.[1] Schultz argues that black women novelists, in contrast, tend to address the element of sexual competition and present friendships that may survive when the women confront their racism. Often, however, the white woman's invocation of power destroys the relationship. Schultz concludes that only Toni Morrison's *Tar Baby* (1981) and Alice Walker's *Meridian* (1976) "establish the open confrontation of racial stereotypes as the necessary bases for an interracial friendship" (82). Even so, such friendships do not develop in either novel.[2]

Among the most extensive treatments of relationships between black and white women in literature is Minrose Gwin's 1985 *Black and White Women of the Old South: The Peculiar Sisterhood in American Literature*.[3] Gwin argues that "cross-racial female relationships during this time and in this place embody psychological and social bases for modern biracial, female experience and its literary reflections" (5). Examining Harriet Beecher Stowe's *Uncle Tom's Cabin* (1852); Mary H. Eastman's *Aunt Phillis's Cabin* (1852), which was written as a response to Stowe's novel; slave narratives; diaries and memoirs of white women who lived through the Civil War; William

Faulkner's *Absalom, Absalom!* (1936); Willa Cather's *Sapphira and the Slave Girl* (1940); and Margaret Walker's *Jubilee* (1966), Gwin concludes that

> White women—fictional or actual, writers or subjects—rarely perceive or acknowledge . . . the humanity of their black sisters. Most of these white women in life and literature see black women as a color, as servants, as children, as adjuncts, as sexual competition, as dark sides of their own sexual selves—as black Other. They beat black women, nurture them, sentimentalize them, despise them—but they seldom see them as individuals with selves commensurate to their own. (5)

In contrast to the "sentimental visions of female bonding" that Gwin finds in the novels by Stowe, Eastman, and Walker, women's autobiographical writings show that black and white women "often viewed one another as missing pieces of a female identity denied them by the patriarchal culture. Female narrators of the slave narratives reveal their yearning for the chaste respectability of their white sisters, while the diaries and memoirs of the white women show their intense jealousy of the stereotypical sexuality of the slave woman" (11). Gwin's work thus shows how the nineteenth century's bifurcation of female identity along racial lines affected individual women's conception of their own identity as well as their relationships with women of a different race. In subsequent chapters I argue that this tendency to identify with women across racial lines continues to characterize white women's relationships with African American women in contemporary novels and autobiographies by white authors. The white women in these more recent works, however, look to black women not for sexuality but for more abstract qualities they appear to embody, such as authority, morality, strength, and love. The physicality attributed to black women has clearly been retained even in relationships not defined by sexual jealousy.

Cather's *Sapphira and the Slave Girl* exemplifies the historical pattern of women's interracial relationships for both Gwin and Toni Morrison. Applying her findings regarding nineteenth-century women's autobiographical writings to this novel, Gwin asserts that "Sapphira . . . becomes, at once, the black woman's nightmare of the jealous cruel mistress and the mistress's view of herself as a woman of good will but trapped in a system which denies her sexuality and humanity" (14). The plot's final resolution, however, minimizes consequences and denies the long-term effects of slavery. Sherley Anne Williams's *Dessa Rose* (1986), which I discuss in chapter 6, recuperates this negative stereotype of the white mistress by isolating her from white society and making her dependent on free blacks. In *Playing in the Dark* (1992), Morrison characterizes *Sapphira and the Slave Girl* as "Cather's inquiry into . . . the reckless, unabated power of a white woman gathering identity unto herself from the wholly available and serviceable lives of Africanist others" (25). Morrison draws attention to the novel's focus on bodies, both through the mistress's need for the slave woman to care for her incapacitated body and through her appropriation of Nancy's young and able body. Sapphira, Morrison argues, "escapes the necessity of inhabiting her own body by dwelling on the young, healthy, and sexually appetizing Nancy. . . . The surrogate black bodies become her hands and feet, her fantasies of sexual ravish and intimacy with her husband, and, not inconsiderably, her sole source of love" (26). Part of Morrison's project is to call attention to how whiteness is constructed. The construction of white womanhood is readily apparent in the autobiographical texts Gwin examines, and, as Morrison shows, this construction is still evident, though typically neglected by critics, in texts such as Cather's novel. That white women and black women came to be defined in oppositional terms during the nineteenth century determined many aspects of their relationships. What has come to be called the Cult of True Womanhood demanded that white women deny their bodies, especially sexual desire.[4] Conversely, black women were defined as overtly sexual. These racial stereotypes persisted throughout the twentieth century, despite the civil rights and feminist movements.

By linking Western European medical and aesthetic discourses, Sander Gilman has traced how black women came to represent sexuality, particularly sexual deviance, over the course of the nineteenth century. The black woman and the prostitute served as the icons of sexualized women, but whereas the prostitute was seen as a deviant form of white womanhood, black women were seen as fundamentally sexual. As scientists sought to establish a biological rationale for racism based upon the "primitive" sexuality of Africans, and as they simultaneously tried to show that white prostitutes were physically different from other white women, the prostitute became discursively linked with the figure of the Hottentot Venus, which had been made emblematic of black female sexuality. Gilman cites key studies and events to account for the development of the Hottentot Venus as an icon of black women's sexuality. Eighteenth-century Europeans described the excessive sexuality of certain peoples in southern Africa, called Hottentots. In 1810 Saartjie Baartman, or Sarah Bartmann, was exhibited in London as the "Hottentot Venus"; other women were similarly displayed. Following Bartmann's death in 1815, her body was autopsied and her genitalia displayed (232).

Karla F. C. Holloway argues that Gilman's comparison of prostitutes and black women is unbalanced, and she points out that his work unfortunately replicates the "first colonizing act" (63) in its reproduction of the nineteenth-century drawings of African women: "Particularly disturbing to me is the fact that Gilman's generously illustrated scholarly text repeats the Victorian exhibit, in a manner discomfitingly parallel to its voyeuristic thesis" (63). By using the drawings that claimed to represent African women's abnormal sexual anatomy, Gilman reinscribes the racist iconography he details. Holloway acknowledges that because black women have been limited to this one sexualized position, "whoever tells this story, the victims or the voyeurs, risks this danger" (64). To demonstrate that the iconography of black women's bodies continues to overshadow the words and identities of actual black women in public discourse, Holloway discusses a number of events both literary and political, including the judiciary hearings of Phillis Wheatley, Anita Hill, and Zora Neale Hurston, and the media's treatment of Whoopi Goldberg and of Professor Lani Guinier when she was nominated by President Clinton to be the U.S. assistant attorney general for civil rights. She points out that the discourse surrounding these women's bodies supplants discussion of the relevant issues. Moreover, the stereotypes affect not only external but also internal assessments, or the ways black women see themselves: "In American culture, and in the imaginative representations of that culture in literature, our compromised environments often allow publicly constructed racial and sexual identities to supersede private consciousness" (45). Both Gilman's and Holloway's works, as well as the imaginative literature and literary criticism devoted to interracial relationships, show how pervasive racist iconography continues to be, even long after the racist and sexist ideologies that created it have come to seem absurd.

Literary analyses of women's interracial relationships focus on a subset of the larger body of literature devoted to women's relationships. Among the earliest critical approaches to women's friendship in literature is Barbara Smith's 1977 "Toward a Black Feminist Criticism," in which Smith confronts the "invisibility" and "massive silence" surrounding black women—especially lesbians—in literary criticism. She defines the task of the black feminist literary critic: "Beginning with a primary commitment to exploring how both sexual and racial politics and Black and female identity are inextricable elements in Black women's writings, she would also work from the assumption that

Black women writers constitute an identifiable literary tradition" (174). Furthermore, "the critic [should] look first for precedents and insights in interpretation within the works of other Black women . . . and not try to graft the ideas or methodology of white/ male literary thought upon the precious materials of Black women's art" (174–175). For Smith, black feminist criticism should maintain its political emphasis and make its connection to political goals explicit: "The Black feminist critic would be constantly aware of the political implications of her work and would assert the connections between it and the political situation of all Black women" (175).

Smith uses novelist and critic Bertha Harris's definition of lesbian literature to create a woman-centered criticism with which to approach novels where women's relationships are central:

> Bertha Harris suggested that if in a woman writer's work a sentence refuses to do what it is supposed to do, if there are strong images of women and if there is a refusal to be linear, the result is innately lesbian literature. As usual, I wanted to see if these ideas might be applied to the Black women writers that I know and quickly realized that many of their works were, in Harris's sense, lesbian. Not because women are "lovers," but because they are the central figures, are positively portrayed and have pivotal relationships with one another. The form and language of these works are also nothing like what white patriarchal culture expects. (175)

Following this approach, Smith determines that Toni Morrison's *Sula* works as a lesbian novel "not only because of the passionate friendship between Sula and Nel but because of Morrison's consistently critical stance toward the heterosexual institutions of male-female relationships, marriage, and the family. Consciously or not, Morrison's work poses both lesbian and feminist questions about Black women's autonomy and their impact upon each other's lives" (175). Deborah McDowell's 1980 "New Directions for Black Feminist Criticism" criticizes Smith's definition of lesbian literature as too broad and argues that it is "a reductive approach to the study of Black women's literature" (190). Although use of the term "lesbian" to include nonsexual relationships or identifications has become dated,[5] Smith's essay helped pave the way for literary critics to focus on women's relationships with each other.

Criticism that focuses on the roles of women's friendships in literature tends to coalesce around questions of sameness and difference, or identification and othering. In "(E)Merging Identities: The Dynamics of Female Friendship in Contemporary Fiction by Women" (1981), Elizabeth Abel argues that whereas film and literature tend to use pairs of women to explore different options for women's lives, thereby implying that women seek friends with traits different from their own, "[s]erious novels that focus on the actual friendships of women . . . suggest that identification replaces complementarity as the psychological mechanism that draws women together" (415). Applying to friendship Nancy Chodorow's self-in-relationship model of female development, which Chodorow bases on the mother–daughter relationship, Abel interprets novels in which the process of identifying with other women helps women develop as complete selves. She asserts that "friendship becomes a vehicle of self-definition for women, clarifying identity through relation to an other who embodies and reflects an essential aspect of the self" (416). Abel notes, however, that "because this identification process can engulf as well as shape identity, its course is smoothest when the object of identification is remembered or imagined rather than physically present. The portrayal of a friendship's actual evolution uncovers the tensions generated by the conflict between identification and autonomy" (426). Thus when Abel suggests replacing the developmental model of separation and independence with a relational model of identification for analyzing characters, she complicates rather than dismisses the notion of autonomy.

Replying to Abel's article, Judith Kegan Gardiner suggests that the social contexts of friendships need to be considered and that "we can supplement Abel's focus on the relationships between characters by looking at the ways in which each fictional relationship mirrors the author's relationship to her characters and our relationship to both" (437). She furthers Abel's recognition of relational conflicts by suggesting that rather than privileging commonality as the foundation of friendship, "we focus on commonality/complementarity as fluid processes" (436). She elaborates: "There is a constant interplay between sameness and difference between the two [characters]. Often the women are treated by others as the same but feel themselves to be different" (437). She argues that the fusion of identity that Abel and the characters in the novels she discusses present as idyllic and as necessary to the development of identity as self-in-relationship may also threaten the development of individual identity. Recognizing both aspects of the relationship, identity and separation, Gardiner proposes that "this broader focus will highlight the complexity and ambivalence of relationships between women" (442).

In *Sororophobia: Differences among Women in Literature and Culture* (1992), Helena Michie also explores the uses of the concepts of sameness and difference in women's relationships, focusing on British and American literature by women writing in the nineteenth and twentieth centuries. Working from debates in feminist and lesbian communities, Michie finds that the reliance on concepts of sameness and difference can create a double bind. Whereas difference tends to be interpreted as "other" and is thus an alienating concept, the demand for similarity as the basis of a relationship tends to deny, obscure, or even prohibit difference. Attempting a more complex understanding of female relationships, she defines sororophobia as "a matrix against and through which women work out—or fail to work out—their differences" (10). Michie contends "that all differences between women, from the competition between Victorian sisters, to debates between contemporary feminist theorists, to more overtly 'sexual' conflicts between, say, cultural feminists and lesbian sadomasochists, partake in the eroticized idiom of sexual difference between women" (108). This eroticization of difference often, as Michie attests, diverts attention from other differences among women, such as race and class.

Michie points out that the ambivalent dynamics between white and black women pervade even a term as fundamental to feminist discourse as "sister":

> The word "sister" in its political context, has, of course, its roots in the civil rights movement and in black culture. The uneasiness of the translation of the term into white culture should remind white feminists of those roots, those debts, and the historical and cultural specificity of the term. To the extent that the word does evoke the civil rights movement and blackness for white feminists, I think it very often calls up a fantasy version of black sisterhood that serves white feminism in two ways. If we think of black women as somehow more intimately bonded to each other, less different from each other than "we" are, we can simultaneously simplify the position of black women in our culture and envy them a unity and direction that compensates for that dismissal. The notion of unity among black women . . . simplifies and contains guilt over racism by projecting onto black women a personal, political, and mythic power which suggests that we need not work with them to overcome racism. (137)

In the above passage, Michie surveys many of the racial tensions in feminism, but this passage also enunciates the allure of literature by African American women writers for white feminist literary critics and the problems African American feminist literary critics identify in the resulting white women's interpretations. White women writers' projections onto black women may similarly infuse their portrayals of black women in fiction and memoirs.

Jean Wyatt uses a Lacanian psychoanalytic model for her extended examination of the role of identification in women's relationships in *Risking Difference: Identification, Race, and Community in Contemporary Fiction and Feminism* (2004). She points out that "identifications with others prove both deep and lasting, causing changes in one's behavior, motivations, and self-representation as one molds oneself to resemble the admired model" and asserts that "the desire to be the other remains a motivating force in human relations throughout life" (2). One of the strengths of Wyatt's study is that she "adapt[s] Lacan's three registers—the imaginary, the symbolic and the real—to social and political uses," thus bridging the gap that so often exists between psychoanalytic and cultural interpretations. Moreover, Wyatt shows how identification can itself impede both relationships and political awareness:

> The differences in social pressures on gender formation in white and black families go some way toward explaining the origins of white women's idealizations of black women. But more generally, I argue that it is not only the historical context of power relations in which contemporary race relations are inevitably embedded, nor the racially skewed economic and social structures in which we live, that impede communication between white and black women: processes of idealization and identification also generate misunderstanding and mistrust. Idealizing identifications tend to obstruct a perception of the other as the center of her own complex reality—as, in a word, a subject. And, as black feminists' commentaries on white women's idealizing fantasies of them make clear, they do nothing to change actual power relations or to bring about economic and social justice. Indeed, white feminists' focus on the individual power of a black woman obscures and distorts the power differential between white and black, inadvertently communicates the message that a "strong black woman" does not need any help from white women—in combating racism, for example—and so perpetuates the actual imbalance of power between white and black women. (87)

As Wyatt's work reveals, the problems of white feminists' interpretations of African American women's novels stem from the interracial discord of the feminist movement itself.

RACISM IN THE FEMINIST MOVEMENT

Racism has plagued the women's movement since the nineteenth-century conflicts between abolitionists and suffragists. Although addressed by many, the problem of racism in the twentieth-century feminist movement nevertheless failed to become a dominant concern of white academic feminists until the late 1970s and early 1980s, and for some, such awareness came even later. In the late 1970s, the demands for inclusiveness and attention to racism made by women of color reached a crescendo. Audre Lorde delivered and published many papers emphasizing that open discussions of racism in the feminist movement were crucial to white and black feminists alike. I discuss Lorde's arguments in chapter 4; I want here to list a number of those papers and their dates to indicate their initial availability. All were later published in Lorde's 1984 essay collection, *Sister Outsider*. They include "The Transformation of Silence into Language and Action," first presented at the Modern Language Association's 1977 "Lesbian and Literature" panel and then published in the feminist journal *Sinister Wisdom* in 1978 and Lorde's *The Cancer Journals* in 1980; "The Master's Tools Will Never Dismantle the Master's House," delivered at the 1979 "Second Sex" conference in New York; "Age, Race, Class, and Sex: Women Redefining Difference," given at Amherst College in 1980; and "The Uses of Anger: Women Responding to Racism," the keynote address at the 1981 National Women's Studies Association Conference. In all of these essays, and in others, Lorde powerfully addresses misunderstandings by white women and the barriers to understanding between black and white women. Barbara Smith's 1977 "Toward a Black Feminist Criticism," which I have already discussed in relation to its importance to criticism focusing on women's relationships, similarly decries white women's ignorance of racial issues: "It is galling that ostensible feminists and acknowledged lesbians have been so blinded to the implications of any womanhood that is not white womanhood and that they have yet to struggle with the deep racism in themselves that is at the source of this blindness" (169).

Some white women were also discussing racism as an important feminist issue in the late 1970s. Adrienne Rich's 1978 essay "Disloyal to Civilization: Feminism, Racism, and Gynephobia," for instance, articulates many of the reasons white women attempting to overcome racism do so in a superficial way and explores the particularities of interracial relationships in the United States, given the country's legacy of slavery. Like many of the feminists prioritizing racism as a problem in the feminist movement, Rich identified herself as a radical feminist, and her commitment to fundamental social change is reflected in her statement that she "shall be assuming that black and white feminists have in common a commitment, not to some concept of civil rights within the old framework of capitalism and misogyny, not to an extension of tokenism to include more women in existing social structures, but to a profound transformation of world society and of human relationships" (279). The degree of change Rich desires and assumes that her audience is committed to indicates the extent to which she and these other feminists expect white women to challenge their assumptions and change themselves. These feminists identify the frightening scope and difficulty of such personal change as one of the sources of white women's resistance.

The year 1981 saw the publication of several books with illustrative titles determined to change the direction of the feminist movement. *Women, Race, and Class*, by Angela Davis, analyzes racism and sexism primarily in nineteenth-century institutions and movements as well as in historical accounts of them. Her topics include slavery, abolition, women's rights, education, suffrage, black women's clubs, work, communism, rape, and reproductive rights. *Ain't I a Woman*, by bell hooks, identifies the racism that causes some twentieth-century white feminists to ignore black feminists' work and traces the source of that racism to the condition of black women during slavery. hooks has continued to be among those feminists most dedicated to overcoming the racial divisions between black and white women. In "Where Is the Love: Political Bonding between Black and White Women" (1995), she notes the general resistance to admitting—let alone exploring— the obstacles to women's interracial friendships as well as the scarcity of such relationships. Addressing the failure of the feminist movement to effect interracial bonds, she states that "even though some white women broke through the racist/sexist denial and came to an under- standing of their role in perpetuating racism, they were not willing to give up the privileges extended them by white supremacy" (222). hooks also contends that friendships and political coalitions between black and white women are possible only when women renounce female competition (223).

Another groundbreaking 1981 book was the collection *This Bridge Called My Back: Writings by Radical Women of Color*, edited by Cherríe Moraga and Gloria Anzaldúa. Its aim was literally to incite a new, revolutionary movement by creating a metaphorical bridge unit- ing women of all races. Affirmative as this purpose is, the wary tone of Moraga's introduction reflects the burden of the collection's goal, a burden that stems largely from the antagonism or ignorance of white women. In searching for a publisher, she is aware that the project could be used for motives other than those of the editors: "The feminist movement needs the book. . . . Do I dare speak of the boredom setting in among the white sector of the feminist movement?" (xiii).

Wanting an inclusive movement, she nevertheless, in a meeting between white women and women of color to discuss racism, wonders, "*How can we—this time—not use our bodies to be thrown over a river of tormented history to bridge the gap?*" (xv). Her question reflects the double meaning of the book's title: the bridge uniting women of all races that the editors want to create and the feeling that white women have built a movement on the backs of women of color.

The following year saw the publication of *All the Women Are White, All the Blacks Are Men, but Some of Us Are Brave: Black Women's Studies*, edited by Gloria T. Hull, Patricia Bell Scott, and Barbara Smith. This anthology sought to call attention to and further the development of black women's studies, which Hull and Smith state in the introduction "can be directly traced to three significant political movements of the twentieth century. These are the struggles for Black liberation and women's liberation . . . and the more recent Black feminist movement" (xx).

In her 1983 article "White Women/Black Women: The Dualism of Female Identity and Experience in the United States," Phyllis Marynick Palmer compares twentieth-century white women's use of black women as examples to nineteenth-century white women's dependence on Sojourner Truth as the spokesperson for women's strength and capabilities at the 1851 Women's Rights Convention in Akron, Ohio, where she gave the legendary "Ar'n't I a Woman?" speech recorded by Frances Gage.[6] Palmer states that white feminists "have used Sojourner Truth's hardiness and that of other black women as proof of white women's possibilities for, and performance of, productive work" (152). Although certain black women and the strong black woman stereotype have served as symbols of strength, Palmer asserts that black women have also functioned symbolically for white women as "America's most oppressed group" (153). Palmer points to two paradoxes these uses create in the feminist movement. First, despite their reliance on black women as symbols, "white women have not . . . sought out or attracted large numbers of black women to the women's movement" (154), largely because they have ignored the issues most pressing to black women and because they have treated race and class as secondary concerns. One benefit is that "the emphasis on sexism enables white women to deny their own history of racism and the benefits that white women have gained at the expense of black women" (155). Second, "black women . . . are criticized [by white women] for their failure to support the movement" (155). Palmer connects white women's ignoring black women to the nineteenth century's cultural bifurcation of womanhood into good and bad categories, which in America was translated into racial difference (157). She argues that until American women rid themselves of this moral overlay, prejudicial in itself, white women will not be able to form successful coalitions with black women. Palmer contends that white women must work to end racism and to further the political goals of black women because "white women will not be free of the fear of their own economic self-reliance and psychological independence until they work with black women to raise the status of women who symbolized and displayed female strength, and suffered its burdens" (166).

Despite the outpouring, beginning in the late 1970s, of writings about racism and feminism—writings that themselves often updated problems that had been lingering since the nineteenth century's women rights movement—white feminist awareness came slowly in many circles. The writings on race that my review only briefly describes came primarily from radical feminists, but I have included the many titles and dates to emphasize the existence and availability of that body of work, for the topic of racism in feminism is one that seems perpetually to be discovered anew, by white women. And so when Jane Gallop, Marianne Hirsch, and Nancy K. Miller, in their published conversation "Criticizing Feminist Criticism," say that in the late 1980s they feel pressured to consider race, whereas in the early 1980s the pressure they felt was to use post-structuralist theory, they seem to have missed a great deal of urgent writing on racism that preceded Adrienne Rich's 1984 "Notes Toward a Politics of Location," which Miller credits her 1986 reading of as her personal impetus to consider race in her work.[7] Granted, Miller admits that her racial awareness came late, but the conversation seems to imply that racism gained urgency for *feminists* in the late 1980s, not that it became compelling for a certain strand of white feminist literary critics at that time. As a result, the history of feminist thought dealing with race seems to get lost. Working from Miller's date and a cluster of publishing events, Elizabeth Abel chooses 1985 as the date for a much more specific event. She declares it "a watershed year that marked the simultaneous emergence of what has been called postfeminism and, not coincidentally, of pervasive white feminist attention to texts by women of color" (485). Noting that "the end of the most confident and ethnocentric period of the second wave (roughly 1970–1985) has interestingly collapsed postfeminism and prefeminism as the ideological frameworks in which white women turn to black women to articulate a politics and to embody a discursive authority that are either lost or not yet found," Abel emphasizes the political motivations behind white women's sudden awareness of writings by women of color ("Black Writing, White Reading" 485).

Almost two decades later, the ambivalence of some white critics is still evident in the chapter of Susan Gubar's *Critical Condition: Feminism at the Turn of the Century* entitled "What Ails Feminist Criticism?" Outlining four stages of feminist literary criticism as "critique," "recovery of female literary traditions," "the engendering of differences," and "metacritical dissension," Gubar proclaims that the last stage has created a "language crisis," which she metaphorically treats as a disease (115–18). She identifies two strands of critique in this phase: "On the one hand, feminist criticism was disparaged by some African-American and postcolonial thinkers as universalizing a privileged, white womanhood; on the other, it was maligned by several poststructualists as naively essentialist about the identity of women" (118). For Gubar, such criticisms pose a real threat, and she describes the rancor that fueled her first version of the chapter: "Originally, when this essay was a talk entitled 'Who Killed Feminist Criticism?,' I relished the idea of a rousing arraignment in which I dramatically pinned the blame for the problems currently facing feminist criticism on a host of nefarious culprits—some of them the most prestigious people in the field" (113). And in the section of the chapter devoted to race-based criticisms of feminism, Gubar seems to have chosen the most acrimonious examples. Certainly such criticisms have often been fueled by painful experiences, but rather than interpreting their tone as expressions of the authors' passion or as the performative reversals of exclusionary and demeaning attitudes they appear to be, Gubar responds to them as attacks, though she does concede the historical context of "a slave past that had set in place black women's subjection to white women and . . . the unconscious racism permeating the women's movement from its inception in the nineteenth century" (120).

What is perhaps most intriguing about the chapter is Gubar's vacillation between an angry and an appreciative tone, for she emphasizes her indebtedness to the contributions of both African American critics and poststructuralist theorists. Their thinking she values; it is their influence on critical language she regrets: "the brilliance of their conceptualizations paradoxically contributed to their regrettable stylistic influence over numerous practitioners in the field of feminist studies. . . . together their words combined to make 'women' an invalid word" (119). The problem is not the influential figures themselves but "the debilitating rhetorics of critical election, abjection, and obscurantism" (134) that she perceives as the effect of their work on feminist criticism at the end of the twentieth century.

INTERRACIAL READING

Many feminist literary critics have begun to theorize how racial identity inflects literary interpretation, or, put more specifically, how white women read—or misread—works by and about black women. Critics of both races have analyzed why those readings, well intentioned and otherwise intelligent, too often tend to reinscribe the invisibility and objectification of racism. The problems of interracial reading, like the problems of interracial relationships, stem from both the different historical experiences of African American women and white women and the oppositional historical definitions of black and white womanhood. The debates center on the questions of who white women identify with when they read black women's works and how white feminists use the works of black feminists. In both cases, invisibility results from the loss of the historical specificity of black women's experience. Conversely, the recognition of black women's strength may too easily lead to stereotypical conceptions that deny black women their individuality and the full complexities of their existence. When readers ignore the historical specificity of black women's experience or fall back on the symbolic power stereotypically accorded black women, they replicate the same objectification and invisibility they set out to overcome.

A central issue in discussions of how white women read texts by black women is which characters white women identify with and how they do it. In her 1988 article "A Theory of Black Women's Texts and White Women's Readings, or . . . The Necessity of Being Other," Minrose Gwin suggests that white women may need to reconsider their approach to negative portrayals of white women when they read black women's stories. She asserts that "such reading . . . must . . . become a reflexive process which not only reads its own cultural assumptions . . . but . . . also turns back upon itself to read itself as white *other* in many black women's texts." For Gwin this process means being open to seeing what black women see in the "signifier *white women*" (22), and she acknowledges that such an openness appears antithetical to the feminist reading practice of refusing to accept woman's position as *other* in texts, a praxis developed to answer the frequent othering of women in writing by men.

Her attempt to practice such a reading method led Gwin to the recognition of "a pattern which seems at the very heart of black women's distrust of white women, and one which emerges again and again in the writing and thinking of African-American women. . . . A construction which may be called 'White Woman as the Breaker of Promises' " (25). Gwin points out that although this is not the only role of white women in black women's works, it does occur frequently in black women's accounts of the feminist movement (26).

In her response to Gwin's essay, Barbara Christian analyzes Gwin's epigraph, taken from Alice Walker's *Meridian*, which reads as follows:

> But what had her mother said about white women? She could actually remember very little, but her impression had been that they were frivolous, helpless creatures, lazy and without ingenuity. Occasionally, one would rise to the level of bitchery, and this one would be carefully set aside when the collective "others" were discussed. Her grandmother—an erect former maid who was now a midwife—held strong opinions, which she expressed in this way: 1. She had never known a white woman she liked after the age of twelve. 2. White women were useless except as baby machines which would continue to produce little white people who would grow up to oppress her. 3. Without servants all of them would live in pigsties. (108)

Christian points out that Walker's passage "highlights so sharply those 'essential' characteristics attributed to 'real' white women by their own society. . . . For white Southern society from slavery on, had distinguished between black and white women in sexual terms" (33). "But because Meridian's maternal ancestors are at the bottom of society's rung, they can see what white women above them may not see, that white women's privilege is rooted in *their* society's definition which demeans *them* by denying them sensuality, an essential part of themselves" (33–34). Christian further explains that "expos[ing] white women's real position in their own society [is] a byproduct that often results when black women write from their own point of view" (34).

Christian states that Gwin's proposal, that white women read themselves as *other*, "sounds like an alienating process in which one encounters oneself as an object" (34). She points out "that to read is . . . to participate in 'the other's' view of the world, the writer's view" (34) and that "the opportunity to enter into other worlds results in a widening of the self" (35). Nevertheless, she acknowledges that "such a reward for the reader is difficult to appreciate, it appears, when one is from a traditionally higher status than the writer" (35). Moreover, "the possibility of widening the self, perhaps, is even more fraught with obstacles if from a societal perspective the reader is both different from and yet the same as the writer" (35). However, Christian contends that the difficulty arises not "because the reader encounters herself as an object but rather because her sense of who she is, as subject, is disrupted" (35). Christian modifies Gwin's suggestion, saying that white women should read black women's works "not as 'white *other*' . . . but as white women, which, after all, is who they are." She adds that they need to realize that they too have a racial identity and that "in actively choosing to look out at the universe, and really know it they may *need* to know our point of view, and perhaps see themselves in ways that they had not before, thus refining their definition of that concept, *woman*" (36). White women need to learn that "neither gender nor racial categories are pure ones; instead they are always interactive" (36).

Valerie Smith, in her 1989 essay "Black Feminist Theory and the Representation of the 'Other,' " argues that both white feminist and African American literary critics have used black women's works to rematerialize or historicize their methodologies:

> At precisely the moment when Anglo-American feminists and male Afro-Americanists begin to reconsider the material ground of their enterprise, they demonstrate their return to earth, as it were, by invoking the specific experiences of black women and the writings of black women. This association of black women with reembodiment resembles rather closely the association, in classic Western philosophy and in nineteenth-century cultural constructions of womanhood, of women of color with the body and therefore with animal passions and slave labor. Although in these theoretical contexts the impulse to rehistoricize produces insightful readings and illuminating theories, and is politically progressive and long overdue, nevertheless the link between black women's experiences and "the material" seems conceptually problematic. (45)

Smith points out that such critical moves are analogous to popular movies' use of black women characters solely to help white women develop their full selves. Black feminist literary theory, on the other hand, "seeks to explore representations of black women's lives through techniques of analysis which suspend the variables of race, class, and gender in mutually interrogative relation" (48).

In "Black Writing, White Reading: Race and the Politics of Feminist Interpretation" (1993), Elizabeth Abel uses her own reading of Toni Morrison's short story "Recitatif" to investigate the effect of racial stereotypes on white women's interpretations of literature by or about black women. She asks, "If white feminist readings of black women's texts disclose white critical fantasies, what (if any) value do these readings have—and for whom? How do white women's readings of black women's biological bodies inform our readings of black women's textual bodies?" (477). Abel admits that when she read Morrison's story, which never reveals the racial identity of the two main characters, she believed Roberta to be the black character because she appears to have "a more compelling physical presence that fortifies her cultural authority" (473). Analyzing her reading, Abel realized that she had succumbed to "a white woman's fantasy (my own) about black women's potency" (474). She surveys a number of feminists' works on race and concludes that they "do indicate certain pervasive tendencies among white feminists, who have tended to read black women's texts through critical lenses that filter out the texts' embeddedness in black political and cultural traditions and that foreground instead their relations to the agendas of white feminism, which the texts alter, or prefigure, but ultimately reconfirm" (496).

Ann duCille also explores the repercussions of white feminists' interest in African American women's texts in her 1994 essay "The Occult of True Black Womanhood: Critical Demeanor and Black Feminist Studies." She argues that "much of the newfound interest in African American women that seems to honor the field of black feminist studies actually demeans it by treating it not like a discipline with a history and a body of rigorous scholarship and distinguished scholars underpinning it, but like an anybody-can-play pick-up game performed on a wide-open, untrammeled field" (603). She points out that "[racial and gender] biases are ideologically inscribed and institutionally reproduced and as such are not easily elided—not even by the most liberal, the most sensitive, the most well-intentioned among us" (612). Among duCille's criticisms is that African American women's works and history tended to be granted authority only when they became the critical province of men or white women, even when black feminist critics had previously written academic works covering the same ground. Furthermore, African American women's fictional writings tend to be valued by men and white women for elucidating their own (men's and white women's) experience. Certainly, this function is one inherent in imaginative literature: readers read for lessons useful to their own lives. However, duCille attests that some male and white readers make this usefulness the only function of African American women's stories: "This, then, is the final paradox and the ultimate failure of the evidence of experience: to be valid—to be true—black womanhood must be legible as white or male; the texts of black women must be readable as maps, indexes to someone else's experience, subject to a seemingly endless process of translation and transference" (623). Jean Wyatt calls "the sequence of white idealizing statements and black feminist critiques . . . a failed dialogue" (101), but I would argue that those white critics who have begun to question how their own racial identity affects their literary interpretations, as well as the white novelists who posit an emerging critical awareness of whiteness as a racial identity as necessary to their characters' development, indicate a progressive change in literary race relations.

WHITENESS

When Barbara Christian suggests that white women read *as* white women, she explicitly asks them to be aware that white is a racial identity, as black is. The task she sets, however, proves more difficult than it perhaps at first appears. For one of the fundamental characteristics of whiteness is its invisibility, its claim to be unmarked. Although people of color have been calling attention to the peculiarities of whiteness since at least the nineteenth century, the meanings of whiteness as a racial identity have only recently begun to be studied extensively. The objective of whiteness studies is to dismantle the power of whiteness by analyzing white as a racial category and specifically as a cultural construction designed to ensure the dominance of one group of people.

Marilyn Frye was one of the first scholars to analyze whiteness.[8] Her influential chapter "On Being White: Thinking Toward a Feminist Understanding of Race and Race Supremacy" in her 1983 *The Politics of Reality: Essays in Feminist Theory* laid the groundwork for later examinations of whiteness, particularly in its focus on the power granted to and wielded by white people. An important aspect of Frye's work is its emphasis on the intersection of whiteness with gender and, to a somewhat lesser extent, with heterosexual and class dominance. Indeed, she begins the chapter by acknowledging that white feminists began attending to race largely "because women of color have demanded it," and this acknowledgment becomes her first example of the power conferred by whiteness: white women could choose whether to listen to those demands (111).

Similarly, white people determine who is and who is not white. Frye compares white people's tendency to presume light-skinned people to be white to heterosexuals' tendency to assume other people to be heterosexual. She notes that within these groups exist self-appointed skeptics who vigilantly watch for those who are supposedly trying to "pass" as white or heterosexual. Frye argues that both assumptions are "arrogant" in "asserting that defining is exclusively their prerogative," but she also contends "that almost all white people engage in the activity of defining membership in the group of white people in one or another of these modes, quite un-self-consciously and quite constantly. It is very hard, in individual cases, to give up this habit and await people's deciding for themselves what group they are members of" (116–117). Race in particular is one of the first ways we identify people, based on their skin color, though having light skin is not sufficient to guarantee inclusion in the group "white."

The tendency to assume the power to define other people's identity categories is closely related to white people's "habit of false universalization" (117), the presumption that speaking for one's group is speaking for all of humanity. Frye uses feminism as one example: "Much of what we [white feminists] have said is accurate only if taken to be about white women and white men within white culture (middle-class white women and white men, in fact). For the most part, it never occurred to us to modify our nouns accordingly; to our minds the people we were writing about were *people*. We don't think of ourselves as *white*" (117). Recognizing white as a racial category is a necessary step to counteract false generalization, as Frye states: "It is an important breakthrough for a member of a dominant group to come to know s/he is a member of *a group*, to know that what s/he is is only *a part* of humanity" (117). This recognition is the core tenet of whiteness studies; to dismantle racial oppression, white people must recognize that they have a race, but because white is the dominant race, it has been far too easy for white people to assume that their experience is representative of all humanity.

One implication of defining whiteness as a constructed group to which certain people belong or hold membership is that race loses its apparent inevitability. Frye uses the social construction of race and the choices granted by whiteness—particularly choosing who is or is not a member—to suggest that theoretically the option of choosing not to belong exists. As Frye puts it, "we are not white by nature but by political classification, and hence it is in principle possible to disaffiliate" (118). For Frye, white women's feminism necessitates the attempt to disaffiliate (she does not argue, however, that such a disaffiliation is actually possible), for if white women retain their racial privilege, then their attempts to overcome gender oppression amount to merely the attempt to achieve parity with white men. Because of their connections to white men, white women accrue certain racial privileges, including "access to material and educational benefits and the specious benefits of enjoying secondhand feelings of superiority and supremacy" (125). But Frye warns that such privileges are insidious to women who are not white:

> We [white women] also have the specious benefit of a certain *hope* (a false hope, as it turns out) which women of subordinated races do not have, namely the hope of becoming actually dominant *with* the white men, as their "equals." This last pseudo-benefit binds us most closely to them in racial solidarity. A liberal white feminism would seek "equality"; we can hardly expect to be heard as saying we want social and economic status equal to that of, say, Chicanos. If what we want is equality with our white brothers, then what we want is, among other things, our own firsthand participation in racial dominance rather than the secondhand ersatz dominance we get as the dominant group's women. (125)

Frye logically concludes that because "race is a tie that binds [white women] to [white] men," white feminists must "give up trading on our white skin for white men's race privilege" in order "not to be bound in subordination to men" (125). Eradicating racial oppression is necessary to eradicate gender oppression. Thus, Frye exhorts women to be "disloyal to Whiteness." Noting that "one must never claim not to be racist, but only to be anti-racist . . . [because] racism is so systematic and white privilege so impossible to escape, that one is, simply trapped" (126), she nevertheless urges white people to "set [themselves] against Whiteness" (127). The fact that privileges accrue to white people in a racist, white-dominated society is inevitable, but white people can analyze such privileges and attempt not to wield the attendant power.

Abolishing racism (and in Frye's argument, sexism) would necessitate that whiteness, as the construct that confers privilege to white people, be abolished. White people cannot simply choose not to be white, however, even if they can, as Frye suggests, attempt to refuse some of the privileges of being white. Peter Erickson addresses this conflict and the dangerous critical position the desire to eradicate whiteness has led some critics to in his essay "Seeing White" (1995). Erickson makes a distinction similar to Frye's between those writers who advocate white people's being "critically conscious" of their whiteness (the stance he favors) and those writers who seem to believe that white people can abolish whiteness:

> Let us assume that there are two basic approaches to the issue of what form a political critique of white privilege should take. The first imagines a redefinition or reconstitution, a transformation even, of whiteness, with the aim of establishing new, critical, white identities. Such

identities, regardless of how fundamentally transformed, at no point engage in a denial of whiteness. By contrast, the abolitionist perspective hypothesizes the total erasure of whiteness. (184)[9]

Although Erickson provides neither an example nor a description of what "new, critical, white identities" would be, his distinction shows that critiques of whiteness often replicate the privileges of whiteness they attempt to abolish. First, they may gratify "romantic white fantasies of oneness with blacks that tacitly erase all differences of historical and social experience" (184). Second, Erickson contends that critiques may imply a slippage from " 'I reject received versions of whiteness' [to] 'I have (therefore) become nonwhite, I am black.' " "This conflation," Erickson points out, "is more than harmless white escapism because the second entails an excessive, unwarranted identification that effectively impedes the formation of cross-racial political coalitions" (184). Presuming that white people can shed their racial identity—something no other racial group can do—replicates the privilege of deciding who is and is not white that Frye discusses. The dangerous identification that Erickson refers to is similar to the problematic identification that black women have criticized in white women's interpretations of black women's texts: when white women readers identify with black women protagonists, they often erase that character's racial identity and thereby betray the literary text.

Among the strengths of Richard Dyer's *White* (1997) is that he addresses both the ways white differs from other racial categories and the gender differences in the ideology of whiteness. "There is a specificity to white representation, but it does not reside in a set of stereotypes so much as in narrative structural positions, rhetorical tropes and habits of perception" (12). For instance, Dyer argues that "questions of colour elide with questions of morality"; the symbolic moral meanings attributed to black and white as colors inevitably affect how we perceive racial categories (62). Dyer elaborates that "any simple mapping of hue, skin and symbol on to one another is clearly not accurate. . . . [Nevertheless,] a white person who is bad is failing to be 'white,' whereas a black person who is good is a surprise, and one who is bad merely fulfils expectations" (63). The question of morality is particularly related to women and embodiment: that "whiteness aspires to *dis*-embodiedness" (39) makes sexuality troublesome, and white women are not supposed to experience sexual desire (27–28).

With respect to embodiment in particular, he describes how white racial characteristics are defined in opposition to blackness. He traces the concept of whiteness as "something that is in but not of the body" to Christianity's concept of incarnation. He thus provides an alternative or complementary genealogy for the association of black people with their bodies and white people as distinct from their bodies. He connects this belief to the common assumptions that race means "black" and that whites have no race: "Black people can be reduced (in white culture) to their bodies and thus to race, but white people are something else that is realised in and yet is not reducible to the corporeal, or racial" (14–15). However, this very definition of whiteness causes psychological conundrums for whites who feel separated from their bodies:

> The corporeality of whites [being] less certain . . . fed into the function of non-white, and especially black, people in representation of being a kind of definite thereness by means of which white people can gain a grounding in materiality and "know who they are.". . . At the level of representation, whites remain, for all their transcending superiority, dependent on non-whites for their sense of self, just as they are materially in so many imperial and post-imperial, physical and domestic labour circumstances. Such dependency could form the basis of a bond, but has more often been a source of anxiety. (24)

Whites thus turned to blacks for spiritual nurturance:

> Many whites . . . have considered that blacks were more spiritual. . . . It is not spirituality or soul that is held to distinguish whites, but what we might call "spirit": get up and go, aspiration, awareness of the highest reaches of intellectual comprehension and aesthetic refinement. Above all, the white spirit could both master and transcend the white body, while the non-white soul was a prey to the promptings and fallibilities of the body. (23)

That dependency of whites upon blacks for spiritual connection—which we will see in Faulkner's Temple Drake, in Hellman's reminiscences of black female domestics, and in Ellen Foster's reliance on her black friend Starletta—creates both white characters' sense of bonding with black women and their anxiety about their relationships with black women. The reliance on black people for material reality is an objection raised by black women to white feminists' use of black women's work, as discussed in the criticism by Morrison, Valerie Smith, and others. Moreover, the sense of dependency helps account for white women's frequent view of black women as authoritative, despite the fact that the white women are often in the more powerful position and are often presuming their authority even as they define the role of black women.

In chapter 2, I argue that although William Faulkner's *Requiem for a Nun* establishes that women's strategies for feminist resistance are circumscribed by both race and class, it nevertheless suggests that the connection of women across differences has the potential to counteract disciplinary social narratives. The structure of the novel—a two-act play centering on Temple Drake and Nancy Mannigoe, interspersed within three long, meditative prose sections that recount the history of Jefferson, Mississippi—effectively places the women at the center of Jefferson's history, emphasizing the centrality of the construction of women's lives to the culture as a whole. Critics have tended to describe the form of the novel as experimental, although Faulkner denied the characterization, declaring that "the hard simple give-and-take of dialogue . . . seemed the most effective way to tell that story"—as if he had to give Temple and Nancy the power of first-person speech in order to discover what they could achieve with words (Gwynn and Blotner 122). To me, the novel is an experiment in finding out what two marginalized women could achieve using language. We have become accustomed to recognizing such projects in women's writing, and the feminist critical tools that enable us to analyze works in terms of how the conventions of women's life stories limit narrative possibilities for female characters' lives, and of how authors confront and overcome those limitations, appear to provide the most apt approach to Faulkner's novel.

Chapters 3 and 4 address women's autobiographical writings. Interracial relationships in autobiography reflect the author's complex process of reading and textualizing other women's races and identities. Accounts of women's interracial relationships in autobiographies might, therefore, illuminate the problems of interracial reading by dramatizing the processes of interpreting race and relating across racial boundaries. Conversely, theories of interracial reading can help us analyze autobiographers' processes of reading and writing women of another race. Furthermore, these relationships show the importance of race as a factor in the author's own identity formation. I modify Abel's question about reading—"How do white women's readings of black women's biological bodies inform our readings of black women's textual bodies?" ("Black Writing, White Reading" 477)—to apply to writing. How do women write women of another race, and how do they imagine those women's perceptions of themselves, the writers?

In these two chapters, I examine the interracial relationships in autobiographical writings by Lillian Hellman and Audre Lorde. These two women of different generations, races, sexualities, and political commitments make an unlikely pairing. Hellman, born in 1905, was a playwright who believed that the problem of women's liberation could be reduced to the question of whether a woman could earn as much money as a man (Bryer 149); Lorde, born almost thirty years later, in 1934, was a self-described "black woman warrior poet" (*Cancer Journals* 21) for whom feminism meant a total political commitment to other women and to working for radical social change. My juxtaposition, then, forces these two women into a conversation that is in some ways unimaginable. Nevertheless, both women's autobiographical writings confront the difficulties of racial difference in women's relationships. Although Hellman's *An Unfinished Woman* and *Pentimento* reveal that she romanticizes black women as sources of nurture and authority, the memoirs also show that her relationships with the two black women domestics who played important roles in her life challenged her assumptions and made her confront her own racism. Lorde, in *The Cancer Journals* and *Zami*, exposes racism in the feminist movement and uses narrative strategies to reconfigure race relations by overturning the primacy of racial concepts of identity and emphasizing the interconnectedness of all oppressions.

Chapter 5 returns to fiction. I read Kaye Gibbons's *Ellen Foster* as an analysis of the detrimental effects of whiteness on Southern women and the racism inherent in aspiring to middle-class values. Similar to *Ellen Foster*, Elizabeth Cox's *Night Talk* makes an interracial friendship central to the white adolescent protagonist's development, thereby suggesting that white women must overcome their own racism to form coherent subjectivities. Chapters 6 and 7 examine novels in which the authors return to the source of the paradigm for relationships between African American and white women in the nineteenth century; the neo-slave narratives by Sherley Anne Williams and Toni Morrison reimagine the possibilities of both women's relationships and their racial identities. *Dessa Rose* provides a sustained relationship between a former slave mistress and a former slave through a plot that allows Williams to analyze the barriers to interracial relationships in both the nineteenth and twentieth centuries. Although the main characters' relationships with whites serves primarily as background in *Beloved*, reading those relationships within the context of Morrison's other works shows her continued interest in the fluidity of the meanings ascribed to race. Her short story "Recitatif" evokes readers' racial assumptions by making racial difference a point of conflict between the two main characters without identifying which woman is white and which is black. Similarly, in *Paradise*, which of the women who live at the convent is white is never explicitly revealed. The ambiguity foregrounds the conflation of racial and class markers, as does the role of the white indentured servant Amy Denver in *Beloved*. The Morrison chapter, then, returns to the emphasis on economic class and historical patterns of race relations established in the Faulkner chapter. Finally, in the "coda," I discuss *Living Out Loud*, a film that explicitly addresses the stereotypical fantasies white women can have about black women.

CHAPTER 2

"Sisters in Sin": Discourse, Discipline, and Difference in *Requiem for a Nun*

In *Requiem for a Nun* (1951), William Faulkner undertakes what has been construed as the feminist project of many women novelists: to ask how women whose lives have been made into social narratives can counteract those narratives and reclaim their own subjectivities, or, put another way, how two disempowered women can change their lives through language.[1] Returning to the story of Temple Drake, whose brutal rape, abduction, and imprisonment in a Memphis brothel are the subject of *Sanctuary* (1931), Faulkner links Temple's story to that of Nancy Mannigoe, the African American prostitute in "That Evening Sun" (1931). Eight years after the events of *Sanctuary*, Nancy is employed as a nanny by Temple and Gowan Stevens, and the dramatic portion of the novel opens with Nancy's sentencing for murdering the couple's baby daughter. Both Temple and Nancy, renowned "whores" in the local lore, try to maintain their subjectivities despite the public narratives that constrain their identities. By situating these women in the judicial system, Faulkner makes explicit the effect of these repressive cultural narratives on their lives.[2]

In trying to reclaim their stories from those with legal and cultural power, the women use different strategies because of their disparate social positions. Class and racial privilege give Temple access to social power that is denied Nancy. Using her identity as Mrs. Gowan Stevens, Temple tries to manipulate the interpretations of her life story in order to control her fate and free Nancy. With far less access to power, Nancy protects her subjectivity by refusing to acknowledge others' power over her, as when she refuses to respond to the judge before he pronounces a sentence of death by hanging in the first dramatic scene. She thereby parodies the judicial system.[3] Both women's strategies for counteracting the narratives of public identity fail, but their relationship, which arises out of their similar experiences of misogynist violence and which their class and racial differences would ordinarily preclude, offers a potential source of resistance that is more powerful than either woman's singular efforts. Despite their ultimate separation and failure, the novel thus suggests that the alliance of women across racial and class differences empowers their resistance and is a necessary precursor to social change.

Temple's strategies for freeing Nancy literally and herself figuratively are determined by public identity narratives. The sexual transgression forced upon her has rendered her "unfit" for the role of the chaste, pedestalled wife, and public discourse has divided her identity into two separate characters, Temple Drake and Mrs. Gowan Stevens. The language and narrative surrounding sexual acts in her past have come to constitute her identity as Temple Drake, whereas her "redeemed"-through-marriage identity as Mrs. Gowan Stevens demands that those sexual acts never be spoken of. She is well aware of discourse's power to constrain women within their roles by punishing deviation with verbal or written gossip. In a mocking tone, she reveals to the governor how rumor exacerbated the trauma of her rape and imprisonment:

> You remember Temple: the all-Mississippi debutante whose finishing school was the Memphis sporting house? About eight years ago, remember? Not that anyone, certainly not the sovereign state of Mississippi's first paid servant, need be reminded of that, provided they could read newspapers eight years ago or were kin to somebody who could read eight years ago or even had a friend who could or even just hear or even just remember or just believe the worst or even just hope for it. (551)

As a part of legend, Temple is herself already a text that is interpreted—often, as she points out, by those who desire the most lurid story. Her story speaks to a common female experience within patriarchal society: that of the woman labeled "whore." Although her experience is extreme, it reflects the psychological violence enacted upon women by a culture that defines them as virgins, mothers, or whores.

Temple's reaction to her predicament is to try to control her public identity by anticipating other people's interpretations of her behavior and then presenting a public self that leads to an interpretation she prefers. She admits to Stevens, for example, that she played the role of the "bereaved mother" at the trial (527). In this sense, public narratives, having split her identity into Mrs. Gowan Stevens and Temple Drake, have created her tendency to speak of both in the third person.[4] She herself attempts to suppress Temple Drake, preferring to perform Mrs. Gowan Stevens, the identity she feels she can control. This bifurcation leads to several verbal conflicts with Gavin, her uncle by marriage and Nancy's lawyer, who insists that she *is* Temple Drake, as when she returns from California to try to save Nancy:

> STEVENS: Yet you invented the coincidence [that brought her back from California].
> TEMPLE: Mrs Gowan Stevens did.
> STEVENS: Temple Drake did. Mrs Gowan Stevens is not even fighting in this class: This is Temple Drake's.
> TEMPLE: Temple Drake is dead.
> STEVENS: The past is never dead. It's not even past. (535)[5]

Temple wants to control her name because she believes her identity as Mrs. Gowan Stevens can exorcise her past.[6]

Temple cannot completely control her identity, however, even by cleaving to her Mrs. Gowan Stevens persona, because she cannot control all the narratives surrounding her. Her past continues to circulate in public conceptions of her identity, regardless of the persona she adopts or how faithfully she executes her role. As her rape and brothel imprisonment became public knowledge through Goodwin's trial in *Sanctuary*, her sexual past functions as an "open secret," as Eve Kosofsky Sedgwick describes it. Sedgwick maintains that the secrecy of the closet has specific meanings for homosexual identity: "Vibrantly resonant as the image of the closet is for many modern oppressions, it is indicative for homophobia in a way it cannot be for other oppressions" (75). Nevertheless, I want to suggest that the structural effects of the open secret implicate Temple as well, particularly because sexual acts have been made a constituent part of her identity and because of the transgressive, and therefore threatening and disruptive, nature of those acts. The rape, the bondage, and the brothel lend to Temple's past the aura of the illicit, which is powerful because it suggests the existence of further illicit details that are not publicly known. A "whore's" identity, as Sedgwick states of homosexual identity, exists in an atmosphere of "crystallizing intuitions or convictions . . . [with] their own power-circuits of silent contempt, silent blackmail, silent glamorization, silent complicity. After all, the position of those who think they *know something about one that one may not know oneself* is an excited and empowered one . . . [even if that knowledge is] that one's secret is known to them" (80). Furthermore, the details of Temple's past, especially the time spent in the brothel, act as what Sedgwick terms a "pathogenic secret," which carries with it "the consciousness of a potential for serious injury that is likely to go in both directions [to the revealer and the revealed-to]" (80). The weight of this secret has been hurting Temple and Gowan and has the potential to do more harm if revealed—in other words, if Temple "outs" herself by verbalizing the details of her sexual experiences. Again borrowing from Sedgwick:

> The double-edged potential for injury in the scene of coming out . . . results partly from the fact that the erotic identity of the person who receives the disclosure is apt also to be implicated in, hence perturbed by it. This is true first and generally because erotic identity, of all things, is never to be circumscribed simply as itself, can never not be relational, is never to be perceived or known by anyone outside of a structure of transference and countertransference. (81)

Here one thinks of Gowan, who, by his uncle Gavin's arrangement, sits silently hidden in the governor's chambers as Temple confesses; he is more or less responsible for Temple's ordeal and has expressed doubt that he is Bucky's biological father.

What is the secret, beyond the public assumption of lurid details, that has such explosive and destructive potential, even for Temple and Gowan, the two people most intimately involved in the past events and their repercussions? The most transgressive, most taboo element of Temple's experience in *Sanctuary*, because it is the most forbidden, is her open expression of insatiable sexual desire for Red. In *Requiem*, that desire is contained in the letters she wrote him; thus, her sexuality is explicitly connected to the act of writing. Initially posed by the letters, the threat soon becomes the possibility that Temple will choose a life in which she may again openly express her sexuality. Pervasive cultural fear of unrestrained female sexuality operates much as the homophobia Sedgwick discusses, making it especially problematic for Temple to integrate past and present, public and private, into a coherent subject position from which to speak and act.

Temple's struggle to regain control of her narrative is expressed mainly through her conflict with Gavin over how her story will be told. Although Gavin insists his goal is the "truth" and making Temple tell it, he constantly interrupts her and creates parts of her story himself. Temple rebukes Gavin for his desire to control her story.

When he treats its narration as a game—"Wait. Let me play too"—she "bitterly" responds, "You too. So wise too. Why cant you believe in truth? At least that I'm trying to tell it. At least trying now to tell it" (558). Silenced by all the retellings of her story by others, Temple resents the appropriation of her story by the man who coerced her into telling it. The nature of the truth that Gavin desires remains elusive. He seems to long for that single, transcendent, redemptive truth, the truth that heals, that "sets free." However, as Michel Foucault argues, "truth is not by nature free— . . . its production is thoroughly imbued with relations of power" (*History of Sexuality* 60). The power Gavin derives from his role as Temple's confessor must make us question his motivation. Foucault's description of the confessor's role indicates the extent of this power, which may itself be Gavin's chief reward:

> the revelation of the confession had to be coupled with the decipherment of what it said. The one who listened was not simply the forgiving master, the judge who condemned or acquitted; he was the master of truth. His was a hermaneutic function. With regard to the confession, his power was not only to demand it before it was made, or decide what was to follow after it, but also to constitute a discourse of truth on the basis of its decipherment. (*History of Sexuality* 66–67)

Furthermore, Foucault's comments on the purpose served by confession help illustrate what may be Gavin's more hidden motive: "it is in the confession that truth and sex are joined, through the obligatory and exhaustive expression of an individual secret. *But this time it is truth that serves as a medium for sex and its manifestations*" (*History of Sexuality* 61, my emphasis). Gavin wants to force sex into discourse. He, too, wants the lurid details of Temple's past to be spoken— whether to hear them, to know all of them, to witness others hear them in his presence, or just to make Temple say them for the suffering that is accorded such redemptive value throughout the novel—for, as Foucault argues, in the confession "investigation and punishment become mixed" (*Discipline and Punish* 41).

In contrast to Gavin's ostensible desire for an existential freedom that can be achieved through language, Temple focuses on the practical, social effects of language and tries to get Gavin to do so as well. She wants to save Nancy and believes legal discourse can effect that. She wants to say the necessary words that will get Gavin to create the necessary paperwork: "All we need is an affidavit. That she is crazy. Has been for years" (528). Despite the fact that Gavin tells her they cannot save Nancy, Temple persists: "what you will need will be facts, papers, documents, sworn to, incontrovertible, that no other lawyer trained or untrained either can punch holes in, find any flaw in" (533). Her desperation to save Nancy, for which she tells Gavin she "will do anything, *any*thing" (532), is what makes her vulnerable to Gavin's power, to his demand for her confession. She keeps asking him, "How much will I have to tell?" (538). She resists resurrecting Temple Drake, realizing that to submit to Gavin's demand for confession requires her to accept the rape as a meaning that both defines and emanates from her essential identity. To believe that the rape resulted from something within her would be to accept that the rape was her fault—to say she "wanted it." Temple mocks Gavin's purported purpose—the truth: "For no better reason than that. Just to get it told, breathed aloud, into words, sound. . . . Why blink your own rhetoric? Why dont you go on and tell me it's for the good of my soul—if I have one?" (533).[7] Nevertheless, perhaps compelled by what Foucault has shown to be the pervasive drive within individuals to turn sex into discourse, she comes to need to tell her story, even after it is clear that she cannot prevent Nancy's execution. She tells the governor, "I've got to say it all, or I wouldn't be here. But unless I can still believe that you might say yes [that he will save Nancy], I dont see how I can" (559).

Temple's need to save Nancy is, in fact, her need to save herself; their identities and destinies have become enmeshed.[8] As Temple Drake and Mrs. Gowan Stevens, she inhabits both ends of the oppositional definition of woman. She is committed to performing the Mrs. Gowan Stevens social identity, which disciplines her subjectivity and by definition precludes her sexuality. Nancy enables Temple to maintain another subjectivity, one that allows her sexuality—is, in fact, defined by it. That subjectivity seems to promise more freedom, because it seems to be less normalized. Resistance, however, is an inevitable component of any power relation and is often contained by the dominant system.[9] This alternative, seemingly resistant identity, then, is just as normalized as the Mrs. Gowan Stevens identity, at least to the extent that being Temple Drake means inhabiting the identity defined by all the lurid stories. Temple's alternative subjectivity has been coopted by the label "whore": discourse exercises power, making her the site of her own discipline. The label "whore" thus serves as an ontological category, making her essential identity out of a sexual act or acts presumed to have been done to or by her, and thereby determining the range of her possible actions.

Forms of resistance are given a specifically female history in the prose sections of the novel. The women in these sections, who contextualize Temple and Nancy culturally and historically, establish a women's culture that both resists and informs the dominant culture. The repetition of the Southern women's refusal to accept defeat by the North as the outcome of the Civil War becomes a refrain and emphasizes this heritage of resistance: "only the undefeated undefeatable women, vulnerable only to death, resisted, endured, irreconciliable" (629). Women are, in fact, a counterforce, "reversed and irrevocably reverted against the whole moving unanimity of panorama" (633). Their legacy of resistance survives them, and their characteristic description eventually turns into a trait of the town's inhabitants, who become "the irreconcilable Jeffersonians and Yoknapatawphians" (642). Subsumed by the larger culture, however, the legacy is reduced or normalized into class distinctions and social forms: "at last even the last old sapless indomitable unvanquished widow or maiden aunt had died and the old deathless Lost Cause had become a faded (though still select) social club or caste, or form of behavior when you remembered to observe it" (638).

Even though women are sites of resistance, they remain within the roles society ascribes to them. The Southern middle-class white woman's role is represented by Cecelia Farmer, who is described first as the prison turnkey's daughter, "a frail anemic girl with narrow workless hands lacking even the strength to milk a cow," and then as a part of the prison structure: "the old tough logs . . . were now the bower framing a window in which mused hour after hour and day and month and year, the frail blonde girl" (626, 627). Cecelia is framed by both the window and her father's home, which is literally the prison.[10] She is also framed by her cultural role, that of the Southern daughter, placed on the pedestal, who waits, passively and silently, to be carried off and married by a man. Her cultural role is analogous to that of the socially elite Temple Drake.

Cecelia's only autonomous act is "inscribing at some moment the fragile and indelible signature of her meditation in one of the panes of it (the window): her frail and workless name, scratched by a diamond ring in her frail and workless hand, and the date: *Cecelia Farmer April 16th 1861*" (627). While her name is described as "paradoxical and significantless" (629), the act of writing it is not. It is important that Cecelia achieves this act with an object of female inheritance, her grandmother's diamond ring (629), which, paradoxically, symbolizes the cultural exchange of women. Her signature is her assertion of her existence, and through it she writes herself into town legend and makes herself a central figure.[11] Faulkner thus places special emphasis on women's written language as an assertion of subjectivity and a potential means of achieving power. Writing is a private act that allows women to express a subjectivity other than that mandated by the public narrative of their role in society.

Cecelia's signature sets the stage for the love letters Temple wrote to Red after their enforced liaisons while she was held prisoner in the Memphis brothel. These letters, creative acts through which she maintained her subjectivity, enable Temple to imagine an identity that is not socially mandated. Through the letters, Temple achieved what Hélène Cixous theorizes in "The Laugh of the Medusa": "by writing her self, woman will return to the body which has been more than confiscated from her, which has been turned into the uncanny stranger on display" (880). At the time Temple wrote the letters, they were a means of controlling her situation by writing the narrative of her relationship with Red. Created out of her sexuality, which she has suppressed to some extent to enact the socially defined role of Mrs. Gowan Stevens, the letters now provide Temple access to a former sense of freedom and control. She emphasizes the importance of the letters when she tells the governor about her relationship with Red: "I fell what I called in love with him and what it was or what I called it doesn't matter either because *all that matters is that I wrote the letters—*" (572, my emphasis). She focuses on her authorship: "So I wrote the letters. I would write one each time . . . afterward, after they—he left, and sometimes I would write two or three when it would be two or three days between, when they—he wouldn't—" (527, ellipsis in text). What the governor hears is that two men were visiting Temple, but she highlights her creativity. When he seeks clarification of events, she continues to discuss the letters. She tells him four times that they were good letters, even alluding to Shakespeare: "you would have wondered how anybody just seventeen and not even through freshman in college, could have learned the—right words. Though all you would have needed probably would be an old dictionary from back in Shakespeare's time when, so they say, people hadn't learned how to blush at words" (574). Writing has been for Temple what Cixous projects it can be:

> An act which will not only "realize" the decensored relation of woman to her sexuality, to her womanly being, giving her access to her native strength; it will give her back her goods, her pleasures, her organs, her immense bodily territories which have been kept under seal; it will tear her away from the superegoized structure in which she has always occupied the place reserved for the guilty. (880)

By focusing on her writing, Temple is able to integrate her past experience with her present and gains access to a subjectivity that, even though its effects remain private (the governor and Gavin remain unmoved), is not coopted in the way that her attempt to reclaim the identity "whore" is.[12]

Just as Cecelia corresponds to Temple, Mohataha, mother to Ikkemotubbe, "the last ruling Chickasaw chief" (618), provides the background for Nancy. Both are illiterate women of color who commit the acts that ostensibly allow their displacement by white society. The description of Mohataha has similarities to that of Nancy; her expression is unreadable, just as Nancy's is at the trial, and as Nancy is repeatedly described as a whore, Mohataha is compared to a madam:

> the inscrutable ageless wrinkled face, the fat shapeless body dressed in the cast-off garments of a French queen, which on her looked like the Sunday costume of the madam of a rich Natchez or New Orleans brothel, sitting in a battered wagon inside a squatting ring of her household troops, her young men dressed in their Sunday clothes for travelling too: then she said, "Where is this Indian territory?" And they told her: West. "Turn the mules west," she said, and someone did so, and she took the pen from the agent and made her X on the paper and handed the pen back and the wagon moved . . . herself immobile beneath the rigid parasol, grotesque and regal, bizarre and moribund, like obsolescence's self riding off the stage. (619)

Mohataha's "capital X on the paper which ratified the dispossession of her people forever" (618) shows that a woman's writing can serve to enforce cultural hegemony. Mohataha's signature, however, is merely the symbolic act of her people's already inevitable dispossession; it is causal

> apparently and apparently only, since in reality it was as though, instead of putting an inked cross at the foot of a sheet of paper, she had lighted the train of a mine set beneath a dam, a dyke, a barrier already straining, bulging, bellying, not only towering over the land but leaning, looming, imminent with collapse, so that it only required the single light touch of the pen in that brown illiterate hand, and the wagon did not vanish slowly and terrifically from the scene to the terrific sound of its ungreased wheels, but was swept, hurled, flung not only out of Yoknapatawpha County and Mississippi but the United States too, immobile and intact. (621–622)

Nancy's murder of the baby—her one signifying act by which she both becomes a part of the town's written record and history and allows for her own eradication by that town—is also accomplished by a "brown illiterate hand" and similarly completes an apparently inevitable end. She fulfills for Temple's daughter what may seem to her the inescapable, violent destiny of a woman, in which her life and Temple's have been cast. Her act reveals the devaluation of life that the violence in her own life has taught her. Throughout the novel, Faulkner emphasizes the cultural forces that impinge upon people's actions, as the portrayal of Mohataha's act shows. Nevertheless, and despite the alignment of Nancy with Mohataha, we must resist the urge to interpret Nancy's action as equally inevitable and determined. Why Nancy kills the child is the irresolvable enigma in the novel.[13] Certainly it serves as a plot device, creating the need for Temple to save Nancy, placing the story within the construct of the judicial system, and inciting the suffering in Temple and Gowan that ruptures the structure of their marriage—the roles they played in it and the suffering they had learned to endure as the result of their circumstances. The fact that the baby is never named, in a novel obsessed with the importance of naming, distances the reader from the reality of her life and supports the murder's greater role as plot function than as moral dilemma.

Placing Temple and Nancy's relationship in its cultural context is important for any interpretation of the murder. Despite Temple's identification with Nancy, their relationship remains largely determined by the Southern social structure within which they live, a structure in which the black woman's role as domestic and nanny is to function as mirror and support for the white woman. The black woman's prescribed role is to assist the white woman in fulfilling her role in society as a white woman.[14] Interestingly, Faulkner does not address this historical and cultural role in the prose sections; yet it fits Temple and Nancy's relationship perfectly, as Temple's description of Nancy for the governor shows:

> nurse: guide: mentor, catalyst, glue, . . . holding the whole lot of them [Temple, Gowan, and their children] together—not just a magnetic center for the heir apparent and the other little princes or princesses in their orderly succession, to circle around, but for the two bigger hunks too of mass or matter or dirt or whatever it is shaped in the image of God, in a semblance at least of order and respectability and peace; not ole cradle-rocking black mammy at all. (579)

In trying to emphasize Nancy's importance, Temple reverts to a definition of the mammy stereotype. Her statement also indicates her restricted ability to imagine possibilities for her relationship with Nancy that extend beyond the limits imposed by that image and narrative, possibilities that break out of the boundaries of disciplined penitentiary space and into a space in which they would no longer have to be what Foucault terms "docile bodies."

In a sense, Nancy fulfills her role by demanding that Temple fulfill her maternal role. When Temple tries to leave with Pete, Nancy repeatedly reminds Temple of her duty to her children. Her exhortations fail, and Nancy sacrifices her own life and that of Temple's infant to ensure that Temple will stay with her family, will continue to enact her role as Mrs. Gowan Stevens. In meeting this requirement, Nancy, as Richard Moreland attests, "betrayed the typical role and trust assigned to her ideologically and economically by her race and gender: to care for people in this predominantly white society in their most vulnerable and dependent stage of life (just as in her previous role as black 'tramp' she was expected to cater to white men in their most socially vulnerable moments of sexuality)" (209). Nancy thus puts her duty to the unity of the family and to the eldest son ahead of her duty to the younger, female child. Nancy is also perhaps asking Temple not to abandon her—is in effect saying, "don't leave me." This possibility depends on whether Temple's need for Nancy is reciprocated. Although Nancy may need Temple to ensure her employment, the cultural definition of their relationship as employer/employee works against an equitable reciprocity. Temple's identification with Nancy and the isolation that dominated Nancy's existence before her life in the Stevenses' home, however, suggest mutual need is a possibility.

Nancy's motivation aside, the murder forces her and Temple to negotiate separately within the judicial system, which then mediates their relationship. Nancy's attempts to use language as a form of resistance, which are informed by Mohataha's use of language, differ from Temple's strategies. As the extreme outsider, being black, poor, female, and a prisoner, Nancy maintains her integrity by refusing to answer to the justice system. When her sentence is passed down, she "quite loud in the silence, to no one, quite calm, not moving" directs her response to God: "Yes, Lord" (507). When she is recounting Nancy's response to the charge of murder, Temple recognizes and respects Nancy's subversion: " 'Guilty, Lord'—like that, disrupting and confounding and dispersing and flinging back two thousand years, the whole edifice of corpus juris and rules of evidence we have been working to make stand up by itself ever since Caesar" (607). As Jay Watson observes, Nancy "short-circuits (and puts in its place) the unfeelingly efficient protocol of the judicial ceremony" (183). Moreland, noting that Nancy's answer follows the judge's invocation of God, furthers that interpretation: "she dramatizes again how such deferrals to higher authorities both insulate those present and also show their need to insulate themselves from a more compromising understanding of, involvement in, perhaps complicity in, the apparent anomaly of her crime" (209–210). Nancy is employing the strategy Luce Irigaray terms "mimicry," which is for a woman

> to resubmit herself . . . to "ideas," in particular to ideas about herself, that are elaborated in/by masculine logic, but so as to make "visible," by an effect of playful repetition, what was supposed to remain invisible: the cover-up of a possible operation of the feminine in language. It also means "to unveil" the fact that, if women are such good mimics, it is because they are not simply resorbed in this function. *They also remain elsewhere.* (76, emphasis in text)

By refusing complicity in the court's judgment, Nancy not only critiques the judicial system, she also shows that her subjectivity—if not her body—remains beyond the reach of its power.

In the novel's final scene, Temple and Gavin's visit to the prison, where Nancy at last gets to speak for herself, she again employs this strategy of resistance.[15] Refusing to be restricted to a single coherent meaning, Nancy finally reduces her message to one word: "Believe" (662). Her repetition and its simplicity lend her message incantatory power, just as Cecelia's "passivity" invests her continual and impenetrable presence with invincibility. Nevertheless, Nancy's "Trust in Him" (657) is problematic in that she seems to have accepted her subjugation to the ultimate male power. Nancy's consideration of her audience, however, affects her message; she makes this and related statements before Gavin drops out of the conversation, before the conversation is carried out solely between her and Temple. Furthermore, because the power over her is male, Nancy assumes she will have to "get low for Jesus" (656). To Nancy, men and women have very different expectations. Her distinction between how men and women listen reveals the impact of her consideration of her audience: "Jesus is a man too. He's got to be. Menfolks listens to somebody because of what he says. Women dont. They dont care what he said. They listens because of what he is" (656). Her statements are therefore addressed to an audience that includes men, and she expects Temple to listen not to the content of her words but to the presence of her being, out of the knowledge of who she is.

Temple and Nancy's relationship is central to the novel; they are identified with each other throughout, particularly by Temple, whose first words echo Nancy's words in the courtroom: "Yes, God. Guilty, God. Thank you, God" (509).[16] Such an echo could be taken merely as mockery if Temple did not persistently align herself with Nancy, as when she refers to the governor as "the first paid servant, a part of whose job is being paid to lose sleep over Nancy Mannigoes and Temple Drakes" (551). A large part of Temple's identification with Nancy is based on the fact that they are both considered "whores."[17] Temple reclaims the word "whore" as their shared identity. By continually referring to them both as "whores," Temple achieves two things. First, she distances herself from her own situation and, paradoxically, from Nancy so that she can maintain the control that her feelings for Nancy threaten. Second, she appropriates society's label for them in order to show her contempt for the misogyny inherent in society's conceptions of women.

Temple's relationship to the word "whore" is complex, however: despite her anger, she has to some extent internalized the moral judgment inherent in the word. (Indeed, her role as Mrs. Gowan Stevens requires her to make that judgment.) Thus, when Temple first decides that she can no longer stand the burden of maintaining her Mrs. Gowan Stevens persona, she feels that her only choice is to reclaim the identity of Temple Drake by running away with Pete, thereby fulfilling the role of "whore."[18] As she puts it, describing for the governor her reaction to Pete's blackmail, "being Temple Drake, the first way to buy them [the letters] back that Temple Drake thought of, was to produce the material for another set of them" (575). The label "whore," by making an act (whether her rape, and thus not her act at all, or her sexual desire for Red) her identity, casts Temple as the enforcer of her own confinement within that role and makes her the site of her own discipline. Temple accepts, under great pressure from Gavin, the essentialized nature of evil: she states, "Temple Drake liked evil," and "the bad was already there [in her] waiting" (564, 574). This self-blame gives her the illusion of control by making her agent rather than victim, but ultimately it keeps her contained within the hegemonic patriarchal constructs and definitions. Temple's own language constricts her narrative. Her vocabulary for women's options is inadequate to provide her with more positive choices.

Temple and Nancy's social identity as "whores" gives them an equality that would not otherwise exist in the relationship of a white woman and a black woman who works for her, a fact that Temple acknowledges even as she tries to assert her superiority, calling Nancy's reasoning "whore morality": "But then, if I can say whore, so can you, cant you?" (597). Temple sets up a parallel between the two of them when she describes the young Temple as "the all-Mississippi debutante" and then says that Nancy "made her debut into the public life of her native city while lying in the gutter with a white man trying to kick her teeth *or at least her voice* back down her throat" (554, my emphasis). Gavin makes the parallel between Temple and Nancy explicit by echoing these words when he describes Temple's plan to run off with Red's brother Pete, "who wouldn't even bother to forgive her if it ever dawned on him that he had the opportunity, but instead would simply black her eyes and knock a few teeth out and fling her into the gutter: so that she could rest secure forever in the knowledge that, until she found herself with a black eye and or spitting teeth in the gutter, he would never even know he had anything to forgive her for" (588). Clearly, the shared experience of misogynistic violence forges the deep bond Temple feels with Nancy.

Whereas Temple relates the violence to an attempt to destroy a woman's voice, she describes her relationship to Nancy in terms of their ability to share language. She tells the governor that she hired Nancy "to have someone to talk to" (554), stating, "it wasn't the Gowan Stevenses but Temple Drake who had chosen the ex-dope-fiend nigger whore for the reason that an ex-dope-fiend nigger whore was the only animal in Jefferson that spoke Temple Drake's language" (579).[19] The sharing of language takes on a spiritual significance for Temple; she describes their communication in religious terms: "acolyte," "sisters," "avocational," "worshipper," "worshipped," and "idol." She is acolyte to Nancy's nun:

> A confidante. You know: the big-time ball player, the idol on the pedestal, the worshipped; and the worshipper, the acolyte. . . . You know: the long afternoons, with the last electric button pressed on the last cooking or washing or sweeping gadget and the baby safely asleep for a while, and the two sisters in sin swapping trade or anyway avocational secrets over coca colas in the quiet kitchen. (579–580)

An idealized unity manifested in a shared language and arising out of a shared gender experience is posited, in many feminist theories, as the potential source of resistance, transformation, and change. Cixous, for example, states that "Everything will be changed once woman gives woman to the other woman" (881). Such theories have been criticized for eliding crucial race and class differences among women in an attempt to forge gender unity.[20] Although race and class differences ultimately separate Temple and Nancy in Faulkner's text, I hope to show that those differences are what make their unity a form of resistance that has not already been coopted and contained, precisely because it has remained unimagined.

Temple and Nancy's shared language is never represented in the text. According to Irigaray's concept of patriarchal language, women's language is by definition unrepresentable because the category woman, as other, remains "unimaginable" (85). The interchange between Temple and Nancy that immediately precedes Nancy's suffocating the baby is in the language not of their idealized relating but of "the phallocentric economy" (Irigaray 78). By agreeing to run off with Pete, Temple denies her subjectivity because she accepts the role of commodity within that economy. As Nancy informs her, Temple's relationship to him is explicitly economic: he will demand money of her. Her acceptance of that commodified role propels the two women back into patriarchal space. It is here that Nancy tries to keep Temple within the nuclear family structure by withholding her money and warning her of the dangers of her precarious position with Pete (596). Here that Nancy accuses Temple: "It was already there in whoever could write the kind of letters that even eight years afterward could still make grief and ruin" (596–597). Here that Temple pulls class rank on Nancy, condescendingly distinguishing them: "Maybe the difference [between us] is, I decline to be one [a whore] in my husband's house" (597). Here that Nancy makes explicit the violence that maintains such hierarchical distinctions, offering, "Hit me. Light you a cigarette too. I told you and him [Pete] both I brought my foot. Here it is" (599). Here that they express the hatred Cixous describes as "the greatest crime against women," which has "led them [women] to hate women, to be their own enemies, to mobilize their immense strength against themselves" (878).

In contrast, the resistant female space created through the relationship between two women who are multiply othered—as women, as "whores," in Nancy's case as an African American and a drug user, and in Temple's case as a woman with sexual subjectivity—constitutes what Irigaray imagines as "an 'outside' that is exempt, in part, from phallocratic law," an outside from which it is possible "to disconcert the staging of representation according to exclusively 'masculine' parameters, that is, according to a phallocratic order" (68). This is the space that she describes as excluded by patriarchal language, in which "there is no possible place for the 'feminine,' except the traditional place of the repressed, the censured," in which "the question of the woman still cannot be articulated" (68). The power of Temple and Nancy's differences—from other women and from each other—is crucial to the resistant power of this space. The text's suggestion that women's differences are necessary for resistance goes against the tendency of some feminist theories to universalize gender experience.

That the possibility of Temple and Nancy's discourse has remained unimagined means it is uncontained. Discourse between two women of Temple's social class, which is described as "young couples or families who can afford to pay that much rent in order to live on the right street among other young couples who belong to the right church and country club" (508), would be the scripted language of the patriarchy because these women are invested in the privilege that ensues from their identities, which are defined by their relationships to men. Within such space, Irigaray argues, "women's social inferiority is reinforced and complicated by the fact that woman does not have access to language, except through recourse to 'masculine' systems of representation which disappropriate her from her relation to herself and to other women" (85). In Foucault's terms, these women are disciplinary sites of their own normalization; thus they maintain their normalized identities and perpetuate hegemony when they are together, even when they are not being observed. Although this would not necessarily be the case if they rejected their prescribed identities, if they were not invested in the system and the privilege it provides, their rebellion would remain contained within the dominant system of power, which has provided space for resistance. Two poor African American women such as Nancy would also be contained; denied access to the power structures, they are rendered invisible, voiceless, and therefore powerless. The problem, therefore, is how to find a way out of contained space, and not just into another already defined space.

As genuine connection and communication across racial and class boundaries has been impeded by the forces of hegemony, Temple and Nancy's discourse has remained unimagined and undefined. It therefore has potential power. Temple and Nancy's challenge, as they attempt to resist hegemony and claim subjectivity, is one not just of language, but of narrative, just as the dominant discourse that constrains them operates by reading women as texts not only on the level of language (through labels such as "whore" and "nigger dope-fiend whore") but also on the level of narrative, by controlling their possible stories and how those stories are told. Their problem is the one Carolyn G. Heilbrun raises as a question to all women: "How can we find narratives of female plots, stories that will affect other stories and, eventually, lives?" (42).

Ultimately, Temple and Nancy's language fails them, not because it lacks power, but because they are separated. The failure is anticipated by Temple's limited conception of the possibilities of their interaction. For her, Nancy is the listener that everyone needs:

> Somebody to talk to, as we all seem to need, want, have to have, not to converse with you nor even agree with you, but just keep quiet and

listen. Which is all that people really want, really need; I mean, to behave themselves, keep out of one another's hair; the maladjustments which they tell us breed the arsonists and rapists and murderers and thieves and the rest of the anti-social enemies, are not really maladjustments but simply because the embryonic murderers and thieves didn't have anybody to listen to them. (580)

The solution Temple proposes for people's need for listeners—"if the world was just populated with a kind of creature half of which were dumb, couldn't do anything but listen, couldn't even escape from having to listen to the other half" (580)—reveals how one-sided her interaction with Nancy has been. Temple's description of the evolution of a murderer implicates her in Nancy's guilt for the murder of her own child; she failed to fulfill her responsibility to listen to Nancy. (Temple's statement also indicates her tendency to assume too much guilt.) This failure of reciprocity—Temple's failure to transcend her own racist assumptions, which have led her to believe that Nancy will listen but prevented her from realizing that Nancy has subjectivity and thus has her own story to tell—contributes to their failure to tap the potential power of their relationship. The failure is not theirs alone, however, but clearly lies primarily in the conditions surrounding their relationship; the hope promised by their connection across racial difference, their love and ability to communicate, is torn apart by the hegemonic social structure. At the end of the play, Temple has called out longingly to Nancy, has desperately tried to hear what that woman has to say. In another textual move that asserts the similarities of their gendered experience, Nancy is enclosed in the prison, in Cecelia's former place, awaiting her execution. Temple acquiesces to Gowan's command for her presence, "Temple" (664), and leaves, contained between two symbols of patriarchal power, the husband and the lawyer. The final scene, therefore, fails to go beyond the two conventional endings of women's plots: marriage and death.

In the final prose section of the novel, which precedes Temple and Gavin's conversation with Nancy in the jail, Faulkner instructs readers in how to read. In this tutorial, Faulkner presents the idea of a living history by directly addressing and then leading the reader, as a stranger, on a journey of discovery into the prison, through the feminine space of the jailor's wife's kitchen, to the window with Cecelia Farmer's signature. The stranger creates a revisionist history of Cecelia Farmer, starting once again with the Civil War women's irreconcilability that had become a part of the mainstream culture: "instead of dying off as they should as time passed, it was as though these old irreconciliables were actually increasing in number" (642). The narrative projects that after a century, in 1965,

> not merely the pane, but the whole window, perhaps the entire wall, may have been removed and embalmed intact into a museum by an historical, or anyway a cultural, club of ladies,—why, by that time, they may not even know, or even need to know: only that the window-pane bearing the girl's name and the date is that old, which is enough; has lasted that long: one small rectangle of wavy, crudely-pressed, almost opaque glass, bearing a few faint scratches apparently no more durable than the thin dried slime left by the passage of a snail, yet which has endured a hundred years. (643)

In this way, Faulkner portrays women as the bearers of culture; they maintain its artifacts and pass down its oral history. The host thus answers the stranger's questions "out of the town's composite heritage of remembering that long back, told, repeated, inherited to him by his father; or rather, his mother: from her mother: or better still, to him when he himself was a child, direct from his great-aunt: the spinsters, maiden and childless out of a time when there were too many women because too many of the young men were maimed or dead" (644–645).

The host and the reader/stranger focus on Cecelia Farmer's signature, and the reader (the character in the text and, by implication and use of the second-person pronoun, the person reading the text) becomes a part of the history by becoming one of the creators of it:

> the faint frail illegible meaningless even inference-less scratching on the ancient poor-quality glass you stare at, has moved, under your eyes, even while you stared at it, coalesced, seeming actually to have entered into another sense than vision: a scent, a whisper, filling that hot cramped strange room already fierce with the sound and reek of frying pork-fat: the two of them in conjunction—the old milky obsolete glass, and the scratches on it: that tender ownerless obsolete girl's name and the old dead date in April almost a century ago—speaking, murmuring, back from, out of, across from, a time as old as lavender, older than album or stereopticon, as old as daguerrotype itself. (643–644)

Cecelia's writing has become active, moving, meaning creating. Indeed, the reader is described as having "heard that voice, that whisper, murmur, frailer than the scent of lavender, yet (for that second anyway) louder than all the seethe and fury of frying fat" (644). Cecelia's voice has become the embodiment of that elusive quality that draws people to live in towns such as Jefferson. The stranger imagines the soldier "drawn . . . by that impregnable, that invincible, that incredible, that terrifying passivity" of Cecelia's look (645). But Cecelia's passivity is an irreconcilable paradox for the stranger, whose created story is insufficient to explain "that passivity, that stasis, that invincible captaincy of soul which didn't even need to wait but simply to be, breathe tranquilly, and take food,—infinite not only in capacity but in scope too" (646–647). Through the stranger's interpretation, Cecelia becomes a strong, autonomous being with an "invincible cap-taincy of soul" who contrasts sharply with the frail, static girl bound by the prison window. By re-presenting Cecelia in this way, Faulkner highlights both the impact of point of view on historical representation and the importance of recovering female texts, hearing female voices, and reimagining female plots, thereby inviting a woman-centered reading of the novel.

The extended description of the stranger's interpretation of Cecelia Farmer also reveals how men read women as texts.[21] The stranger's imagination expounds until the image of Cecelia's face becomes "Lilith's lost and insatiable face drawing the substance—the will and hope and dream and imagination—of all men (you too: yourself and the host too) into that one bright fragile net and snare" (647). Suddenly the weak, anemic, almost ephemeral girl has become a fear-some trap. Men's compulsion to read women evokes a catalog of interpretations:

> among the roster and chronicle, the deathless murmur of the sublime and deathless names and the deathless faces, the faces omnivorous and insatiable and forever incontent: demon-nun and angel-witch; empress, siren, Erinys: Mistinguette too, invincibly possessed of a half-century more of years than the mere three score or so she bragged and boasted, for you to choose among, which one she was,—not *might* have been, nor even *could* have been, but *was*: so vast, so limitless in capacity is man's imagination to disperse and burn away the rubble-dross of fact and probability, leaving only truth and dream. (648)

Despite all these negative and ambivalent associations, Cecelia's signature is finally interpreted as a proclamation of identity: " '*Listen, stranger; this was myself: this was I*' " (649). Cecelia established her identity, and her existence in history, by writing her name.[22] The clear implication here is that women need to be read from a sympathetic, women-centered perspective and that women need to read themselves and write themselves. This call and the novel's association of violence against women's bodies with their exclusion from language anticipates Cixous: "Woman must write her self: must write about women and bring women to writing, from which they have been driven away as violently as from their bodies—for the same reasons, by the same law, with the same fatal goal. Woman must put herself into the text—as into the world and into history—by her own movement" (875). Cecelia's assertion of identity reverberates in Temple's deeply felt pride in the letters she wrote to Red. The writing, then, frees these white women's subjectivities from the public disciplinary narratives. That freedom parallels the independence Nancy achieved by refusing to answer those in the judicial system on their own terms. As the novel shows, however, such a liberation of the private self, while a necessary precursor to the transformation of those public narratives, is insufficient in and of itself to effect social change. The novel suggests that the connection of women across differences has the potential to counteract those narratives, to bring private liberation to a public space.

"The Image of You, True or False, Last[s] a Lifetime": Lillian Hellman's Memories of Black Women

Judith L. Sensibar attributes much of Faulkner's impetus for writing about race to his childhood relationship with Caroline Barr, the woman he called "Mammy" and to whom he dedicated *Go Down, Moses* (1942). She states:

> Much of Faulkner's racial unconscious springs (like that of most white middle- and upper-class Mississippians of his generation), from his doubly mothered childhood. Cultural conventions prevented him from ever fully acknowledging one of the two women who nurtured him. Often they required that she be demeaned. In contrast to Faulkner's eulogy for Caroline Barr, a public act conforming to those conventions, *Go Down, Moses*, a fiction, is both an act of true mourning and, in rare unguarded moments, of the liberation that true mourning brings. (110)

Reading his fiction through this biographical lens—and his biography through his fiction—Sensibar is able to unpack some of the complexities of Faulkner's presentation of racial issues. Interpreting both *Go Down, Moses* and the reason fiction enabled Faulkner to break out of the prescribed codes that constricted his public statements about Barr, she argues that the novel allowed Faulkner to explore his loss of Barr as well as his earlier loss stemming from his denial of his love for her:

> To identify not only with the feminine but with the black feminine is so shameful and so taboo that the feeling part of the self has to be killed. That loss, because one is never permitted to mourn for it, is always felt as a loss. . . . But his exploration throughout this novel and throughout

the record of *his writing* of this novel is, as always, fraught with an ambivalence often articulated as blatant racism. (108)

If, as Sensibar attests, fiction freed Faulkner to explore the relationships of white children and black maternal figures, the autobiographical mode appears to have enabled Lillian Hellman's exploration of her own passionate relationships with black women. The two authors were close in age: a mere eight years separates Faulkner's birth in 1897 from Hellman's in 1905. Faulkner's masterpiece *Absalom, Absalom!* appeared in 1931, three years before Hellman's first play, *The Children's Hour* (1934). However, more than three decades passed before Hellman changed genres and began writing autobiographically, and it is in those later works that she most clearly explored the meanings of her personal relationships. I examine her portrayals of her relationships with the two black women she discusses at length in her first two memoirs, the 1969 *An Unfinished Woman* and the 1973 *Pentimento*. Hellman's loving portraits of Sophronia, her childhood nurse, and Helen, the black woman who worked for years as her domestic, replicate much of the racism and sentimentality that Sensibar and others describe. Hellman's autobiographies are among the first to explore the complexities of such relationships at length, however. Although her conceptions of these women remain bound by cultural stereotypes of black women, Hellman's accounts reveal her own struggles with racism—struggles spurred first, perhaps, by her relationships with these women.[1]

I first wanted to include Lillian Hellman in my study of black and white women's relationships because of an image I remembered from "Pentimento," the chapter that concludes the book with the same title: Helen watching Hellman stare at a window in the building where she had planned for the ill and aging Dashiell Hammett to convalesce while she taught at Harvard. That particular form of grieving—Hellman's need to look at something connected to Hammett, even though he never stayed there—and Helen's watching Hellman compelled me. What did Helen see? And what did Hellman see, as she wrote the scene, recreating the moment?

The problem that arose when I went to write about that scene is that it does not exist. There is no moment in "Pentimento" when Helen watches Hellman stare at the nursing home in the wee hours of the morning. Hellman does tell us of her habitual insomnia-induced late-night walks to the hospital to stare at the window that she imagined would have been Hammett's room, but on the night she discovers that Helen has been following her, she turns back before she reaches the hospital and sees Helen standing with her friend Jimsie. This scene opens "Pentimento," the title chapter of Hellman's second autobiographical work, which she subtitled "A Book of Portraits." With her black domestic worker Helen, Hellman has moved to Cambridge, Massachusetts, to teach at Harvard. Dashiell Hammett was to move with them but died shortly before the trip. Although the image I remembered is not a part of the text, Hellman's reaction when she sees Helen epitomizes the complexities of her portrayal of her relationships with the two black women domestics she writes about extensively in her memoirs: "Long before I reached our corner I saw Helen, looking very black in her useless summer white raincoat, standing with a tall boy who was holding a motorcycle. I felt the combination of gratitude and resentment I had so often felt for her through the years, but I didn't want to waste time with it that night" (590). Hellman's dependence upon Helen's emotional support reveals that Helen's job entailed more than domestic chores, but Hellman's combination of "gratitude and resentment" also shows her ambivalence about her need for Helen and the limitations she placed on their intimacy.

Race is not the only problematic issue for Hellman as memoirist. A more visible pattern as she discusses her childhood and her relationship with her parents is the conflict she experiences between masculine and feminine, a conflict that inflects her choices throughout *An Unfinished Woman* (1969).[2] She presents her parents as rivals for her affections, which went primarily to her father and his family, people with whom her mother's family compared poorly. Although her idolized father provides a heroic figure and a standard for her own judgment and behavior, his necessarily masculine model leaves gaps for a female child, and Hellman does not find among the women in her extended family a role model that appeals to her. Within her immediate family, however, the mother–father dyad is complicated by the presence of Sophronia Mason, the African American woman who was Hellman's nurse in early childhood.[3] This triangle of caretakers affects her developing sense of identity. The history and culture of the South into which Hellman was born taught her to hold different definitions, perceptions, and expectations of white women and black women, but Hellman repeatedly turns first to Sophronia for guidance, approval, and love.

Sophronia is often the ideal for the young Hellman, whose love for this woman is the most strongly expressed emotion in the work. Hellman's relationship with Sophronia, then, is embedded in a complex web created by her parents' relationships to her and each other and by the gender and racial divisions and stereotypes of the time and place. Throughout the work, Hellman repeatedly characterizes herself as a rebel, and her first rebellion is her refusal to deny the importance of Sophronia in her life. In her 1949 *Killers of the Dream*, Lillian Smith says of the racist lessons she learned as a child, "Neither the Negro nor sex was often discussed at length in our home. We were given no formal instruction in these difficult matters but we learned our lessons well. We learned the intricate system of taboos, of renunciations . . . of manners, voice modulations, words, and feelings" (18). Smith also addresses the conflict white children cared for by black women experience when they realize that white social norms demand they deny their love for these women:

> I knew that my old nurse who had cared for me through long months of illness, who had given me refuge when a little sister took my place as the baby of the family, who soothed, fed me, delighted me with her stories and games, let me fall asleep on her deep warm breast, was not worthy of the passionate love I felt for her but must be given instead a half-smiled-at affection similar to that which one feels for one's dog. I knew but I never believed it, that the deep respect I felt for her, the tenderness, the love, was a childish thing which every normal child outgrows, that such love begins with one's toys and is discarded with them, and that somehow—though it seemed impossible to my agonized heart—I too, must outgrow these feelings. I learned to use a soft voice to oil my words of superiority. I learned to cheapen with tears and sentimental talk of "my old mammy" one of the profound relationships of my life. I learned the bitterest thing a child can learn: that the human relations I valued most were held cheap by the world I lived in. (28–29)[4]

Unwilling to deny her feelings and her need for Sophronia, Hellman rejects instead the racism she sees and rebels against the pressures to separate herself from her beloved caretaker, both physically and mentally. In her memoirs, she tries to revive that relationship.

Hellman's need for Sophronia is fueled, in part, by her need to distance herself from her parents, who she felt failed her in different ways, though she reports that she was far more critical of her mother. Hellman begins her account of her lineage by describing her mother's family. She portrays her maternal grandmother, "the silent, powerful, severe woman, Sophie Newhouse," as a fearsome matriarch who ruled her children's lives. "Her children, her servants, all of her relatives except her brother Jake were frightened of her, and so was I. Even as a small child I disliked myself for the fear and showed off against it" (13). Hellman's grandmother is just one of the sources of her ambivalent feelings toward these relatives, feelings that carry over into her concept of herself. Her visits with her mother as "the poor daughter and granddaughter" highlight for the child the family's preoccupation with class and finances and foster her resentment. She reports that the family homes "made me into an angry child and forever caused in me a wild extravagance mixed with respect for money and those that have it. The respectful periods were full of self-hatred and during them I always made my worst mistakes" (15). Family gatherings seemed more like board meetings, ruled by her grandmother and Uncle Jake, both "given . . . to breaking the spirit of people for the pleasure of the exercise" (14). The family members' repetitive contentious discussions of anticipated inheritances and current purchases annoyed Hellman and would later become sources for the satirical drama *The Little Foxes* (1939).

In contrast, Hellman's paternal aunts' stories created a far more favorable picture. They told of a venerable, lovable patriarch. Her aunt Hannah assured Hellman that her grandfather had allowed and even encouraged his children's individuality: "although whatever he said had been law, he had allowed my father and aunts their many eccentricities in a time and place that didn't like eccentrics, and to such a degree that not one of his children ever knew they weren't like other people" (26). The contrast between the two families was no doubt heightened by a child's limited perceptions, which Hellman admits distanced her from her mother: "It was not unnatural that my first love went to my father's family. He and his two sisters were free, generous, funny. But as I made my mother's family all one color, I made my father's family too remarkable, and then turned both extreme judgments against my mother" (15). Hellman's perception of the two families as antagonists was increased by her parents' rivalry, and her maternal family's flaws tarnished her mother's image just as her paternal aunts' adoration of her father polished his.

Hellman recognized that part of her parents' power struggle was conducted through efforts to win their only child's favor. She states:

> I was thirty-four years old, after two successful plays, and fourteen or fifteen years of heavy drinking in a nature that wasn't comfortable with anarchy, when a doctor told me about the lifelong troubles of an only child. Most certainly I needed a doctor to reveal for me the violence and disorder of my life, but I had always known about the powers of an only child. I was not meaner or more ungenerous or more unkind than other children, but I was off balance in a world where I knew my grand importance to two other people who certainly loved me for myself, but

who also liked to use me against each other. I don't think they knew they did that, because most of it was affectionate teasing between them, but somehow I knew early that my father's jokes about how much my mother's family liked money, how her mother had crippled her own children, my grandmother's desire to think of him—and me—as strange vagabonds of no property value, was more than teasing. He wished to win me to his side, and he did. He was a handsome man, witty, high-tempered, proud, and—although I guessed very young I was not to be certain until much later—with a number of other women in his life. Thus his attacks on Mama's family were not always for the reasons claimed. (18)

Her parents' struggles thus led Hellman to distance herself from her mother. Aligning herself with her father, she tended to view her mother largely from his perspective, and his stories of her mother's family clearly heavily influenced Hellman's perception. Partly because of her father's misogyny, the young Hellman interpreted her mother's femininity as weakness and refused to view her mother as a role model; she turned instead to her father and Sophronia.

Hellman uses the activity of writing her autobiography, in part, as an opportunity to reevaluate her mother's circumstances and actions from an adult's perspective. By balancing contrasting views from different periods of her own life, Hellman reimagines her mother, constructing a recuperative portrait of a woman that she can value. The autobiographer is able to see the paradoxical strength in her mother's apparent and sometimes transparent weakness that confused Hellman as a child: "simple natures can also be complex, and that is difficult for a child, who wants all grown people to be sharply one thing or another. I was puzzled and irritated by the passivity of my mother as it mixed with an unmovable stubbornness. . . . Mama seemed to do only what my father wanted, and yet we lived the way my mother wanted us to live" (16). Hellman also conveys the contradictions of her mother's character by presenting—yet simultaneously undercutting—the perspective of her aunts, with whom she and her mother lived for the half of each year that they did not spend in New York with her mother's family. Hannah and Jenny treated their sister-in-law as an exquisite guest in the boarding house they ran:

It was strange, I thought then, that my mother, who so often irritated me, was treated by my aunts as if she were a precious Chinese clay piece from a world they didn't know. And in a sense, that was true: her family was rich, she was small, delicately made and charming—she was a sturdy, brave woman, really, but it took years to teach me that—and because my aunts loved my father very much, they were good to my mother, and protected her from the less wellborn boarders. I don't think they understood . . . that my mother enjoyed the boarders and listened to them with a sympathy Jenny couldn't afford. (23)

The apparent contradiction and modification Hellman adds to her aunts' perspective is characteristic of the portraits she creates in her memoirs. Rather than give a static, definite interpretation, she juxtaposes illuminating moments and characteristics from her subjects' lives that capture a fluid range of behavior and traits, creating a more fully developed character.

When Hellman turns to her college years—a brief discussion that provides the transition from her childhood to adulthood, beginning with her first job—she again employs a maternal frame. By using her mother's reactions to contextualize her college experience, she illustrates the contradictions of their relationship: "My mother had gone to Sophie Newcomb College in New Orleans, and although the experience had left little on the memory except a fire in her dormitory, she felt it was the right place for me" (40). Despite the rather lackluster impression the college had left, her mother not only wanted Hellman to attend the same college but also evidently had the power to make the choice. However, her mother's falling ill kept Hellman in New York, at an extension of New York University, and her cursory description of her experience there is summed up in her statement that "college would mean very little to me" (41). She left without a degree because, as she puts it, "In my junior year, I knew I was wasting time." She withdrew, and her mother's reaction seems to contradict her initial investment in Hellman's choice of school: "My mother took me on a long tour to the Midwest and the South, almost as a reward for leaving college" (42).

Perhaps what Hellman most admires in her mother is the defiant fortitude she showed in marrying the man she loved, despite her own mother's disapproval: "My father had not been considered a proper husband for a rich and pretty girl, but my mother's deep fear of her mother did not override her deep love for my father, although the same fear kept my two aunts from ever marrying and my uncle from marrying until after his mother's death" (16). What makes Hellman's mother sympathetic to the reader, even more than Hellman's assertions of the woman's real strength, are the difficulties of her life as revealed through the details Hellman provides. A husband who not only cheated on her and competed with her for their daughter's love but who also failed to take her seriously, fostered contempt for her family, and thought her foolish; the unsettledness of living in two cities, with her own home in neither; and a lack of purpose or meaningful work, even when her child was very young, because Sophronia performed the child-care labor, constitute a portrait of a very lonely life. Hellman portrays her mother as kind but naïve; an eager but not astute "sympathetic listener" to the stories of strangers. Her penchant for bringing home strangers reveals the deep loneliness of her life: "sad, middle-aged ladies would be brought home from a casual meeting on a park bench to fill the living room with woe: plain tales of sickness, or poverty, or loneliness in the afternoon often led to their staying on for dinner with my bored father" (16). She clearly longed for the companionship of contemporaries, women friends with whom she could share her life, but such relationships would have been difficult to maintain, as she alternated living in New Orleans and New York.

Hellman conveys her mother's loneliness as a pastoral nostalgia, stating, "She liked a simple life and simple people, and would have been happier, I think, if she had stayed in the backlands of Alabama riding wild on the horses she so often talked about, not so lifelong lonely for the black men and women who had taught her the only religion she ever knew" (15). This projection of emotional and spiritual qualities onto blackness, imbibed from her Southern cultural heritage, translates, to some extent, into Hellman's own situating of morality in Sophronia and, later, Helen, the woman Hellman employed for years as a live-in domestic worker. Just as Hellman appears to believe that an African American presence would cure her mother's loneliness, she turns to black women to assuage her own. The strongest statement of Hellman's relationship with her mother abruptly culminates a humorous anecdote spun out of an account of her mother's naïveté: "My mother was dead for five years before I knew that I had loved her very much" (17). The statement contrasts starkly with her description a few pages later of Sophronia as "the first and most certain love of my life" (24).

A sense of loss pervades Hellman's memoirs and seems to stem from her longing not just for a closer relationship with her own mother but also for a model of womanhood that did not require the deceptive performance of weakness.[5] Among the women in her family, Hellman was unable to find an acceptable female role model. Her own mother, viewed partially from her father's perspective, was a confusing mix of pleasant flightiness, quotidian neuroses, and a determined will. Sophie Newhouse's domineering manner made her unappealing. And her strong and capable aunts Hannah and Jenny, a mutually supportive pair who together ran a boarding house that kept them at the center of a perpetually changing community, led single, hard-working lives that Hellman could not imagine for herself, though she loved and respected them both. As a child Hellman felt closest to her black caretaker, Sophronia, and turned to her for guidance.

Hellman recognizes the common cultural pattern of black women taking care of white children. She describes Sophronia as "a tall, handsome, light tan woman—I still have many pictures of the brooding face—who was for me, as for so many other white Southern children, the one and certain anchor so needed for the young years, so forgotten after that" (24). Hellman adamantly denies that such a rejection applies in her own case, however, adding parenthetically, "It wasn't that way for us: we wrote and met as often as possible until she died when I was in my twenties, and the first salary check I ever earned she returned to me in the form of a gold chain" (24–25). It is difficult to know how to interpret this exchange, which Hellman chooses as a way of signifying their continued attachment. Hellman's sending her first paycheck to Sophronia suggests the urgency with which she seeks Sophronia's approval in her childhood and indeed throughout her memoirs: Sophronia's reaction is often Hellman's first concern. Perhaps Hellman's wanting Sophronia to be proud of her is the reason she sent the actual check rather than a gift. Perhaps Sophronia's gift of the gold chain—an extravagant gift—was a sign of her affection and pride, a well-deserved reward, but given the taciturn personality that comes across as Sophronia's in the memoirs, it is difficult not to read her return of the gift as a rebuke too, a sign that she found Hellman's sending her money condescending. As is evident in her later relationship with Helen, Hellman is often blind to the inequities of race and class and fails to recognize that her status as employer (or employer's child) was one of the principal forces delineating her relationships with both women. Hellman's failure to realize the extent to which economics limited her personal relationships with Sophronia and later Helen often impeded her understanding of these women's perspectives. Hellman does not seem to realize that her generosity did not eliminate the power structure of the employer–employee relationship or the inequities between different socioeconomic classes. She persistently believes that she can exempt herself from the dominant racism of her culture through the force of her own will.

If Hellman's mother did not meet her child's emotional needs, neither did her father, whose adulteries and fights with his wife ultimately undermined his child's trust in his moral authority, despite her alliance with him. Hellman's relating to Sophronia as a maternal figure illuminates a common cultural pattern of black women caretakers as substitute mothers, but Hellman also found in Sophronia the stable authority and constancy sometimes lacking in her father. Hellman's frequent opposition of Sophronia's authority to her father's is telling. Hellman's narrative portrayal of her father indicates that he was aware of an unforeseen rivalry with the black woman he once employed. Although he could be assured of his victory over his wife, his preeminence in his daughter's affections remained insecure because of her love for Sophronia. Hellman's comments indicate that her father often resented Sophronia's power over his daughter, especially when it usurped his own: "Years later, when I was a dangerously rebellious young girl, my father would say that if he had been able to afford Sophronia through the years, I would have been under the only control I ever recognized" (24).

In a later chapter on Helen, at a point when Hellman is trying to figure out that woman's racial anger, Hellman returns to her memories of Sophronia and tells a story that is the first indication of Sophronia's own anger. The incident Hellman recounts illuminates not only Sophronia's character but also Hellman's parents', as well as her father's exasperation with his daughter's idolization of Sophronia. While Hellman and her father are waiting for a train, they see two white men taunting, circling, and finally catching a young black woman. The assault is both sadistic and sexual; the man who grabs the woman "put the lighted matches to her arm before he kissed her" (256–257). Hellman's father intervenes, wards off the men, and corrals the woman and his daughter onto the train, only to realize he does not know the whereabouts of his wife. Hellman's mother, undaunted, is returning the woman's possessions to her suitcase. Invoking her full racial and class privilege, she intimidates the men into submission:

> My mother was on the ground repacking the girl's valise. The two men were running toward her but she smiled and waved at my father and put up her hand in a gesture to quiet him. She had trouble with the lock of the valise but she seemed unhurried about fixing it. My father was halfway down the train steps when she rose, faced the two men and said, "Now you just step aside, boys, and take yourselves on home." I don't know whether it was the snobbery of the word "boys" or the accents of her native Alabama, but they made no motion as she came aboard the train. (257)

The incident reveals what Hellman worked so diligently to show in the earlier portion of *An Unfinished Woman*—that her mother knew how to use her Southern lady demeanor to achieve her ends and that she often displayed courage in doing so. Hellman's response to the incident, however, elicits her father's anger; she tells him, "You're a hero. Sophronia will be pleased" (257). Her father, annoyed, responds, "To hell with Sophronia. I don't want to hear about her anymore" (256).

When Hellman tells the story to Sophronia, the woman is at first silent, though with some prompting, she acknowledges Hellman's father's courage. When Hellman asks Sophronia what is wrong, Sophronia answers, "Things not going to get themselves fixed by one white man being nice to one nigger girl." Hellman writes that she "thought long and hard about that, as I thought about everything she said" (258), and she reports, as if it were a direct consequence of those words, that the following year she refused to move to the back of the bus, holding Sophronia by her. She screams at the conductor, "We won't move. This lady is better than you are—." As Sophronia gets off the bus, Hellman screams at her, "Come back, Sophronia, don't you dare move. You're better than anybody, anybody—" (258). A white woman hits Hellman and the conductor grabs her until Sophronia pulls her off the bus. Their conversation following this incident, as Hellman reconstructs it, reveals the tenderness of their relationship, the intensity with which the young Hellman looked to Sophronia for advice and guidance, and the severity of Sophronia's anger, realizing as she does the dangerous position her charge has put her in:

> After a while she said, "Crybaby."
> "I did wrong?"
> It was an old question and she had always had a song for it:
> > *Right is wrong and wrong is right*
> > *And who can tell it all by sight?*
> I said, "Sophronia, I want to go away with you for always, right now. I've thought a lot about it all year and I've made up my mind. I want to live with you the rest of my life. I won't live with white people any-more—"
> > She put her hand over my mouth. When she took it away, I knew she was very angry. She said, "I got something to tell you, missy. There are too many niggers who like white people. Then there are too many white people think they like niggers. You just be careful." (259)

Hellman's impulse to reject whiteness and embrace blackness angers Sophronia, who recognizes the fantasy as a product of racism.

After this exchange, Hellman is even more upset, because she fears Sophronia is rejecting her. She goes to her and asks, "Aren't you going to see me anymore?," to which Sophronia enigmatically replies, "I got a no good daughter and a no good son" (260). This invocation of familial relationships may suggest that Sophronia felt such a tie to Hellman, though what we have is Hellman's writing of her memory of the incident, so it may be Hellman's intent or subconscious that desires the implication. Hellman elicits the following explanation from Sophronia: "I mean you got to straighten things out in your own head. Then maybe you goin' to be some good and pleasure me. But if they keep pilin' in silly and gushin' out worse, you goin' to be trouble, and you ain't goin' to pleasure me and nobody else" (260). These comments are filled with contempt for the ways white people raise their female children. Clearly Sophronia did not want Hellman to embody the type of weakness that Hellman herself could not stand in her own mother, but interpreting the words in her autobiography, Hellman both renders the attack impersonal and ignores its racial content:

> Many years later, I came to understand that all she meant was that I might blow up my life with impulsiveness or anger or jealousy or all the other things that she thought made a mess, but that day, in my thirteenth year, I shivered at the contempt with which she spoke. (And there I was not wrong. I came to know as she grew older and I did, too, that she did feel a kind of contempt for the world she lived in and for almost everybody, black or white, she had ever met, but that day I thought it was only for me.) (260)

Hellman resists being made aware of Sophronia's racial anger and her critique of the construction of white femininity.

More comfortable with Sophronia's love than with her anger, Hellman instead clings to her romantic vision of their special relationship. Hellman describes her feelings as "maybe the kind of pain you feel when a lover has told you that not only does the love not exist anymore, but that it possibly never existed at all" (260–261). Hellman retorts, "You mean I am no good and you don't want to see me anymore. Well, I won't hang around and bother you—," but Sophronia tells her, "You all I got, baby, all I'm goin' to have." Similar to the previous incidents, this one closes with one of the acts of physical intimacy that Hellman describes as rare but that appear to have cemented moments into her memory. "Then she leaned down and kissed me. She hadn't kissed me, I think, since I was three or four years old. Certainly I have had happier minutes since, but not up to then. We shook hands and I went back to the park bench [where they had been meeting] the next day" (261). Such moments of emotional intimacy are conspicuously lacking in Hellman's descriptions of her interactions with her parents and are no doubt among the reasons for Sophronia's importance to her.

Given Hellman's father's ambivalence toward Sophronia, it is significant that her first act in Hellman's text is to reinforce his authority. The incident that leads to Sophronia's introduction in the text is Hellman's "accident" after she sees her father getting into a taxi with a woman from her aunts' boarding house and realizes that he is betraying her mother. The contextualization Hellman provides illuminates not only her parents' relationship but also the pain and confusion their antagonisms caused their child:

> there were two faded, sexy, giggly sisters called Fizzy and Sarah, who pretended to love children and all trees. I once overheard a fight between my mother and father in which she accused him of liking Sarah. I thought that was undignified of my mother and was pleased when my father laughed it off as untrue. He was telling the truth about Sarah: he liked Fizzy, and the day I saw them meet and get into a taxi in front of a restaurant on Jackson Avenue was to stay with me for many years. I was in a black rage, filled with fears I couldn't explain, with a pity and contempt for my mother, with an intense desire to follow my father and Fizzy to see whatever it was they might be doing, and to kill them for it. An hour later, I threw myself from the top of the fig tree and broke my nose, although I did not know I had broken a bone and was concerned only with the hideous pain. (24)

This response to the violence aroused in her by anger at others—releasing the emotional pain by inscribing it as physical pain on her own body—is, regrettably, one that Hellman will later repeat.

Although Sophronia is now employed by another family, Hellman runs to her. Sophronia is presented as protector, nurturer, source of love and care—embodying all the qualities associated with ideal motherhood when a child is hurt. She is also, however, ultimately presented as a disciplinarian and moral authority. She is, in effect, presented as the ideal parent. Hellman's description shows that Sophronia, like her father, was a hero of Hellman's childhood—and the one who did not disappoint her:

> She came, running, I think for the first time in the majestic movements of her life, waving away the two redheads. She took me to her room and washed my face and prodded my nose and put her hand over my mouth when I screamed. She said we must go immediately to Dr. Fenner, but when I told her that I had thrown myself from the tree, she stopped talking about the doctor, bandaged my face, gave me a pill, put me on

her bed and lay down beside me. I told her about my father and Fizzy and fell asleep. When I woke up she said that she'd walk me home. On the way she told me that I must say nothing about Fizzy to anybody ever, and that if my nose still hurt in a few days I was only to say that I had fallen on the street and refuse to answer any questions about how I fell. A block away from my aunts' house we sat down on the steps of the Baptist church. She looked sad and I knew that I had displeased her. I touched her face, which had always been between us a way of saying that I was sorry.

She said, "Don't go through life making trouble for people."

I said, "If I tell you I won't tell about Fizzy, then I won't tell."

She said, "Run home now. Goodbye." (25)

Hellman's romantic portrait of Sophronia's attention idealizes her; her advice is nevertheless difficult to accept, perhaps particularly for a reader with a twenty-first century perspective.[6] Her imposition of silence demands that Hellman accept and enact patriarchy's silence regarding men's adultery, thereby devaluing and dismissing Hellman's own pain as well as her mother's. The silence also reinforces Hellman's masochistic act of inflicting violence upon herself to release her anger at her father, even though Sophronia herself disapproved of that response. Sophronia's advice is practical; knowing when to keep silent is a useful survival skill, and one that is no doubt particularly crucial in her profession. Following the advice uncritically, however, creates confusion for Hellman, who diminishes the incident—"In any case, I soon forgot about Fizzy" (26)—to which she had first attributed such significance: "the day I saw them meet and get into a taxi in front of a restaurant on Jackson Avenue was to stay with me for many years" (24). The contradiction between these two statements shows the tremendous influence Sophronia exerted and the degree to which Hellman filtered her own reactions through Sophronia's eyes. Even much later, as she is writing her memoirs, Hellman accepts Sophronia's judgment; her idealization of Sophronia prevents her from considering why Sophronia gave her that advice.

The stoicism Hellman learned from Sophronia and the more evident strength of Sophronia's demeanor made her a more acceptable model of womanhood to Hellman than her own mother, whose endurance was cloaked in delicacy and the appearance of passive acquiescence. For Hellman, the alternative to such a weak stance was her anger, which she repeatedly values as a sign of strength. On this occasion, however, her anger is translated into silence, used not to give her the strength to express her emotions but to shield her from having to deal with them directly, or with the consequences that expression would have incurred. She learns to silence her anger at men's betrayal.

Years later, when Hellman is herself married, her father's promiscuous infidelities are again revealed to his wife and daughter, and Hellman once again is discomfited at her mother's response. A restaurant owner who knew her father in New Orleans jokes with him "about 'seven girlies' in . . . three days." Hellman reports that her

> mother's pleasant face changed so sharply that I thought she was sick. She went to the ladies' room and I followed her there. She was sitting in a chair, staring at the floor. I don't think we spoke, but I remember thinking that I had never in my life been jealous about a man and had contempt for what I was watching. A few years later, when I had gone to live with Dashiell Hammett, I remember being ashamed of that contempt and always wishing to apologize to my mother for it. (71)

Growing up, Hellman resisted identifying with her mother partly because she saw weakness and victimhood in her mother's pained reactions to her husband's infidelities. Reading the surface demeanors of the adults around her, she did not see that Sophronia's position as employee gave her far less power than her mother, whose powerlessness Hellman the autobiographer acknowledges was often a façade.

Hellman's account of her menarche, a passage into womanhood, again positions her father in opposition to Sophronia, as if Hellman felt that as a child she had to choose between them. The story she tells ends Hellman's Sophronia-influenced childhood and precedes her entrance into the predominately male work environment, whose "masculine" values Hellman's memoir has been criticized for endorsing.[7] The fourteen-year-old Hellman runs away from home following a particularly bitter fight with her father, who has returned from the jeweler angry at his daughter. He has discovered that the watch he gave her stopped working because she had put a boy's lock of hair in its back. Her refusal to explain what she has done increases his anger. Hellman parenthetically notes, "My father was often angry when I was most like him" (30), identifying her own stubbornness with his, and thereby praising the quality. The women in her family accede to her father's power and leave her to fight her battle on her own: "My mother left the room when my father grew angry with me. Hannah, passing through, put up her hand as if to stop my father and then, frightened of the look he gave her, went out to the porch" (31).

Hellman identifies the incident with her first awareness of the power of her own anger. She describes its power to control her but also implies that her anger gives her power.

> I tried to get up from the couch, but one ankle turned and I sat down again, knowing for the first time the rampage that could be caused in me by anger. The room began to have other forms, the people were no longer men and women, my head was not my own. I told myself that my head had gone somewhere and I have little memory of anything after my Aunt Jenny came into the room and said to my father, "Don't you remember?" I have never known what she meant, but I knew that soon after I was moving up the staircase, that I slipped and fell a few steps, that when I woke up hours later in my bed, I found a piece of angel cake—an old love, an old custom—left by my mother on my pillow. (31)

The women of her family have neither abandoned nor betrayed her, and Jenny, in fact, rescues her in a way by calling up some family knowledge, shared with her brother, a reference that curtails his anger, or calls his attention to the emotional state of his child. Hellman's mother's leaving the cake is a symbolic action of nurturance and solidarity. Nevertheless, the women's support neither questions nor overturns the father's authority, nor does it satisfy Hellman, who, upon awakening, leaves home.

She wanders around New Orleans, spends a night in a child's playhouse, and then goes to the train station, where she is too frightened to purchase a ticket. She spends her second night sleeping behind a shrub. The onset of cramps sends her to hide in a restroom. "After a while the cramps stopped, but I had an intimation, when I looked into the mirror, of something happening to me: . . . I had gotten older" (34). Afraid she will be recognized if she continues to wander the streets, she goes to a black neighborhood where she had gone as a child with Sophronia and where she remembers a clean and inviting boardinghouse with a pink door. Her initial attempts to gain entrance into the boardinghouse through thinly veiled lies are rejected. As Hellman recounts the dialogue, the woman dealing with her, frustrated, sends her away, stating, "This is a nigger house. Get you off. *Vite*," to which Hellman answers, "in a whisper, 'I know. I'm part nigger.'" She adds, " 'Please'—and then, 'I'm related to Sophronia Mason. She told me to come. Ask her' " (35). What comes across in this account is Hellman's desperate need to identify with Sophronia—to have some tangible connection, to have Sophronia be a recognizable, manifest part of her own identity in the way that family is. Her longing to hold on to her relationship with Sophronia is perhaps in part a longing to hold on to her childhood by clinging to the woman who nurtured her during her early years. Her willingness to cross the racial barrier—to claim that she embodies the miscegenation so taboo in her culture—also reveals a romanticization of blackness and the idealism of a child who believes that her culture's exclusive racial dichotomies are traversable.[8]

When the man who opens the door for her, suspicious because she has no suitcase, tells her to leave, Hellman relies on her status as a white woman to counter his command. He tells her, "I say you lie. I say you trouble. I say you get out." Hellman responds, "And I say you shut up." Hellman acknowledges her invocation of white privilege: "Years later, I was to understand why the command worked, and to be sorry that it did, but that day I was very happy when he turned and closed the door" (36). The incident reveals that although her longing for blackness may have involved a rejection of certain aspects of whiteness, it did not include a willingness to relinquish racial privilege. Rather, her assumption of her freedom to choose to cross racial lines is itself an expression of white privilege.

The next morning, both her father and Sophronia are there to order her home. When her father tells his crying daughter to "get up," she says she cannot, but when Sophronia tells her to, she comes out into the hall. Her father holds the position of authority, but Sophronia has the power to make Hellman move. Sophronia points to the door, signaling for Hellman to follow her father outside, but Hellman responds, "He humiliated me. He did. I won't . . ." When Sophronia makes what to Hellman is the ultimate threat—"Get you going or I will never see you whenever again"—Hellman hurries out, and the three of them walk to the streetcar. Hellman moves to go with Sophronia, but is turned away: "Sophronia bowed to us, but she refused my father's hand when he attempted to help her into the car. I ran to the car meaning to ask her to take me with her, but the car moved and she raised her hand as if to stop me" (37).

Her father mends the breach in their relationship with a joke, and Hellman confides in him that she is "changing life" (39). In the memoir, the event serves to reconcile the tension between Hellman's attempts to identify with both Sophronia and her father and marks her alignment with her father. This choice provides the transition to Hellman's adulthood and first job, where she works within the predominant white masculinist values. The acceptance of these values continues to cause conflicts for her conception of herself as a woman, and she will turn, toward the end of *An Unfinished Woman*, to another black woman as she attempts to come to terms with her mortality, her identity, and the importance of these two women, Sophronia and Helen, in her life.

In *An Unfinished Woman*, Hellman focuses on Helen, the employee who lived with her for many years, in her attempt to reconcile her sense of self with the cultural definitions of women.[9] Here, she presents her ruminations as the result of unconscious forces, "the digging about that occasionally happens when I am asleep" that produces "an answer to a long-forgotten problem, clearly solved" (250). Her revelation concerns the meaning for her of the two black women who were close presences in her life. She reflects, "Of course, one has been dead three years this month, one has been dead for over thirty, but they were one person to you, these two black women you loved more than you ever loved any other women, Sophronia from childhood, Helen so many years later" (250). Hellman has imaginatively combined these two women into one strong, nurturing, and stable moral presence. She wonders how she could conflate the identities of two women with such different personalities, and surely one answer is through their symbolic presence as black women. Hellman's awareness of the powerful symbolism attributed to black women's bodies comes across in her explanation of people's fondness for Helen despite the woman's brusque manner. She attributes that fondness mostly to the symbolism of Helen's body:

> The enormous figure, the stern face, the few, crisp words did not seem welcoming as she opened a door or offered a drink, but the greatest clod among them [Hellman's guests] came to understand the instinctive good taste, the high-bred manners that once they flowered gave off so much true courtesy. And, in this period of nobody grows older or fatter, your mummie looks like your girl, there may be a need in many of us for the large, strong woman who takes us back to what most of us always wanted and so few of us ever had. (254–255)

In Hellman's imagination, the comforting stereotype of the black mammy has in some ways superseded the qualities of the real woman she lived with for years. The women continue to return to Hellman in her dreams and force her to reckon with her own mortality:

> for weeks later, and even now, once in a while, I have dreamed of Sophronia and Helen, . . . I feel guilty because I did not know about Sophronia's death for two years after it happened, and had not forced Helen into the hospital that might have saved her. In fact, I had only been angry at her stubborn refusal to go. How often Helen had made

me angry, but with Sophronia nothing had ever been bad. . . . But the answer there is easy: Sophronia was the anchor for a little girl, the beloved of a young woman. (251)

Hellman's memories of these women are affected by her guilt, which is both racial guilt and the perhaps inevitable retrospective wish of the survivor that she had done more for them.

Hellman's relationship with Helen is far more conflicted than her relationship with Sophronia, and thus her memories of Helen reflect more than her longing for a nurturing presence. Frequently condescending to Helen, Hellman presents her understanding of the black woman's feelings as more accurate than the woman's own—as in her description of the older woman shortly before her death:

> marrow-weary with the struggle to live, bewildered, resentful, sometimes irrational in a changing world where the old, real-pretend love for white people forced her now into open recognition of the hate and contempt she had brought with her from South Carolina. She had not, could not have, guessed this conflict would ever come to more than the sad talk of black people over collard greens and potlikker, but now here it was on Harlem streets, in newspapers and churches, and how did you handle what you didn't understand except with the same martyr discipline that made you work when you were sick, made you try to forgive what you really never forgave, made you take a harsh nature and force it into words of piety that, in time, became almost true piety. (251)

Hellman also recounts two bitter fights she and Helen had about racial issues. These accounts reflect Hellman's attempt to confront the subject of race with Helen, but they also reveal Hellman's condescension to Helen, though Hellman admits that Helen's "feelings for white people and black people were too complex to follow, because what had been said on one day would be denied the next" (255).

Rather than pursue the complexities of Helen's attitudes and thereby credit Helen's thought and reflectively assess their relationship, Hellman slips back to a discussion of Sophronia. When Helen refuses to express anger toward white people, Hellman again presents her own understanding of Helen's feelings as more perceptive than that of the woman herself. Hellman is annoyed by what she calls "the Uncle-Tomism" of Helen's recollections of her childhood in the home of the Southern white family who employed her mother as a cook. When Helen says, "I ain't ever hated," Hellman's response reveals her insecurity about Helen's feelings toward her, an insecurity perhaps rooted in an awareness of the inequities in their relationship and the lingering racism she could not admit to herself: "I said, too fast, 'Yes, you have. You just don't know it—' and stopped right before I said, You often hate me, I've known it for years and let you have it as a debt I wouldn't pay anybody else but Sophronia" (255). Rather than explore the complexities of their feelings for each other, she falls into a reverie about Sophronia, for whom Hellman's feelings are less complicated by antagonisms.

Hellman's passionate longing for Sophronia erupts through the controlled voice of her text: "Oh, Sophronia, it's you I want back always. It's by you I still so often measure, guess, transmute, translate and act. What strange process made a little girl strain so hard to hear the few words that ever came, *made the image of you, true or false, last a lifetime?*" (255–256, my emphasis). This apostrophe enacts the same return of repressed desire as the dreams she describes at the beginning of the chapter, which bring back her memories of the women; it creates an intimate, emotional tone. This meditative tone does not necessarily represent a more authentic voice than the dominant, harder-edged one, though it certainly leads the reader to such a conclusion. Although it is indicative of the content's emotional import for Hellman, the exclamation also masks Hellman's evasiveness.

Her memory of Sophronia leads into the bus station story I have already discussed. The incident seems strangely placed in the chapter on Helen, rather than in the earlier chapters in which Hellman tries to show Sophronia's importance to her development. However, this incident presents a different picture than the earlier, idealized image of a strong, nurturing, dependable, and loving nurse; it reveals instead Sophronia's racial anger and her ambivalence toward her role in raising a child who is maturing into a white woman. Racial issues were the most heatedly problematic between Hellman and Helen, and in trying to come to terms with their arguments over race, Hellman must acknowledge and deal with Sophronia's anger as well.

Hellman fails to apply Sophronia's lesson in her interactions with Helen. The transition back to Helen immediately follows the happy closure of Hellman's account of her conflicts with Sophronia. In the scene Hellman sets, Helen stands holding a picture of Sophronia. Hellman identifies the woman and says that she herself as a girl was "trouble." Helen's response, "She didn't think so," enables Hellman to see the picture from a fresh perspective: "for the first time in the forty years since it had been taken, [I] saw the affection the woman had for the child she stood behind" (261).

When Helen mentions that Sophronia "was a light-skinned woman," Hellman becomes defensive, remarking in the memoirs,

"I know about that question, I've known about it all my life," and telling Helen that "she didn't use it, if that's what you mean" (261–262). When the topic becomes Sophronia's age, the conversation turns bitter. Helen says, "Black women get old fast," (262). Hellman grows angry when Helen refuses to criticize white women and turns the conversation into an ugly fight by bringing up slavery: "Colored women who cook as well as you do never had a bad time. Not even in slavery. You were the darlings of every house. What about the others who weren't?" (262). Helen answers, "You mean the good house nigger is king boy" (262). Hellman replies, "I mean a house nigger pay no mind to a field hand," at which Hellman says Helen "laughed at the words we had both grown up on," apparently ending the conversation (262). Hellman recounts this exchange without gloss. The irrationality of it—over and beyond a white woman's accusing a black woman somehow of being guilty for being the type of woman who was not treated as badly during slavery as other women of her race (as if that were not ludicrous enough)—is that historically slaves with lighter skin tended to be the ones chosen to work in the house. Sophronia's skin color might have been more beneficial than Helen's.

That Helen's laughter masks her anger becomes clear when later that day she tells Hellman, "You ain't got no right to talk that way. No right at all. Down South, I cook. Nothing else, just cook. For you, I slave. You made a slave of me and you treat me like a slave" (262). Calling Helen a liar, Hellman orders her to move out. She then goes to Hammett's, and it is his interpretation with which she agrees. He tells her she should not talk to Helen about the South, and that as she had as a child with Sophronia, Hellman has taken the exchange as a summation of the woman's feelings toward her. "I didn't think she hated me," she tells him. He corrects her: "She doesn't. She likes you very much and that scares her, because she hates white people. Every morning some priest or other tells her that's not Christian charity, and she goes home more mixed up than ever" (263). Both Hellman and Hammett interpret the fight through their understanding of race relations rather than listening to what Helen said and realizing both that Hellman made inappropriate accusations and that she was treating her employee unfairly. They enact their racial privilege in their presumption that they understand Helen's feelings better than she does herself.

Hellman's feelings upon her return home reveal her emotional need for Helen. She says that "on that day I did not wish to see the kitchen without Helen, did not want to face a life without her" (264). Helen is there and is formally cordial. That Hellman did not learn the lessons Sophronia realized she needed and hoped she would learn is evident not only in the manner in which she uses Sophronia—specifically by aligning herself with a product of Sophronia's body—to exempt herself from her own guilt but also in her condescension toward Helen in her final remarks about this fight:

> We did learn something that day, maybe how much we needed each other, although knowing that often makes relations even more difficult. Our bad times came almost always on the theme of Negroes and whites. The white liberal attitude is, mostly, a well-intentioned fake, and black people should and do think it a sell. But mine was bred, literally from Sophronia's milk, and thus I thought it exempt from such judgments except when I made the jokes about myself. But our bad times did not spring from such conclusions by Helen—they were too advanced, too unkind for her. (264–265)

Hellman assumes that her emotional dependence upon Helen is reciprocal, and she continues to demean Helen with simplistic praise, even though Helen clearly expressed her resentment and her understanding of how racism affected their relationship as employer and employee. Hellman's refusal to entertain the possibility of her own racism and her willingness to appropriate Sophronia's body results in her continued condescension to Helen. Although Hellman is at first annoyed that Helen does not express anger toward white people, she clearly did not anticipate that the anger would be directed at her.

In the final sentence of the paragraph quoted above, Hellman does, however, acknowledge that Helen "did not think white people capable of dealing with trouble," and the incident that follows presents Helen as more aware, knowledgeable, and capable than Hellman. That the specialized knowledge Hellman attributes to Helen concerns drug use unfortunately reinforces another stereotype. When Hellman went to Washington, D.C., to cover the famous 1963 march for *Ladies' Home Journal*, she was supposed to meet Sophronia's grandson Orin.[10] He was not there, but she met another man, George, who was traveling to New York the next week, and when he did he brought Orin to visit her. A boring man, Orin returns from a trip to the restroom more animated but less coherent. Helen informs Hellman, "He took a shot in the toilet," and when Hellman asks her, "What do you mean?," Helen responds, "A no good punkie-junkie. Maybe heroin." Helen's response startles Hellman: "The words were so modern, so unlike her, that I stared, amused and puzzled that there was a side of her I didn't know" (268). Hellman does not immediately believe her, but when they return to the room, Orin is playing music loudly, dancing, and acting even more bizarrely. Helen takes charge, confident that she can handle the situation, but she orders Hellman to leave: "She crossed to him, pulled his arms behind his back, and stepped to one side as he tried to kick her. She held him easily, gracefully, as she pulled him toward a chair. She said to me, 'Go for a walk,' and closed and locked the door" (269). When she explains the situation to Hellman, who she clearly felt would not comprehend on her own, Helen says, "You see, things happen to people." Later, she adds, "I locked the door 'cause I wanted you out of trouble," but Hellman states, "No. . . . You just didn't think I'd be any good at it" (269). Helen then reveals that her daughter, too, had a drug problem, and her attitude toward the South becomes clearer: "No good for colored people to come North, no good. . . . Live like a slummy, die like one. South got its points, no matter what you think. Even if just trees" (269).

A friendship develops between Helen and George, and he visits at Hellman's when he is in town. Through George, Hellman learns how little she really knows of Helen's life—that, for instance, every week she sent money to a nearby family who had been abandoned by the father. George's visit to Hellman the night of Helen's funeral closes the chapter. Hellman resists George's assertion that Helen knew she was going to die, until he tells her of all the errands Helen had him do for her in her last days, settling her accounts and sending away her clothes. And he tells her that Helen still occasionally gave money to Orin, who Hellman believed had long since disappeared. These details, and Hellman's contact with Helen's family members, reinforce for Hellman how little she knew of Helen's life.

The final, title chapter of *Pentimento* opens with the fact of Hammett's death and the scene I discussed at the beginning of this chapter. The grieving tone follows smoothly from the previous chapter, "Turtle," in which Hellman tells the story of how a turtle that she and Hammett trapped and that proved difficult to kill caused her to meditate on the meaning of life and death, and to question whether Hammett would be there for her when she died. Just as "Turtle," which opens with Hellman's recounting an incident of almost drowning and is framed by contemplations of death, is more revealing about Hellman's relationship with Hammett, "Pentimento," though framed by Hellman's mourning Hammett, actually centers on her relationship with Helen.

After finding Helen and Jimsie on her return home from the nursing home, Hellman says merely, "bad night," as she passes them and then goes to her room and "closed [her] own door against whatever she might say to me" (590), clearly wanting neither to explain her own behavior—the strange midnight walks—nor to share her grief. Although she has counted on Helen, and earlier in her life and to a greater extent, Sophronia, for moral advice, Hellman is now resistant, perhaps afraid that Helen knows her too well or will tell her what she does not want to hear. A few days later, Helen says only, "Death ain't what you think," to which Hellman responds, "I don't know what it is, do you?" Helen says, "A rest. Not for us to understand." Hellman reports that Helen began to elaborate but stopped herself: " 'You go stand in front of that place because you think you can bring him back. Maybe he don't want to come back, and maybe you don't—' she shrugged, always a sign that she had caught herself at something she considered unwise or useless to continue with" (591). In recounting this dialogue, Hellman conveys her respect for Helen's knowledge, despite her earlier frequent condescension. Her ambivalent feelings are matched by the odd mixture of awareness and ignorance about their relationship. She states, "It was a long time before I knew what she had been about to say," but she never tells the reader what it was.

Instead, she discusses Jimsie, who, on another night, follows her home after her vigil at the nursing home. On the way, Hellman says to him, "pentimento"; when he asks what the word means, she tells him not to follow her anymore. Hellman defines "pentimento" and its relationship to her work in the epigraph to the book:

> Old paint on canvas, as it ages, sometimes becomes transparent. When that happens it is possible, in some pictures, to see the original lines: a tree will show through a woman's dress, a child makes way for a dog, a large boat is not longer on an open sea. That is called pentimento because the painter "repented," changed his mind. Perhaps it would be as well to say that the old conception, replaced by a later choice, is a way of seeing and then seeing again.
>
> That is all I mean about the people in this book. The paint has aged now and I wanted to see what was there for me once, what is there for me now. (309)

When she says the word to Jimsie, it refers to her seeing again her relationship with Hammett, but the word also ends both the chapter and the book, this time when Jimsie refers to the night Hellman said it to him. He and Hellman have eaten dinner together, sometime shortly after Helen's death. Again Hellman turns to a male friend of Helen's only to find out how little she knew of Helen's life. When Jimsie says he loved Helen, Hellman responds, "Too bad you never told her so. Too late now" (599). However, Hellman is the one who never told Helen how she felt and who never reconciled their relationship, in all its intimacies and antagonisms, until she wrote about them in her memoirs.

CHAPTER 4

"The Very House of Difference": Audre Lorde's Autobiographies

Whereas Hellman's facing her own mortality leads to her reminiscences of Helen and Sophronia as she tries to construct a meaningful past, Lorde, in *The Cancer Journals* (1980), uses her illness, which forces her to confront her mortality, as a transformative experience through which she can construct a meaningful politics. She uses racial and gender analysis to understand her experience as a cancer patient; conversely, she uses that experience to develop her politics. In *An Unfinished Woman,* Hellman states that "by the time I grew up the fight for the emancipation of women, their rights under the law, in the office, in bed, was stale stuff. My generation didn't think much about the place or the problems of women, were not conscious that the designs we saw around us had so recently been formed that we were still part of the formation" (45). However, her account of her experiences proceeds to emphasize gender politics; likewise, her concerns with race and civil rights develop out of her need to understand her relationships with Sophronia and Helen. Whereas race and gender issues arise in Hellman's autobiographies as by-products of her experience, Lorde's emphasis on gender and race stems from the primacy of her commitment to feminist and antiracist politics. In both *The Cancer Journals* and *Zami: A New Spelling of My Name* (1982), she confronts race as one of many differences that divide women and forestall political activism.

In these works, Lorde uses different means to overcome racial divisions between women. In *The Cancer Journals,* while analyzing the intersections of gender and racial oppression, she tries to overcome the power of race to divide women by refusing to identify the race of the individual women in her stories. In this way, she counteracts the primacy that race is usually accorded in American culture. At the same time, her evasiveness about racial identity, by creating in the reader a desire to know the women's racial identity, emphasizes how much racial identity usually means.[1] By using this strategy in a text that emphasizes both the impact of race on lived experience in America and the problems of racism in the feminist movement, Lorde avoids replicating the erasure of race as an important component of identity, which is a problem in those attempts to unify women that universalize the experience of being a woman. *Zami*, on the other hand, addresses racial divisions largely by revealing Lorde's frustration when white women ignored racial difference and acted as if race did not matter. Lorde's aim is neither to ignore race nor to allow it to undermine unity. As Elizabeth Alexander states, "Lorde names differences among women . . . as empowering rather than divisive forces" (695). Referring to Lorde's simultaneous effort to recognize the many components of identity and to make them a unifying force, Alexander argues:

> The implications of this thinking for questions of identity are broad. For the self to remain simultaneously multiple and integrated, embracing the definitive boundaries of each category—race, gender, class, et cetera—while dissembling their static limitations, assumes a depth and complexity of identity construction that refutes a history of limitation. For the self to be fundamentally collaged—overlapping and discernibly dialogic—is to break free from diminishing concepts of identity. (696)

For Lorde, recognizing the overlapping aspects of identity requires a political stance that accounts for the intersections of oppressions.[2]

The Cancer Journals serves many of Lorde's political goals: uniting women in a feminist politics that recognizes the interconnection of all oppressions, emphasizing the importance of women's analyzing their own bodily experiences in the United States, and identifying the silencing forces of the dominant culture that disempower women. Cancer, in the text as in her life, is the impetus for cultural analysis; Lorde writes illness as political manifesto. She encourages other women to analyze their bodily experience, as her cancer has forced her to. Just as women have been alienated from the experience of their own bodies, they have been alienated from each other. They have been taught to interpret certain differences between women—such as race, class, and sexuality—as threats and insurmountable divisions, and the culturally mandated silence about these issues ensures their perpetuation.

For Lorde, recognition of the unity of experience of all women who have had breast cancer is a precursor to political action.

Beginning with her experience, and the political meanings it has for her, Lorde extends the concept of unity to include potentially all women. As Lorde states her purpose in the introduction:

> For other women of all ages, colors, and sexual identities who recognize that imposed silence about any area of our lives is a tool for separation and powerlessness, and for myself, I have tried to voice some of my feelings and thoughts about the travesty of prosthesis, the pain of amputation, the function of cancer in a profit economy, my confrontations with mortality, the strength of women loving, and the power and rewards of self-conscious living. (9–10)

This statement of purpose both makes important distinctions about the unity she establishes and gestures to the tensions that the remainder of her text will confront. Aware of the problems of universalizing statements, she cannot claim to speak for "all women." Nor can she ignore those differences—of race, class, sexuality—that carry significant cultural valence, usually to separate women. To work against those divisions, throughout the work when she speaks of the community of women who supported her, she specifies that those women "were black and white, old and young, lesbian, bisexual, and heterosexual" (20). Nevertheless, she recognizes the impact of women's differences and does not want to elide them. Rather, she interrogates the meanings and effects of those differences, and she groups women instead according to what she believes is politically important. She writes for those women "who recognize that imposed silence about any area of our lives is a tool for separation and powerlessness." She uses that belief throughout in an attempt to unify women as well as to convince women of the dangers of silence.

Even within the distinction she makes according to political belief, Lorde tries to avoid making the distinction antagonistic because she wants to respect those women who have made choices different from her own. In the work she powerfully analyzes how the presumed and pressured choice to wear a prosthesis as a curative return to normalcy that erases bodily difference for the postmastectomy woman serves to alienate women from their own bodies, dissuade them from analyzing—and hence acting upon—their experience, and render cancer victims invisible and thus powerless; nevertheless, she acknowledges and respects the strength of women who have chosen prosthesis "in a valiant effort not to be seen as merely victims" (9). For Lorde, wearing a prosthesis results in a denial of pain and a concomitant denial of the strength to be gained from the cancer experience. Despite her clear judgment of that choice and her earlier limitation of her audience, she attempts to assert the existence of a community of "all women with breast cancer":

> There is a commonality of isolation and painful reassessment which is shared by all women with breast cancer, whether this commonality is recognized or not. It is not my intention to judge the woman who has chosen the path of prosthesis, of silence and invisibility, the woman who wishes to be "the same as before." She has survived on another kind of courage, and she is not alone. Each of us struggles daily with the pressures of conformity and the loneliness of difference from which those choices seem to offer escape. I only know that those choices do not work for me, nor for other women who, not without fear, have survived cancer by scrutinizing its meaning within our lives, and by attempting to integrate this crisis into useful strengths for change. (10)

Lorde's attempt at such broad inclusiveness fails, however, because her arguments against prosthesis and all it implies for her are so strong.

In her attempt to assert an absolutely inclusive community of all cancer survivors *and* maintain her political purpose, Lorde constructs a group that in some ways ignores women's own interpretations of their experience: women who have chosen prosthesis are included in the group "whether this commonality [with other cancer survivors] is recognized or not." That inclusion denies other women's subjectivities; they cannot choose not to be in the group. Although Lorde qualifies her criticism of prosthesis by stating that her rejection of it is her own personal choice, that rejection seems crucial to the "painful reassessment" by which she defines the group. Even as Lorde attempts to validate the bravery and survival of women who choose prosthesis and to cast herself as nonjudgmental, her judgment is clear. And indeed those choices—of prosthesis, silence, invisibility, and conformity—become the meaningful differences with which Lorde describes women in the work. All the choices except prosthesis implicate all women, not just those who have had cancer, and, in fact, given the interconnectedness of oppressions Lorde stresses throughout *The Cancer Journals*, prosthesis can be read as not merely the prosthetic breast but also the symbol of all the devices and means women use to try to make their bodies conform to cultural standards of normalcy and beauty. Silence, the overarching theme with which Lorde characterizes the effect of all such choices of conformity, becomes the resonant destructive force, the choice that is complicit in the perpetuation of all oppression.

In her introduction, Lorde establishes the political connections she makes between breast cancer and other forms of cultural violence largely by including journal entries written during her recovery. The underlying cultural violence Lorde perceives encompasses the environmental causes of her cancer, the lack of research into a cure, the perverse and pervasive commodification of women's bodies, and the brutal slaying of black men. As her experience with cancer holds both personal and political meanings for her, she suffers the pain of both individual and collective loss. Her commitment to her recovery, therefore, becomes an integral part of her political commitment to working to improve the world in which we live. Her individual suffering exacerbates her sense of isolation and despair, as well as her empathic suffering, which she registers as bodily pain:

2/5/79
The terrible thing is that nothing goes past me these days, nothing. Each horror remains like a steel vise in my flesh, another magnet to the flame. Buster has joined the rolecall of useless wasteful deaths of young Black people; in the gallery today everywhere ugly images of women offering up distorted bodies for whatever fantasy passes in the name of male art. Gargoyles of pleasure. Beautiful laughing Buster, shot down in a hallway for ninety cents. (11, journal entries italicized throughout text)

Lorde's montage of painful incidents evokes a visceral reaction to complement her intellectual analysis. The journal entries are among the means by which she avoids letting her argument become abstracted; the abstract principles are always connected to individual, personal, material experience. As Alexander attests, Lorde "in-corporates the intellectual and physical aspects of her life, reminding the reader that the metaphysical resides in a physical space, the body" (697).[3] In her radical feminist interpretation, all the forms of violence are interconnected and require fundamental societal change. Cancer becomes the bridge between private and public that instigates that analysis. The racist and misogynist violence that is the subject of this passage connects breast cancer to the larger question of whose bodies are valued in the culture.

Lorde's holistic vision could, however, be overwhelming for her on a personal level, and one journal entry begins, "*the enormity of our task, to turn the world around*" (11). Her recognition of the interconnectedness of oppressions and the need for unified political commitment is balanced by her awareness that the very cultural forces she is fighting—particularly racism, classism, and sexism—can undermine a political movement's unity. As she expresses her frustration, she focuses on the race and class divisions among feminists:

> 9/79
> *There is not room around me in which to be still, to examine and explore what pain is mine alone—no device to separate my struggle within from my fury at the outside world's viciousness, the stupid brutal lack of consciousness or concern that passes for the way things are. The arrogant blindness of comfortable white women. What is this work all for? What does it matter whether I ever speak again or not? I try. The blood of black women sloshes from coast to coast and Daly says race is of no concern to women. So that means we are either immortal or born to die and no note taken, un-women.* (12)

Mary Daly becomes representative of those feminists who have downplayed the importance of race and class in order to isolate the effects of gender oppression.

Lorde's analysis of race in Daly's *Gyn/Ecology* (1978) lays out many of the issues and arguments developed by later critics who analyze the act of interracial reading, including white critics' ignoring African and/or African American history and culture; selectively using black women as negative examples or appropriating their words to support the aims of white feminism; and treating white women's experience as representative and thus normative for all women, thereby rendering women of color either deviant or invisible. The relevance of those arguments prompts me to digress from *The Cancer Journals* to discuss Lorde's letter to Daly.

Daly sent a copy of her *Gyn/Ecology* to Lorde, who responded with a letter thanking Daly for the book and expressing appreciation for the helpfulness of her work in general but also holding Daly account-able for and asking her to respond to the deployment of race in the book. After four months, having received no reply from Daly, Lorde published her missive as "An Open Letter to Mary Daly." In the let-ter, Lorde asserts her confidence in Daly's "good faith toward all women" and says that she wants to create a dialogue with Daly about race, "a joint clarification of some of the differences which lie between us as a Black and a white woman" (*Sister Outsider* 67). Lorde also refers to their first meeting at a 1977 MLA panel:

> This letter attempts to break a silence which I had imposed upon myself shortly before that date. I had decided never again to speak to white women about racism. I felt it was wasted energy because of destructive guilt and defensiveness, and because whatever I had to say might better

be said by white women to one another at far less emotional cost to the speaker, and probably with a better hearing. (*Sister Outsider* 70)

This passage reveals Lorde's wariness of discussing racial issues with white women and her awareness of the potential personal costs of such interactions.[4] As *The Cancer Journals* makes clear, her stance had changed.

Lorde's letter is rooted in the importance of history—both the effects of the historical relationships of black and white women and the importance of black history. She begins with the impediment the history of black and white women's relationships poses to communication:

> The history of white women who are unable to hear Black women's words, or to maintain dialogue with us, is long and discouraging. But for me to assume that you will not hear me represents not only history, perhaps, but an old pattern of relating, sometimes protective and sometimes dysfunctional, which we, as women shaping our future, are in the process of shattering and passing beyond, I hope. (*Sister Outsider* 66–67)

She criticizes Daly for the racially biased selections in her book: Daly uses only "white, western european, judeo-christian" goddesses in the first section, which discusses myth. Lorde asks, "Where was Afrekete, Yemanje, Oyo, and Mawulisa? Where were the warrior goddesses of the Vodun, the Dahomeian Amazons and the warrior-women of Dan?" (67). Such exclusions, Lorde continues, "dismissed my heritage and the heritage of all other noneuropean women, and denied the real connections that exist between all of us" (68). Lorde asserts that the power of these goddesses, too, should be made available to all women, asserting that "the old traditions of power and strength and nurturance found in the female bonding of African women . . . is there to be tapped by all women who do not fear the revelation of connection to themselves" (69). Lorde thus argues that *Gyn/Ecology* not only excludes many women by making white Western European history normative but also undermines, through its exclusions, the very unity it attempts to create.[5]

Lorde also criticizes the way Daly includes women of color: "dealing with noneuropean women . . . only as victims and preyers-upon each other" (67). She feels that Daly's use of an excerpt from one of Lorde's poems, "A Sewerplant Grows in Harlem, or, I'm a Stranger Here Myself When Does the Next Swan Leave," for the epigram to that chapter appropriates her words:

> Then, to realize that the only quotations from Black women's words were the ones you used to introduce your chapter on African genital mutilation made me question why you needed to use them at all. For my part, I felt that you had in fact misused my words, utilized them only to testify against myself as a woman of Color. For my words which you used were no more, nor less, illustrative of this chapter than "Poetry Is Not a Luxury" or any number of my other poems might have been of many other parts of *Gyn/Ecology*. (68)

Lorde describes Daly's use of epigrams as "another instance of the knowledge, crone-ology and work of women of Color being ghettoized by a white woman dealing only out of a patriarchal western european frame of reference" (68). As she criticizes Daly for employing the words of black women only when the subject is racial, she employs Daly's own terminology, thereby validating the usefulness of Daly's methodology and gesturing toward creating a dialogue that furthers their work and feminism. That dual move—criticism as both corrective and community building—is characteristic of Lorde's work.

In criticizing Daly for tokenism, Lorde distinguishes between mining black women's works to support preconceived ideas and reading them to learn from them. She asks Daly to examine her reading experience: "Have you read my work, and the work of other Black women, for what it could give you? Or did you hunt through only to find words that would legitimize your chapter on African genital mutilation in the eyes of other Black women?" (69). She wants Daly (and by implication other women) to learn from her words, by using them to question their ideas and experiences, not to reaffirm "an already conceived idea concerning some old and distorted connection between us" (68). In this way, she expresses her desire that her literary work will perform the same role that cancer has played in her own life: an impetus for critique that leads to a better understanding of the world. She perceives her writing as an agent for feminist change and warns Daly to

> be aware of how this [dismissal of black women] serves the destructive forces of racism and separation between women—the assumption that the herstory and myth of white women is the legitimate and sole herstory and myth of all women to call upon for power and background, and that nonwhite women and our herstories are noteworthy only as decorations, or examples of female victimization. I ask that you be aware of the effect that this dismissal has upon the community of Black

women and other women of Color, and how it devalues your own
words. This dismissal does not essentially differ from the specialized
devaluations that make Black women prey, for instance, to the murders
even now happening in your own city. When patriarchy dismisses us, it
encourages our murderers. When radical lesbian feminist theory
dismisses us, it encourages its own demise. (69)

Here she makes the same connection between individual and communal
meanings as she makes throughout *The Cancer Journals* regarding her
illness: her cancer is an individual instance of widespread violence and
suffering.[6] Daly's book exemplifies the ignoring of black women; such
ignorance contributes to and allows cultural violence directed against
women of color. Lorde wants white women to interpret the world
with an awareness of the effect of racism, even when race is not the
subject. She wants white women to read black women's works with an
awareness that they are reading across race in a racist culture, and to
be responsible in, and accountable for, their use of the words of
women of color.

Lorde emphasizes that eliding race is problematic for white women
as well as black women because it replicates the invisibility that
enforces the separation of women: "To imply . . . that all women suffer the same oppression simply because we are women is to lose sight
of the many varied tools of patriarchy. It is to ignore how those tools
are used by women without awareness against each other" (67). She
points out that white women's relationships with black women are
not constituted solely of exploitation. Their history is also a history of
affection and love, however limited and complex; therefore "to
dismiss our Black foremothers may well be to dismiss where white
women learned to love" (67). By emphasizing this point, Lorde
stresses that the inclusiveness she asks for is as urgent for white women
as it is for black women. The global scope of Daly's topics indicates
that she had aimed for such inclusiveness; chapter titles include "Indian
Suttee," "Chinese Footbinding," "African Genital Mutilation,"
"European Witchburnings," and "American Gynecology." Lorde's
criticisms indicate both the difficulty of overcoming ethnocentrism
and the limitation of early radical feminism's assertion that gender was
the primary site of cultural oppression.

Exclusion is a social as well as a textual problem, of course, and
much of Lorde's critical work demands that the feminist movement
end its exclusivity, include poor women and women of color, and
recognize the crucial differences between their experience of oppression and that of the middle-class white women whose concerns had

predominated. For Lorde, political unity and community does not mean ignoring difference; rather, she views recognizing difference as necessary for community. The position created by her multiple oppressions gives her a perspective that is constantly questioning even as it subjects her to multiple exclusions:

> 10/3/79
> *I don't feel like being strong, but do I have a choice? It hurts when even my sisters look at me in the street with cold and silent eyes. I am defined as other in every group I'm a part of. The outsider, both strength and weakness. Yet without community there is certainly no liberation, no future, only the most vulnerable and temporary armistice between me and my oppression.* (12–13)

This passage, as well as Lorde's description of her young white friends in *Zami*, indicates the pressure Lorde felt to be strong as a black woman.[7]

The first chapter of *The Cancer Journals*, "The Transformation of Silence into Language and Action," chronicles Lorde's first brush with breast cancer, when she underwent a biopsy that revealed a growth to be benign, and develops the connection Lorde makes between survival and speaking. Originally delivered at the "Lesbian and Literature" panel at the 1977 MLA, the chapter retains the persuasive qualities of a speech. It becomes clear that silence is threatening in the same way that illness is, that silence *is* illness—culturally imposed, psychic and physical. Lorde's brush with mortality forced her to reconceptualize the fear that had kept her silent and to realize that although speaking could at times seem dangerous, silence offers no protection. The experience leads her to emphasize both unity and differences among women. Breaking silences becomes an act that unifies women across difference:

> I was going to die, if not sooner then later, whether or not I had ever spoken myself. My silences had not protected me. Your silence will not protect you. But for every real word spoken, for every attempt I had ever made to speak those truths for which I am still seeking, I had made contact with other women while we examined the words to fit a world in which we all believed, bridging our differences. And it was the concern and caring of all those women which gave me strength and enabled me to scrutinize the essentials of my living.
>
> The women who sustained me through that period [waiting to find out if she had cancer] were black and white, old and young, lesbian, bisexual, and heterosexual, and we all shared a war against the tyrannies

of silence. . . . Within those weeks of acute fear came the knowledge—
within the war we are all waging with the forces of death, subtle and
otherwise, conscious or not—I am not only a casualty, I am also a
warrior. (20–21)

By choosing to identify herself as a warrior and not a victim or
survivor, Lorde links her fight against cancer to political activism. Just
as she questions the efficacy of her culture's language in the introduction, asking, "shall I unlearn that tongue in which my curse is
written?" (11), in this chapter she urges women to find and create the
words they need to describe their experience. She points out
that women have been taught to react to difference with fear and that
this reaction enforces their silence. Linking the personal and political
struggles to language, she challenges her audience to find the
language they need:

What are the words you do not yet have? What do you need to say?
What are the tyrannies you swallow day by day and attempt to make
your own, until you will sicken and die of them, still in silence? Perhaps
for some of you here today, I am the face of one of your fears. Because
I am woman, because I am black, because I am lesbian, because I am
myself, a black woman warrior poet doing my work, come to ask you,
are you doing yours? (21)

By naming and claiming her differences and connecting them to her
identity as a warrior, she appropriates the power of those differences
for her challenge, turning what had been used against her into a
strength. By speaking what is meant to remain unspoken—the
connection of her identity categories to the fear they are meant to
arouse in other women—she disables the power of that fear. She lists
the identifying labels—"woman," "black," "lesbian"—and redefines
their associations by proclaiming herself "a black woman warrior poet
doing my work"; she gives herself an active role and challenges other
women to do the same. Lorde connects the fear that enforces silence
to oppression—explicitly to racial oppression, but by analogy implicitly to gender oppression.[8] She also connects her analysis of silence
to the contradictions of visibility. To remain silent and invisible is to
remain powerless; she acknowledges, however, that being visible and
audible renders one vulnerable:

In the cause of silence, each one of us draws the face of her own fear—
fear of contempt, of censure, or some judgment, or recognition, of
challenge, of annihilation. But most of all, I think, we fear the very

visibility without which we also cannot truly live. Within this country where racial difference creates a constant, if unspoken, distortion of vision, black women have on one hand always been highly visible, and so, on the other hand, have been rendered invisible through the depersonalization of racism. Even within the women's movement, we have had to fight and still do, for that very visibility which also renders us most vulnerable, our blackness. For to survive in the mouth of this dragon we call america, we have had to learn this first and most vital lesson—that we were never meant to survive. Not as human beings. And neither were most of you here today, black or not. And that visibility which makes us most vulnerable is that which also is the source of our greatest strength. Because the machine will try to grind you into dust anyway, whether or not we speak. We can sit in our corners mute forever while our sisters and our selves are wasted, while our children are distorted and destroyed, while our earth is poisoned, we can sit in our safe corners mute as bottles, and we still will be no less afraid. (21–22)

Using the overlapping metaphors of silence and invisibility, Lorde calls attention to the means by which oppression works: because the oppressed are afraid, they keep themselves silent; because their subjectivities are invisible to the dominant culture, they must find new ways of using language in order to be heard.

Lorde calls for other women to break these silences by committing themselves to learning and teaching about women without being intimidated by difference. She connects the need for language to the cause of unity—women's responsibility to their own and one another's words:

And where the words of women are crying to be heard, we must each of us recognize our responsibility to seek those words out, to read them and share them and examine them in their pertinence to our lives. That we not hide behind the mockeries of separations that have been imposed upon us and which so often we accept as our own: for instance, "I can't possibly teach black women's writing—their experience is so different from mine," yet how many years have you spent teaching Plato and Shakespeare and Proust? Or another: "She's a white woman and what could she possibly have to say to me?" Or, "She's a lesbian, what would my husband say, or my chairman?" Or again, "This woman writes of her sons and I have no children?" And all the other endless ways in which we rob ourselves of ourselves and each other. (23)

By stating that we are to examine the words of other women "in their pertinence to our lives," she suggests that women's words are relevant to other women, even across their differences. As Valerie Smith points out, an initial effort in the study of women's literature was the crucial recovery of women's texts, and Lorde's sentiments appear to capture that spirit. However, as later critics have recognized, when women's texts are interpreted solely within the context of their readers' lives, important aspects of difference can be obliterated. Lorde's passage gestures toward that concern. Her reference to Plato and Proust critiques traditional education: Western literature teachers and critics have been trained in Western European men's history and know how to present authors such as Shakespeare in their historical context. Lorde implies that teachers and critics likewise need to learn other cultural contexts.

When Lorde describes her cancer diagnosis and her painful recovery following her mastectomy, she addresses more explicitly the structures that keep women silenced and distanced from their own bodies. Her experience of treatment reveals the institutional forces that resist women's analysis of their experience.[9] She writes: "I want to illuminate the implications of breast cancer for me, and the threats to self-revelations that are so quickly aligned against any woman who seeks to explore those questions, those answers. Even in the face of our own deaths and dignity, we are not to be allowed to define our needs nor our feelings nor our lives" (25). The community of women gathered around her sustains her, but she has difficulty thinking clearly for days after the surgery. The anesthesia, the impersonal protocol of the hospital, the numbing whiteness of the walls, and the antiseptic surroundings conspire with the shock of her loss to keep her from experiencing her emotions or questioning her experience. The physical pain contributes to her inability to think, and Lorde argues that this pain provides the time during which others start trying to determine how she will deal with her mastectomy:

> My main worry from day three onward for about ten more was about the developing physical pain. This is a very important fact, because it is within this period of quasi-numbness and almost childlike susceptibility to ideas (I could cry at any time at almost anything outside of myself) that many patterns and networks are started for women after breast surgery that encourage us to deny the realities of our bodies which have just been driven home to us so graphically, and these old and stereotyped patterns of response pressure us to reject the adventure and exploration of our own experiences, difficult and painful as those experiences may be. (41)

Lorde wants to learn from her experience, but her efforts to do so are repeatedly stymied by those who provide her treatment.

This appropriation of her experience begins with a visit from the official representative of Reach for Recovery, an American Cancer Society program. Lorde describes this woman as one

> of admirable energies who clearly would uphold and defend to the death those structures of a society that had allowed her a little niche to shine in. Her message was, you are just as good as you were before because you can look exactly the same. Lambswool now, then a good prosthesis as soon as possible, and nobody'll ever know the difference. But what she said was, "*You'll* never know the difference," and she lost me right there, because I knew sure as hell *I'd* know the difference?' " (42)

In her description, Lorde emphasizes this woman's choices in terms of Lorde's feminist political beliefs. As she confirms that she cannot tell which of the woman's breasts is prosthetic, she adds, "in her tight foundation garment and stiff, up-lifting bra, both breasts looked equally unreal to me" (42). The differences Lorde establishes are political: "I thought what a shame such a gutsy woman wasn't a dyke, but they had gotten to her too early, and her grey hair was dyed blond and heavily teased" (43). Lorde avoids explicitly naming the woman's race and postpones naming her identity categories; she specifies instead what the woman is not by stating, "I looked away, thinking, 'I wonder if there are any black lesbian feminists in Reach for Recovery?' " (42).

Lorde does not identify the race of other women who visit her. The resulting indeterminacy emphasizes several of Lorde's themes: the definitional division of women that makes race not only the first way we define women but also a necessary thing to know before you can know a woman, the economic division of women that makes it far more likely that a woman can claim some small area of power if she is white, and finally, that the significant difference is a woman's politics—whether she is committed to other women or to the prevailing power structure of the culture. Even given the last difference, the difference that separates women, however, Lorde admires the Reach for Recovery woman's strength and recognizes her as part of the community of women.

Indeed, throughout the discussion of her recovery, Lorde emphasizes the primacy of her connection to other women; "I say the love of women healed me," she states (39). When she discusses the lessons she has learned from other women, she does not limit the teachers to the women she loves; she argues, "one never really forgets the primary lessons of survival, if one continues to survive. If it hadn't been for a lot of women in my lifetime I'd have been long dead. And some of them were women I didn't even like! (A nun; the principal of my high school; a boss)" (39–40).

Lorde continues to be pressured to conform. A nurse forces her to wear the lamb's-wool prosthetic breast when she leaves the hospital, even though she does not want to, and when she arrives at the doctor's office to have her stitches removed, another nurse chastises her for not wearing a prosthesis, telling her, "we really like you to wear something, at least when you come in. Otherwise it's bad for the morale of the office" (59). Lorde records her shock at this "assault on my right to define and to claim my own body" (59), but comes to recognize "that the attitude towards prosthesis after breast cancer is an index of this society's attitudes towards women in general as decoration and externally defined sex object" (60). For Lorde, the fundamental purpose of prosthesis is to hide difference, a purpose that she connects to silence and invisibility. She argues that

> it is that very difference which I wish to affirm, because I have lived it, and survived it, and wish to share that strength with other women. If we are to translate that silence surrounding breast cancer into language and action against this scourge, then the first step is that women with mastectomies must become visible to each other. For silence and invisibility go hand in hand with powerlessness. (61)

Lorde acknowledges that although she was determined to learn and grow from this experience, she also at times wanted not to deal with it, and she criticizes the medical establishment for encouraging this denial by treating breast cancer "as a cosmetic problem" (55). The woman from Reach for Recovery wanted to discuss appearance and embarrassment, not survival.

For Lorde, the "emphasis upon prosthesis . . . encourages [a woman] not to deal with herself as physically and emotionally real" (57). By hiding the physical effects of surgery and concentrating on appearance rather than experience, the medical establishment resists "the need for every woman to live a considered life" (57). A woman then "must mourn the loss of her breast in secret, as if it were the result of some crime of which she is guilty" (57). The focus on appearance also, Lorde argues, keeps women from questioning their cancer treatment:

> For as we open ourselves more and more to the genuine conditions of our lives, women become less and less willing to tolerate those conditions unaltered, or to passively accept external and destructive controls

over our lives and our identities. Any short-circuiting of this quest for self-definition and power, however well-meaning and under whatever guise, must be seen as damaging, for it keeps the post-mastectomy woman in a position of perpetual and secret insufficiency, infantilized and dependent for her identity upon an external definition by appearance. In this way women are kept from expressing the power of our knowledge and experience, and through that expression, developing strengths that challenge those structures within our lives that support the Cancer Establishment. (58)

Lorde connects these efforts to keep women from questioning their cancer experience to a larger cultural effort to prevent women from analyzing their experience of their bodies and the ways women's bodies are treated. She uses her experience of cancer treatment as an example of the ways women are treated in society, and she contrasts that demeaning treatment with her vision of women in active engagement with their lives.

Lorde describes her early lessons about race and racism in her "biomythography" *Zami*. Alexander defines Lorde's experimental genre as "neither autobiography, biography, nor mythology; biomythography is all of those things and none of them, a collaged space in which useful properties of genres are borrowed and reconfigured according to how well they help tell the story of a particular African-American woman's life" (696). In *The Cancer Journals*, Lorde combined journal entries, speeches, personal narrative, and political analysis; in *Zami* she creates a new genre to convey her vision of her life in its connection to other women's stories and cultural myths. As Linda Wagner-Martin has argued, such experimental structures are characteristic of writing by women, who have had to invent ways to tell their stories, which often did not fit into traditional narrative modes: "It [women's fiction] has adopted some distinctive narrative structures. The most obvious is the work that collects fragments of story and juxtaposes them, mixing chronology or narrators or themes, in a design that forces readers to supply personal connections" (*Telling Women's Lives* 29).

Lorde's account in *Zami* of the racism she experienced matches much of the criticism that has been levied against the women's movement by women of color. Her family did not talk about race or racism, so Lorde had no language to describe the racism she experienced in grammar school. AnaLouise Keating connects the confusion her family's silence caused Lorde to her emphasis on the importance of language and her affirmation of difference:

The personal and cultural confusion Lorde describes in *Zami* illustrates an important component of her theory of transformational language, as well as a recurring pattern in her work: The erasure of differences—even when motivated by the desire to establish bonds among differently situated subjects—inadvertently widens the gap between disparate groups. (149)

When Lorde attended a predominately white high school, race remained silenced. All the members of her group of friends, self-named "The Branded," were white, except her, but they

> never talked about those differences that separated us, only the ones that united us against the *others*. . . . We never ever talked about what it meant and felt like to be Black and white, and the effects that had on our being friends. Of course, everybody with any sense deplored racial discrimination, theoretically and without discussion. We could conquer it by ignoring it. (81)

As race was ignored, Lorde reports that she often felt that the reason her friends did not include her in weekend activities or invite her to their houses must have been that something was wrong with her. She still "had no words for racism" (81).

After high school, when Lorde was the only one of the group to get her own apartment and it became the main gathering place for her friends, she continued to blame herself for what happened without considering their contribution. When she fails two courses in summer school, she reports, "it never occurred to me to think that it was because I had spent the summer wetnursing the girls of The Branded in my tiny tenement apartment" (118). Lorde felt separated from her friends and from the other students at Hunter College because of her race, her sexuality, and the economic differences of their lives, now that she was no longer supported by her parents. However, she could not talk about her problems with her friends, who, she says, "saw my house and my independence as a refuge, and seemed to think that I was settled and strong and dependable, which, of course, was exactly what I wanted them to think" (119). Lorde had fallen into two traditional roles of black women, that of taking care of white women and that of providing a model of strong womanhood. Later, Lorde found herself alienated from heterosexual women in the workforce even though she did not reveal her sexuality: "We were good listeners, and never asked for double dates, *but didn't we know the rules?* Why did we always seem to think friendships between women were important enough to *care* about?" (176). In addition to the disparity in priorities, the necessary secrecy with which Lorde guarded her personal life increased her remoteness.

Lorde found that she often felt alienated even in the lesbian community, and she describes the loneliness she and others experienced as a result. She knew very few black lesbians and states that their racial difference was often exoticized: "I didn't know the few other Black women who were visibly gay at all well. Too often we found ourselves sleeping with the same white women. We recognized ourselves as exotic sister-outsiders who might gain little from banding together. Perhaps our strength might lay in our fewness, our rarity" (177). Here the exoticization of blackness discouraged the bonding of black women because they feared losing their value in the sexual economy. Lorde also documents a number of young women whose supposed blindness to color made her and much of her experience invisible to them. White lesbian women who felt their minority status was analogous to hers, and therefore that their experience of oppression was the same, could not hear what was unique to her experience. As she says of one of her white partners,

> Even Muriel seemed to believe that as lesbians, we were all outsiders and all equal in our outsiderhood. "We're all niggers," she used to say, and I hated to hear her say it. It was wishful thinking based on little fact; the ways in which it was true languished in the shadow of those many ways in which it would always be false. (203)

Although Lorde acknowledges some of the similarities of racial and sexuality oppressions, she also states that she and the other black woman in their group

> shared both a battle and a strength that was unavailable to our other friends. We acknowledged it in private, and it set us apart, in a world that was closed to our white friends. . . . And because that world was closed to them, it was easy for even lovers to ignore it, dismiss it, pretend it didn't exist, believe the fallacy that there was no difference between us at all. (203–204)

Nevertheless, Lorde is able to assert, "Lesbians were probably the only Black and white women in New York City in the fifties who were making any real attempt to communicate with each other; we learned lessons from each other, the values of which were not lessened by what we did not learn" (179).[10] The experiences Lorde describes in *Zami* emphasize her arguments in *The Cancer Journals*: that differences must be recognized rather than silenced before unity among women—for personal or political ends—is possible.

CHAPTER 5

"Just This Side of Colored":
Ellen Foster and *Night Talk*

The distinction between autobiography and fiction, like that between the personal and the political, is a fine one.[1] Much of Lorde's feminist politics, including her ideas about difference, grew out of her personal experiences with women and racism. Her politics informed her experiments in *Zami*, for which she created a new genre category, biomythography. Kaye Gibbons's first novel, *Ellen Foster* (1987), also grew out of personal experience, and she even said in an interview on *The Oprah Winfrey Show*, "I am Ellen Foster." The fictional genre provides freedoms that can lead to more extended treatments of individual friendships between black and white women than autobiography allows. Certainly, that has been true in the cases of Gibbons's *Ellen Foster* and Elizabeth Cox's *Night Talk* (1997), both of which make interracial friendships central to their white protagonists' adolescence. Gibbons has said that "the core of the book [*Ellen Foster*] started from this relationship between a white child and a black child" (*Broken Silences* 69), and Cox has said that although her main character "Evie came alive when she was writing letters to her father," Cox soon "realized that the friendship between the two girls was taking over and that the story was about their friendship" (Interview 308).

In their focus on girls' interracial relationships, Gibbons's and Cox's novels overturn the historical construction of the relationship between black and white women and attempt to rewrite white women's identity by deconstructing the historically dichotomous definitions of black and white womanhood. In each novel, racial difference challenges the subjectivity of the protagonist, who must confront the racist stereotypes and blindness of both her culture and her own imagination, not only to continue her relationship with her friend but also to create a viable subject position for herself.[2] Ellen, the abandoned heroine of Gibbons's autobiographical novel, struggles to establish her identity in the absence of sufficient role models. Surrounded by negative, commodified conceptions of white women's bodies and taught to fear black bodies, Ellen nevertheless finds her sole positive model for embodiment in her black friend Starletta, who clearly experiences sensual pleasure through her own body.

Ellen's friendship with Starletta seems to be ending at the close of the novel.[3] Cox, in contrast, attempts to envision the survival of Evie and Jane's friendship into adulthood. Evie's contemplation of the racial tensions between her and Jane as she returns home to Georgia for the funeral of Jane's mother, Volusia, provides the novel's structural frame for the story of their childhood. Even though she grew up sharing a bedroom with Jane, Evie does not fully recognize the extent to which race caused her and Jane to experience growing up differently. The scope of the novel's plot is broad, incorporating the beginning of the civil rights movement, integration, and racial and sexual violence, but the girls' individual experiences of these events remain the novel's focus. Like Ellen, Evie must overcome the definitions of racial difference she has learned from her culture. Evie's reeducation occurs not just through her social observations but mostly through discourse—her nightly talks with Janey-Louise. Because Cox's novel incorporates two time frames, we see that this reinterpretation process continues into Evie's adulthood. Both novels suggest that overcoming the racialized cultural conceptions of women's identities is crucial to white women's ability to define their own subjectivities.

ELLEN FOSTER

Ellen's nuclear family disintegrates early in the novel. When Ellen's mother comes home from the hospital after heart surgery, Ellen tries to protect her from her angry, demanding, and abusive husband. But Ellen's mother's emotional and mental weariness matches her physical weakness, and she swallows most of her potent heart medication. Ellen's father threatens to kill Ellen if she goes to phone for help, and consequently her mother dies in bed with Ellen lying beside her. Ellen takes care of herself for a while, but when she can no longer safely remain at home with her abusive father, she begins to search for a new family. Although she stays with her grandmother and then her aunt for short periods, the members of her extended family are unable or unwilling to provide a nurturing environment for her, and their ineptness is shown to be closely related to their need to assert class and racial superiority. They reject Ellen because they shun her father, and their exclusiveness limits their ability to love. Part of the difficulty of

Ellen's search for a home is that she is unsure what she wants a family to be. Her best examples are her friend Starletta's family and the family of her grandmother's employee Mabel. As both these models of caring families are black, the novel functions as an analysis of whiteness. Gibbons's focus on race in a coming-of-age novel reveals how whiteness structures and distorts not only the idea of family but also the related concepts of identity and sexuality.

That Ellen Foster's world is sharply divided along racial lines is evident from her frequent and often gratuitous use of the adjective "colored." The idea of racial division is omnipresent in her family, and everything is subsumed under it. From her imagining the "two colored boys heaving [her] dead daddy onto a roller cot" (1) as she fantasizes killing her father to her description of her aunt as someone who "could not organize a two-car colored funeral" (14), her repeated use of racial markers as she describes her past in the early pages of the novel indicates the pervasiveness of the racial segregation and racism of her world. "Colored" signifies for her everything that is of a lower status and worth than whiteness, and her racism has clearly been absorbed from her family.

Ellen's relatives depict the dangers of the concept of whiteness for white people. Ellen's grandmother and Aunt Nadine are preoccupied with race and social class. Their sense of their own racial superiority leads them to performances of whiteness that are as detrimental to their own humanity as they are comic, as when Nadine tries to impress the funeral director:

> My aunt is entertaining the smiling man. That is her part-time job. When she is not redecorating or shopping with Dora [her daughter] she demonstrates food slicers in your home. . . . on she will go about sorrow and sin and how is Ellen ever going to make out? Pretty soon she catches onto the sound of what she is saying and she pulls one word out to meet the next and once every sentence or so she will clap. (17)

Nadine's attempts to impress other people and her illusions about herself and her daughter make her appear pretentious and ridiculous to Ellen. Being white is not in itself detrimental—the art teacher Ellen stays with for a short time provides a striking and loving contrast to the members of Ellen's extended family. Rather, her family's preoccupation with their whiteness is what is harmful. Their expressions of racism suffuse their behavior; for instance, Ellen notes that on the way to her mother's funeral, her "aunt is so glad to be out of colored town. She unlocks her car door because now she feels safe" (19).

Ellen's maternal relatives are also protective of their own social status as whites, as their attitude toward Ellen's father shows. One of the disembodied statements about her mother that echoes in Ellen's mind from the day of the funeral is "Marry trash and see what comes of you. I could have told anybody" (14). The family's resentment of her mother's marriage to a man of lower social standing and economic means—an act they perceive as a threat to the social and economic standing of their family—leads them to blame her for her circumstances and even for her own death, and they consequently disparage her at her own funeral.

No one exemplifies the family's racism or hatred for Ellen's father more than her grandmother, who is so angry at him that she "calls him a nigger and trash so long and loud she gets hoarse" (21). The grandmother attributes all of Ellen's father's negative characteristics to his not being white enough; in her perception, even largely unraced characteristics become raced because the conception of racial difference is so powerful. When the grandmother sends one of the women who works for her to collect Ellen's mother's clothes, she also sends a pointed announcement of Ellen and her father's unworthiness: "She said to tell my daddy the message was plain and simple. Now get it right. It was she had rather some real niggers have my mama's things than any of us that drink and carry on like trash" (33).

The phrase "real niggers" implies that Ellen and her father are also a type of "nigger," albeit an inauthentic one because of their white skin. "Trash," short for "white trash," is repeatedly paired with the racial slur "nigger"; the former is intended to evoke the latter. The coupling of the two pejorative terms implies an equivalence that stems from the economic dimension of racism. One intention of the concept of white superiority is to ensure economic dominance. Those white people who lack sufficient economic means threaten the logic of racial superiority; they cannot be authentically "white" without undermining the logic of an essentialized racial superiority. Economically privileged white people must therefore make economically disadvantaged white people an "other" to protect their status and the faulty logic of white superiority. In his 1997 *White*, Richard Dyer argues that one of the sources of the success of whiteness as a system of privilege lies in its adaptability:

> Whiteness has been enormously, often terrifyingly effective in unifying coalitions of disparate groups of people. It has generally been much more successful than class in uniting people across national cultural differences and against their best interests. . . . Whiteness as a

coalition . . . incites the notion that some whites are whiter than others. . . . A shifting border and internal hierarchies of whiteness suggest that the category of whiteness is unclear and unstable, yet this has proved its strength. Because whiteness carries such rewards and privileges, the sense of a border that might be crossed and a hierarchy that might be climbed has produced a dynamic that has enthralled people who have had any chance of participating in it. (19–20)

When Ellen's mother married a man of lower social and economic standing, her mother and sister interpreted her act as a betrayal; after her death, they feel compelled to protect their social standing by assiduously enforcing the boundaries of their caste of whiteness.

Their vigilance has a moral as well as an economic component.[4] One of Ellen's grandmother's reasons for assuming Ellen's father's degeneracy is that he associates primarily with the black men who buy his liquor, and the social integration clearly offends her more than the drinking. Dyer's discussion of the moral connotations of whiteness in Western movies fits this case: "part of the genre's realism [is] to acknowledge the variation in white people; that is, the ways in which some white people fail to attain whiteness. Bad whites in Westerns are often associated with darkness, either in the iconography of black and white costuming . . . or in their association with non-white Others" (35). Just as the association with blackness has been used in movies to connote moral corruption, so Ellen's father's friendship with black men renders him morally suspect to his in-laws.

Her grandmother's "message" to her father confuses Ellen, who tells the reader, "That is hard to figure out because you know I do not drink and I would not even eat in a colored house" (33). Although Ellen does not understand her grandmother's behavior, she has already internalized the proscriptions for maintaining whiteness. Her family's racism has taught her to fear blackness, and that fear manifests itself physically: she is afraid to eat, drink, or sleep at Starletta's house. When she goes there on Christmas day, she thinks, "As fond as I am of all three of them I do not think I could drink after them. I try to see what Starletta leaves on the lip of a bottle but I have never seen anything with the naked eye. If something is that small it is bound to get into your system and do some damage" (29–30). If Ellen has learned that race constitutes an essential ontological difference, she has also learned to fear blackness as if it were a communicable disease. Although she is hungry and food is difficult to procure, she turns down Starletta's offer of a biscuit: "No matter how good it looks to you it is still a colored biscuit," she tells herself (32).

Ellen is also reacting to her grandmother's moral condemnation. More than anything else, perhaps, Ellen wants to dissociate herself from her father, whose association with black men renders him suspect to her grandmother. Ellen's deductive reasoning here produces a preposterous conclusion that is simultaneously funny and heartbreaking. She assumes that her behavior—her refusal of food—means that she does not "act like trash," because she has avoided becoming too physically intimate with black people. Ellen's liminal racial position, as she tries to avoid being "trash," impedes her relationship with Starletta and her family, despite their mutual affection and her need of them, and even though Starletta's parents are the only adults who care for Ellen by helping her and looking after her. The moral judgment is conflated with the association of blackness and dirt; even though racist whites may long for the romanticized notion of a close relationship to the earth, they nevertheless consider black people dirty, both morally and physically. Ellen is not only worried about imbibing something invisible but harmful from Starletta's food; she also demands of her friend, "You got to wash before I will play with you is what I told her" (31).[5]

Despite the racism of both Ellen and her family, however, Ellen turns to Starletta to escape from her own family and to experience vicariously the physical nurture she lacks. When Ellen first enters the church for her mother's funeral, she is overwhelmed by the number of people but finds comfort by watching Starletta and her parents: "I see Starletta and she looks clean. I wish I could sit with her mama and daddy" (20). Watching Starletta's family attenuates the pain of watching her own and relieves the pressure to look at her mother's dead body in the coffin: "There is no reason I have to look at her. It would just give me something else to think about" (20).[6] "Do I have to watch?" (21) becomes a refrain as she tries to resist the implicit demand to look made by her mother's open coffin and subsequent burial. Ellen also resists her relatives' example of family behavior: "I do not want to watch them anymore. What one can hardly wait to say to the other is making them squirm" (14). Indeed, Ellen tries to control her experience and her emotional reaction by controlling what she sees. She tires of watching her own family but revels in watching Starletta's.

The image of Starletta sitting with her mother at the funeral contrasts sharply with Ellen's earlier description of her experience of her own mother. Whereas Ellen feels she must care for and protect her mother, Starletta finds her mother's body a warm and welcoming source of comfort and sustenance. Ellen's and her parents' roles have become reversed. When Ellen's mother comes home from the hospital, she is both physically weak from her heart operation and psychologically vulnerable from years of her husband's mental abuse. Ellen becomes her caretaker, helping her change clothes and putting her to bed. Ellen describes her mother's body as "sore all up through her chest and bruised up the neck" and says, "It makes me want to turn my head" (5). Her mother's body is sick and frightening, but also childlike in its weakness and vulnerability, and Ellen tries to take care of her mother as one would a child. After Ellen chases her drunk and sick father out of the house to sleep in his truck, she thinks of how easy her mother is by comparison: "Mama's easy to tend to. . . . Not a bit of trouble. Just stiff and hard to move around" (6). When her mother overdoses on heart medication, Ellen lies in bed with her, believing her father's promise that her mother can "sleep it off" (9). Ellen longs for connection and security and seeks both in her mother's body:

> I always want to lay here. And she moves her arm up and I push my head down by her side. And I will crawl in and make room for myself. My heart can be the one that beats.
>   And hers has stopped.
>   Damn him to the bottom of hell damn him.
>   What to do now when the spinning starts people will come and they will want to know why and I cannot tell them why. They will not come yet no not for a while. I have her now while she sleeps but just is not breathing. (10)

Blaming her father, and simultaneously realizing and denying her mother's death, Ellen identifies with her mother and wants them to share a unified experience. Addressing her mother, she thinks, "You can rest with me until somebody comes to get you. We will not say anything. We can rest" (11). In her longing for her mother, Ellen attempts to merge their experience. She seeks the nurturing she needs by trying to provide it for her mother.[7]

In contrast to Ellen's efforts and longing for a tangible and secure connection to her own mother, Starletta relates to her mother's body with unselfconscious ease. Secure in her mother's affection and permanence, Starletta experiences being held in the church pew as both comfort and restraint. Ellen focuses on Starletta's experience at the funeral rather than her own: "Starletta is lounging all over her mama. I know it kills her to stay for too long a time in one place. If her mama loosened up on her a little she would roll down the aisle and crawl out the window. In a minute Starletta will get her head thumped" (21). By watching Starletta, Ellen voyeuristically experiences a mother's physical nurturance and avoids seeing her own mother's body dead in the coffin.

The amplitude of Starletta's mother's ability to nurture her daughter is represented for Ellen by their habit of sucking on clay rocks.

> Starletta and her mama both eat dirt. My daddy slapped my face for eating dirt. Oh yes but I have seen Starletta sucking in her face drawing what she can from red clay. My daddy slapped my face and jerked my elbow round to my nose and he ran his finger across my gums feeling for grit. She eats that mess like it is good to her. She sits at the end of the row while her mama chops. She loosens a piece and pops it in her jaw and squeezes. She sits and eats clay dirt and picks at her bug bites. Starletta has orange teeth and she will plait my hair if I ask her right. (20)

Ellen longs for the nourishment she sees Starletta getting from her closeness to her mother—from continual physical presence and from sharing the same habits—but her father punishes her for imitating their behavior. Ellen is admonished for seeking nurturance, and the punishment reinforces the mandate to maintain differences in behavior from black people. Ellen remains transfixed, however, at the pleasure Starletta gets from the clay rocks in her mouth. Her fascination is no doubt fueled by one of the corollaries to Southern American racism: the belief that African Americans have a more intimate and sensual relationship to the earth than white Americans. Foiled in her attempt to share this sensual ritual, Ellen chooses to adopt another characteristic of Starletta, her hairstyle. By getting Starletta to braid her hair as Starletta's mother no doubt braids Starletta's, Ellen establishes a connection to the maternal care she sees in their relationship by creating a symbolic manifestation of it on her own body.

In a similar way, Ellen tries to maintain a connection to her mother after the woman's death by wearing her mother's clothes. Outgrowing her own clothing, she notes that she and her mother are about the same size (23): "I enjoyed wearing my mama's clothes. . . . I decided to wear a little something every day. That worked out fine because the only thing I had left that fit good was socks" (24). The clothing brings her comfort not only for the loss of her mother but also for her developing body in the awkwardness of puberty: "I have a odd shape. But I am not ill formed. My head is too big for the rest of me. Just this side of a defect. When I get a chest and hips I will look weighted down. I have been waiting for some time now" (24). Ellen portrays herself as a head waiting for a body, and that is in some sense what she is. Forced to confront adult concerns to take care of herself, she has relied on her precocious reasoning skills to cope and has sublimated her feelings. The strategy of wearing her mother's clothes works only for a short time, however, until her grandmother sends someone to take the clothes away. Ellen thereby loses her last connection to her mother's body. She displaces her physical needs by focusing on someone else's physical experience, most often Starletta's.

Ellen initially learns what a caring family is from watching Starletta's family. Her account of her Christmas visit with them is, in fact, interspersed with memories from her mother's funeral, signifying the longing for love that they stir within her. Subsequent events in the novel show that Starletta's parents show more concern and care for Ellen than her own family does. Despite her condescension and racial anxieties, Ellen feels safer with them than with her father, more comfortable with them than with her maternal relatives. Unlike Ellen's own angry and often absent father, who leaves her to fend for herself, Starletta's father tends to Ellen's needs: "I hated to see it get cold. Starletta's daddy called the heat man for me and took me to town to get a coat" (25–26). At other times, he takes her to buy her Girl Scout uniform and to go Christmas shopping.

More important, Starletta's father offers security. When Ellen's father is home, she reports that she "always walked in wide circles around him" (25). Her description of Starletta's father emphasizes the contrast with her own and with what racism has taught her to expect of black men: "He . . . has never bothered me and he is the only colored man that does not buy liquor from my daddy" (30). Whereas Ellen's father screams orders at her mother when she comes home from the hospital, Ellen notices that Starletta's parents display mutual affection with ease. While Starletta's mother is cooking, her father "sneaks up behind her and pinches her on the tail. I saw that" (29). Ellen recognizes, however, that their behavior must be modified in public: "They would not carry on like that if they were at the store or working in the field. They walk up the road and pick cotton and do not speak like they know they go together. People say they do not try to be white" (29). To "try to be white" in this context would be to presume to carry on ordinary human relations in public. The statement, in Ellen's matter-of-fact voice, as she reports what she knows but has not yet begun to question, is highly ironic, given that Starletta's parents are the only adults to exhibit decent behavior without ulterior motives thus far in the novel. Ellen even feels that the teacher at school who asks about her mother's death is motivated by her desire for gossip.

As part of her survival strategy, Ellen has become a keen observer of people's behavior, and gradually her experience leads her to question the racism she has learned. She comes to realize that the only disadvantages of Starletta's home compared with her own are material ones: a one-room house with a dirt floor, no indoor plumbing, and no television. Ellen recognizes, but does not fully comprehend, the economic impact of racism. For instance, she says of the quilts Starletta's mother sews: "She sells them to white women from town and they turn around and sell them again for a pretty penny. That would gall me" (30). As a child, she recognizes the unfairness but not the social cause. She has not yet realized that many of the differences she has been taught are racial are in fact economic and largely the result of a racist system. She states that Starletta's family "live regular but most colored people have a grandmama or two and a couple dozen cousins in the same house. A family up the road had fifteen people in one house and when they ran out of plates they ate off records. Records like you play. I know that for a fact" (30). What she sees as eccentric behavior has an economic impetus she does not realize.

When Ellen's home becomes too dangerous, her desire for safety overcomes some of her qualms about staying at Starletta's. When her father comes home drunk on New Year's eve with a bunch of his friends, Ellen overhears one of the men saying about her, "Yours is just about ripe. You gots to git em when they is still soff when you mashum" (37). She hides in her closet until they pass out and then tries to sneak out, but her father catches her and grabs her, mistaking her for her mother. Ellen runs to Starletta's house for safety. "When I got up in the morning I was surprised because it did not feel like I had slept in a colored house. I cannot say I officially slept in the bed because I stayed in my coat on top of the covers" (39). After Ellen's aunt Betsy refuses to take her in, and despite Starletta's mother's frequent offers that Ellen can stay there whenever she wants, Ellen returns home. Escaping from her father becomes increasingly difficult, and when she returns to school a teacher asks her about her bruise: "She asked me how it all happened so I told her my daddy put the squeeze on me and that is how it happened. She was shocked but I told her I was used to it so do not get in a uproar over it. You live with something long enough you get used to it" (44). When Ellen's only suggestion for an alternative place for her to stay is Starletta's, she rightly surmises that that option is unacceptable to the teacher because of race.

For a short idyllic time Ellen lives with her art teacher, and on her birthday Starletta visits. This visit marks a change in Ellen's perception of Starletta. She still uses Starletta to experience vicariously a sensuality that she needs but cannot risk experiencing directly, such emotions appear dangerous to Ellen, both because of her father's sexual aggression and because she still has difficulty believing that she is in a safe environment. The nature of the sensuality, however, has changed; no longer connected to maternal care, the sensual experience of Starletta's that she focuses on is one of pure physical pleasure: "She liked the idea of scratchy carpet on the floor and all into the closet and under the bed she crawled on her stomach. She was in love with rubbing all her body parts on my floor" (50).

Ellen's identification with Starletta remains highly ambivalent, however, because her own sense of superiority as a white person compels her to maintain distance between them. Her attitude is condescending and controlling: "Starletta stared at her slice [of cake] until I told her it was food and to dig in. She did not understand how slices and modest servings go so I had to tell her when to quit eating" (51). Gibbons thus shows that affection is reconcilable with condescension, that well-meaning whites who have overcome some of their racist attitudes may still be paternalistic. Ellen is now proud to have Starletta as a friend, although her pride is proprietary: "Starletta was the only colored girl at the movies and she was mine" (50–51). Even though Ellen has lost many of her misconceptions, she continues to treat Starletta as an object.

A court order forces Ellen to live with her grandmother, who has initiated legal proceedings because she wants revenge: she believes that Ellen colluded with her father in killing her mother. When summer arrives, Ellen's grandmother takes Ellen to the cotton fields to work alongside her black tenant farmers. This experience turns out to be transformative for Ellen, causing her to reevaluate her gender and race identities and giving her time to contemplate what qualities she wants in a family. By giving her this job, Ellen's grandmother has forced her to cross racial lines and perform labor that has been coded black. On the first day, Ellen thinks, "I lived on a farm with my mama and daddy but they hired colored people to do my part of the slave labor. I was too small to work right. I used to play in the fields with Starletta and watch her mama and daddy chop but I never figured it would be me one day" (63). Working in the heat makes Ellen sick, and Mavis looks after her, telling her, "what the bosslady is up to is her business but it must be a mighty bad debt you is out here working off. They is no sense in a white chile working in this heat. I can hardly stands it my own hot self" (64). Mavis seems to accept the racial division of labor, but Ellen questions such arrangements after seeing how Starletta's mother's quilts profit white women. She reports that "she said they were born to chop and that is how they could work so fast and steady. She would say that and laugh but it was not funny to me" (64). Although Mavis's laughter no doubt masks her true feelings about her work, the matter-of-fact Ellen hears no irony in the remark; she does, however, recognize poor working conditions. The time with Mavis is a gift to Ellen, not only because the woman befriends her but also because she knows so much about Ellen's family. When Ellen asks her whether she knew Ellen's mother, Mavis responds, "I was raised up beside her on this farm. I knowed her good as I know my own self. I never knowed anybody sweet like your mama. Smart as a whip too!" (65). Ellen's mother was clearly her own mother's favorite child, and Mavis, confirming Ellen's sense of reality, tells her that after her mother's death, her grandmother "had acted touched" (65).

The work causes physical transformations for Ellen that lead her to rethink her assumptions about gender and race:

> By July I was like a boy. When I started out both my hands were a red blister but then I toughened up good.
>
> I thought while I chopped from one field to the next how I could pass for colored now. Somebody riding by here in a car could not see my face and know I was white. But that is OK now I thought to myself of how it did not make much of a difference anymore.
>
> If I just looked at my own arms and legs up to where my shorts and shirt started I said I could pass for colored now. I was tan from the sun but so dark I was just this side of colored. Under it all I was a pinky white. (66)

The physical changes transform her consciousness. The direction of this effect—external physical changes compelling internal changes of consciousness—corresponds to Elizabeth Grosz's argument in *Volatile Bodies* (1994) that "the social inscriptions of the surface of the body generate a psychical interiority" (115).[8] Grosz's argument overturns the interior/exterior hierarchy; the internal is no longer the privileged site of consciousness. Ellen is proud of the skills, strength, and physical changes she has acquired by performing work that is coded "black." Her "inner" beliefs about race and gender and her own position with regards to them are changed. Race and gender become more permeable categories for her, and she is less invested in maintaining racial and gender boundaries. Whereas racial permeability caused the fears of her grandmother and aunt—the fear of failing to be white that led them to hate her father—for Ellen, who has seen the love in Starletta's and Mavis's families, the suggestion of racial permeability creates the possibility that she is not destined to perform whiteness as her grandmother and aunt have. Instead, not being as white as some whites, such as her grandmother, becomes a positive sign of her strength, resilience, and flexibility.

Grosz connects the deconstruction of the mind/body or interior/exterior duality with the deconstruction of the conceptions of race and gender as dualities (white/black, male/female). If the mind and body are no longer conceived of as distinct entities, then "corporeality must no longer be associated with one sex (or race), which then takes on the burden of the other's corporeality for it. . . . Blacks, slaves, immigrants, indigenous peoples can no longer function as the working body for white 'citizens,' leaving them free to create values, morality, knowledges" (Grosz 22). Thus Ellen's physical change and the resulting change in her racial identity and conception of gender and racial difference would seem to compel a change in her relationships to Starletta and the other African American characters in the novel. The changes do modify Ellen's attitudes toward these characters; her relationships with them, however, retain their basic structure. She watches Mavis's family from a distance, and even though she comes to long to eradicate the distance she had formerly imposed between herself and Starletta, she nevertheless continues to use Starletta to experience sensuality.

Ellen's growth is a result not just of working but also of the care Mavis has shown her. Ellen spends her evenings watching and learning from Mavis's family, though racial stereotypes still largely determine what she sees. To her, "it looked like slavery times with them all hanging out on the porch picking at each other. They fought strong as they played and laughed. . . . I wondered right much about them and the way they got along" (66). Although Ellen is beginning to recognize economic cues, noting that her grandmother "did not pay them [Mavis and her family] doodly-squat" (66), even as a precocious child she lacks an understanding of the systemic effects of racism. She wonders why "Mavis and her family showed up in the field every day when I was thinking of how I would save up my money and leave if I was old as them. I guess it never dawned on them just to pack up and leave" (67). Ellen fails to realize how limited Mavis's family's economic choices are and attributes their acceptance of poor working conditions and low pay to their intellectual or imaginative failure. Gibbons's novel thus simultaneously emphasizes the economic trap of tenant farmers and the flawed assumptions made by many people with better employment opportunities.

Despite the limits of Ellen's awareness, and partially because of the romantic nature of the stereotypes Mavis's family evokes for her, Ellen learns a great deal from them about families, and she begins to consider what she desires in a family in very concrete and particular terms. She still prioritizes race, however: "While I was easedropping at the colored house I started a list of all that a family should have. . . . While I watched Mavis and her family I thought I would bust open if I did not get one of them for my own self soon. . . . I only wanted one white and with a little more money. At least we can have running water is what I thought" (67). Ellen admires Mavis's family, and it becomes her model. In it she sees community, protection, and affection, especially affection for children:

> every night when I went to bed I knew I had found a little something on that colored path that I could not name but I said to myself to mark down what you saw tonight because it might come in handy. You mark down how they laugh and how they tell the toddler babies, you better watch out fo them steps. They steep! Mark all that down and see if you can figure out what made you take that trip every night. Then when you are by yourself one day the list you kept might make some sense and then you will know that this is the list you would take to a store if they made such a store and say to the man behind the counter give me this and this and this. And he would hand you back a home. (93–94)

After her grandmother's death, when Ellen has to go live with her aunt Nadine, she regrets losing her nightly vigils. Ellen describes Nadine's as "a place so far from the house at the end of the colored path" (94), emphasizing what it lacks as a home in comparison to Mavis's.

If Ellen sometimes vicariously experiences sensuality through Starletta, her cousin Dora's discomfort with her body shows that Ellen's reluctance to express sensuality is not only a protective response to her abusive past and insecure circumstances but also a characteristic of whiteness. Indeed, the whiteness to which Nadine, Dora, and Ellen's grandmother aspire requires that women deny their bodies. Ellen has already perceived that one of Nadine and Dora's pretensions is a denial of their bodily functions. Sitting next to Dora in the car on the way to her mother's funeral, Ellen notes, "Dora has soaked the seat of this car. My daddy is not aware of this but I am so I slide closer to the window to put some space between this red suit and Dora. Old as me and wets herself once or twice a day. I know they [Nadine and Dora] expect this dress back dry" (17). Psychically removed from her body, Dora cannot control it. Ellen is also distanced from her own body, worrying not about herself but about the condition of the borrowed dress she is wearing. Nevertheless, the extreme capacity for denial that Ellen attributes to Nadine is comic and telling: "Dora's mama would stand beside Dora dripping and deny her big girl wet herself" (17). Ellen also suspects that she would be blamed, imagining herself answering, "You are right, Aunt Nadine. I promise never to pee in your girl's pants again" (18).

Nadine and Dora's denial of their bodies stems from their aspirations to a particularly commodified and normalized version of femininity, which makes their behavior quite predictable to Ellen. When her aunt and cousin, "dressed up alike" (94), leave Ellen alone in the house, she rummages through Dora's things and reports, "I should not even have to say all that I found. Dora does not have any secrets from me but she has the idea that there is more to her self than there really is. Dora keeping romance books in the back of her underwear drawer was not a surprise. And I was not exactly blowed over by the boy movie star pictures under her mattress" (94–95). Dora's expression of her sexuality takes on a commodified form: the romance novels are tutorial scripts for hegemonic female sexuality, as are the pictures, which direct her sexual desire toward a particular masculine ideal. She must keep both the books and pictures hidden because her sexual desire is not supposed to exist, or can be allowed expression only in ways that indicate shame. As cultural products, the texts themselves are designed to elicit and discipline this shameful, desiring response. But the feminine ideal that Nadine has accepted requires her to deny the possibility of her daughter's sexual desire, and Ellen muses, "I bet her mama would be shocked and she would cry because Dora let her down. And if I was anywhere near she would finally decide that I planted all that nasty stuff there because I am jealous of Dora's good fortune" (95).

Nadine's aversion to bodies makes Ellen suspicious of her aunt's ability to care for the ill. Feeling that she failed to care for her mother adequately causes Ellen to take care of her dying grandmother with particular vigilance. In Nadine's house, she stays in the room that was Nadine's husband's sickroom during the period between his stroke and his death. When Ellen imagines that time, she assumes Nadine's willful denial of reality and inability to nurse an ailing husband: "I feature Nadine hiring a colored woman to look after him and saying impatient to her don't tire me with the details just say FINE when I ask you how he's doing. Nadine would probably not need to hear the truth much less see it for herself. That sums her up" (95). Ellen presumes Nadine's assumption that taking care of sick human beings is work for black women; it is also the work that Ellen did for her grandmother before her grandmother's death. In this scenario, Nadine is also clearly using a black woman to shield her from a reality that she is not strong enough to bear. Again, having done work that is often delegated to black women by privileged white women has given Ellen not only a practical capability but also a critical awareness of the limitations imposed by the narrow and class-conscious definition of white femininity.

In contrast to Dora's hidden teen magazines and romance novels, what Ellen hides from Nadine and Dora are her microscope, the instrument of her scientific curiosity, and her paintings, the products of her emotional expression. These manifestations of Ellen's intellectual and imaginative desire are not merely shocking to Nadine and Dora; they are incomprehensible. Ellen knows they will not understand her art, so when she decides to paint them a picture as a Christmas gift, she chooses kittens as her subject:

> I would really like to paint them one of my brooding oceans but they would miss the point I am sure of how the ocean looks strong and beautiful and sad at the same time and that is really something if you think about it. They would not like the picture because it looks so evil when you first look at it. It is not something that would grow on them. Not like these cats hopping around teasing with a ball of yarn. I like that picture fine except once you look at it one time you have seen and felt everything you will ever see and feel about those cats. (106)

Nadine and Dora are not grateful for the present. On Christmas morning, Ellen watches Dora surrounded by her toys and wishes she were again with Starletta, as she was the previous year. Furious with Dora for mocking the painting she gave them, and envious because Dora has once again received everything she wanted, Ellen thinks, "And all I wonder is why I do not hate Starletta" (110). Ellen has secretly been hoping for Christmas surprises that would show her that Nadine cared for and liked her, so when her only gift is the art paper she has requested, she angrily storms out of the room. She chooses a form of retaliation she knows Dora and Nadine will be susceptible to, heterosexual female competition: "I could only think of one thing Dora did not have and most likely would not ever have and that was a boyfriend. . . . So if I could round me up a boyfriend and sport him around in front of Dora I could bring her down a notch or two and feel pretty good my own self" (111). By creating a fake beau, Nick Adams, to make Dora jealous, Ellen consciously manipulates Nadine and Dora's investment in the heterosexual economy by citing evidence of her own worth—and Dora's implied failure—in that exchange system.

Ellen shows them her microscope as proof, claiming that it is a gift from her boyfriend. Dora is skeptical about the existence of the boyfriend, and she is even more skeptical about the microscope: "She had moved close in on her mama like I was about to bite her. Like she had just found out a dark secret of mine that I kept hid because it likes to hurt pretty girls with blonde curly hair." Nadine is suspicious of Ellen's possession of such a masculine instrument, even if it was acquired from as acceptable a source as a boyfriend; she "says they have those things at the doctor's office and what do I think I'm doing with one whether a boy gave it to me or not?" And when Ellen replies that she "use[s] it to look at paramecia, diatoms, or euglenas," Nadine asks her, "Where are they . . . like I might be hoarding wanted criminals in my closet" (113). Whereas Ellen's painting seems strange to her aunt and cousin, her proclivity for science, to them a clearly masculine domain, renders her downright suspect.

When Nadine tells Ellen she cannot live with them anymore, Ellen walks to the house of the woman with foster daughters she has seen in church.[9] What Ellen wants most after she is settled into her new home is to have Starletta visit for the weekend. The visit seems urgent to Ellen both because she senses that their friendship may soon end and because she wants to make reparations for how she has treated Starletta. In addition to missing Starletta during the time she has lived with her relatives, Ellen sees that her friend's adolescence has caused changes that affect their relationship: "She [Starletta] has hit the growth spurt they talked about in my health book and she is getting tall. . . . I want to press my hands to her to stop her from growing into a time she will not want to play" (83). Starletta is also beginning to be interested in the opposite sex, which is another sign to Ellen that their days of playing together are limited. The boy Starletta has a crush on is white, and Ellen assumes that Starletta's interest in a white boy is economically motivated: "It is no use to snag a colored boy she would think when the white ones are the ones that have the cars and the money to set you up in style. Why do I want to chop all day and make quilts all night? she would think" (84). Ellen's assumptions about Starletta's desire reveal both an assumption that Starletta wants upward economic mobility and that for Ellen, whose pecuniary focus stems from her own limited circumstances, money and sexuality are still tied together—not surprising, perhaps, after her father, in front of her school, offered her money for sex. Although Ellen and Starletta have maintained their connection by making "lists of what [they] need to tell each other," Ellen worries: "I wonder how long she will be interested in keeping the list with me and something tells me inside that one of these days soon she will forget me" (84).

When Ellen decides to ask her "new mama" whether she can invite Starletta for the weekend, she is hesitant because of their racial difference: "That [a black person spending the night in a white person's house] is brave to think about because I am not sure if it has been done before" (85). Ellen, now aware of her racism, wants to make amends to Starletta:

> It was just Starletta the girl I was after and she could tote my bed and my checkerboard curtains back to her house if she felt like it. But it is just Starletta I want to squeeze so hard she will remember that every time somebody loves her good. . . . Then I will not miss her so bad. We will be even friends and I will not need to prove a thing to her ever again. And she will remember me good when she is old enough to think and sort through her own past to see all the ways I slighted her oh not by selling her down a river or making her wash my clothes but by all the varieties of ways I felt God chose me over her. (100)

Ellen wants to merge with Starletta, imagining that her friend can borrow her clothes and thinking, "I wonder if Starletta would let me take a bath with her" (122). She needs to express her feelings for Starletta physically to atone for all her previous physical rejections, such as her refusal to eat in Starletta's home. Ellen's projection of her own desires onto Starletta, despite her love for her friend, remains problematic, as is Starletta's silence in the novel. (Starletta is the one character in Gibbons's novel for whom we have no direct speech.) Gibbons has acknowledged this limitation in an interview, stating, "I got to the end of the book and realized she [Starletta] hadn't talked. . . . I think I put off having her talk until I got to the end of the book and I said, 'Kaye, you've got to say why this girl has not said a word and I said, well she stutters and doesn't like to talk.' I took care of that real quickly" (*Broken Silences* 78). In the same interview, Gibbons admits to her limitations in portraying black characters, and surely that insecurity accounts for Starletta's silence. Gibbons argues that

> it's . . . important that white women learn to portray black women as characters who are not just acting as maids, quiet confidantes, the way I have portrayed black women in my fiction because that's all I know. And as I develop more black friends, I will be able to see the experience and know the experience through something more than the literature of Paula Giddings. And I'll be able to portray—not in a more positive light—I've tried to portray black women in a positive light because the black women I've known have been positive—almost saviors of me. They were. They saved me as a child. (*Broken Silences* 73)

Gibbons's comments reveal that the limitations of fiction often stem from limitations in authors' lives and suggest the same intertwining of life and writing that is more evident in Lorde's explicit blending of genres in *Zami*.

NIGHT TALK

In many stories of interracial friendship between young girls, the relationship does not survive the characters' adolescence. Elizabeth Cox's *Night Talk* is an exception to this rule; primarily a story of adolescence, the novel also shows the difficulties two women face sustaining their interracial friendship as adults. Whereas Ellen leaves her original home and searches for a new and nurturing one, in *Night Talk* Evie Bell's home changes as a result of her father's leaving on his own quest. After her husband leaves, Evie's mother Agnes has Volusia, a black domestic, and her daughter Janey Louise move in. Evie does not have the blatant racist beliefs of Ellen Foster and is eager for Janey Louise to share her bedroom, but the girls have to hide their shared room from other people in the town. Cox reveals the hidden racist assumptions that always informed Evie's relationship with Janey Louise, however, by framing the story of their childhood with an early chapter in which an adult Evie remembers the argument with Jane (as she is called as an adult) that caused the current breach in their friendship. The cumulative effect of Evie's failure to recognize the impact of racial difference on her and Jane's lives threatens to destroy the friendship that has lasted into their adulthood. When a salesclerk eyes them suspiciously, Evie says, "She's being a bitch." Jane replies, "That's *not* it. If you think that's it, I don't even know who you are" (11). Jane insists that they leave the mall, and when Evie complains, suggesting that the salesclerk's rude behavior may not have been racially motivated, Jane tells her, "All of a sudden it seems like you've been stupid all your life" (12). Evie and Jane's argument causes Evie to reevaluate the experiences they shared growing up. It assures readers that Evie will be held accountable for all the ways she betrays Jane as a child by both accepting and not recognizing her racial privilege.

Because Cox frames the story of Evie and Jane's childhood with this argument, leaving the reader unsure of whether the friendship will be repaired and continue, the novel avoids some of the problematic romanticizing of the ability of the girls' friendship to overcome racial barriers. In an interview, Cox tells of one reader's experience that shows how effectively the novel's frame works:

> One woman . . . said, "You know when I went to the library and I found this book, and I read the jacket copy, I thought 'this sounds interesting.' And then I turned to the back and saw a white face and

thought, 'right.' You know, 'what does she know?' " And she said she took it home anyway, but didn't expect to like it. Then she told me, "I want to tell you, you got it right." And I said, "I can't tell you what that means to me to hear that." To hear how she doubted it, and then believed it. But she talked mainly about when the two women were going shopping, and the saleswoman was very suspicious of her [Jane]. (317)

Evie's racial assumptions are clear to the reader in the chapters that cover the girls' childhood experiences, and Cox uses the few reflective chapters written from Evie's adult perspective for Evie to come to terms with her accountability. Returning to Georgia for Volusia's funeral, Evie must try to earn Jane's forgiveness, and she must also rethink her relationship with Volusia. Her first realization about Volusia is that "there were places in her life where she would not allow me to go" (5). As Evie remembers the way Jane was treated by Evie's white friends, the difficulties Jane faced when she began attending Evie's newly integrated school, and the fact they could never sit together in the movies, she also realizes that there were parts of Jane's life that she did not know about, despite their shared home. Although the motivation for Evie's reflections is her love for Jane, realizing her own racism and the effect of society's racism on Jane's life enables her to repair both her relationship with Jane and other relationships in her life. Taking responsibility for her lack of awareness and former racist assumptions prepares her to overcome the emotional obstacles that have been preventing her from committing to marrying and starting a family with the man she loves.

Forms of racism pervade the household, but the restructuring of that household, caused by the father's departure and Volusia and Janey Louise's moving in, destabilizes the typical racial roles and hierarchies of a white Southern home with live-in black employees. When Volusia moves in, she becomes the authoritative presence in the home. She has the authority of a woman who works and is accustomed to running a household. By keeping the home running smoothly and involving everyone in its operations, telling both the children and Evie's mother Agnes what to do, Volusia helps them transition smoothly through the reordering of their lives after Evie's father August's sudden departure. As Evie writes in one of her letters to her father:

Volusha does everything around the house like Mama used to do, and Mama comes home and sits down to supper like you used to do. It is the strangest thing, Mama says, and I agree. But I am not sure why it is strange. Janey Louise says it's because Mama Agnes (that is what she calls Mama) is not a wife anymore, but she is still a mother, and usually those things go together. Volusha says that Janey Louise is exactly right. (25)

Agnes has broken out of her gender role as homemaker, and both Agnes and Volusia take on new responsibilities. As Agnes recovers from her shock, the balance of authority becomes more equitable. Agnes and Volusia share the parenting of Evie, her brother, and Janey. Although they never truly work as equals and Agnes maintains ultimate authority as the employer, the power the women exert in the home shifts with different events. Their relationship becomes more equal as they share their lives. Later in the novel, Agnes and Volusia start a business together, and although there are problems in their relationship, based on Agnes's failure to understand some of the realities of Volusia's life as a black woman, their lives remain intertwined. When Agnes dies, she is, at her request, buried next to Volusia.

Evie and Jane's relationship is also repaired, but not until after Evie learns and realizes the violence that was a part of Jane's life that Evie never saw. Although the novel ends in an idyllic scene, the conversation in which Jane and Evie confront the impact of racial difference on their lives rings more true. Jane tells Evie:

> What you never got . . . was the fact that whenever we were together—walking in town or through the cemetery, anywhere—there was never any doubt in anybody's mind about who was servant and who wasn't. I was always there, because I was with you. I'd like the day to come when I exist for myself, the same as anyone. I'd like for the issue not to be a part of people's minds. I'd even like for it not to be very interesting. (213)

As Evie learns of the racism Jane was always aware of and the antagonism toward Evie she sometimes experienced, Evie "felt as if my years with Jane had been a test, and that I'd failed. I tried to imagine a world in which I had not failed—what would have been different?" (213). If the ending to the novel seems overly optimistic, it is because Cox has portrayed the complex difficulties of interracial friendship so well.

"Who Can You Friend With, Love With Like That?": Sherley Anne Williams's *Dessa Rose*

Though it is set in an earlier century, Sherley Anne Williams's *Dessa Rose*, like Elizabeth Cox's *Night Talk*, shows that black women and white women both must overcome their preconceptions of the other race if they are to be friends. In the "Author's Note" at the beginning of her novel, Williams describes its genesis. Having learned of a pregnant Kentucky slave found guilty of participating in a revolt, whose execution was postponed until after she gave birth, and a North Carolina white woman rumored to shelter escaped slaves, Williams reflected, "How sad . . . that these two women never met" (ix). She creates two characters based on these women, Dessa and Ruth (or Rufel, as she is called for most of the novel), as well as a situation and series of events that would allow these women to overcome their distrust and befriend one another. The ending of the novel is both hopeful and sobering. The black woman and white woman become friends through a set of extraordinary events, yet they realize their unequal social positions prevent their sustaining a meaningful friendship. The fear of difference that fuels their animosity at the beginning of the novel and the barriers to their friendship at its end are depressingly contemporary. That, of course, is the success of the novel's didacticism; it serves as a lesson on the conditions of slavery and connects that history to contemporary antagonisms between African American and white women.

As the novel begins, Dessa has been captured and imprisoned until she gives birth, when she will be executed for participating in a slave revolt in which white men were killed. In the first section, "The Darky," Adam Nehemiah, a figure much like School Teacher in Toni Morrison's *Beloved*, only a pseudohistorian and self-proclaimed expert in plantation management rather than a pseudoscientist, interviews Dessa, wanting to find out about the slave uprising and where she and the other escaped slaves were headed. He plans to write a book based on what he discovers, hoping this text will enable his entrée into plantation society.[1] Nehemiah (or Nemi, as he is later called) is himself thus an outsider to the landed class to which he aspires. In this section of the novel, his thoughts and his conversations with Dessa are interspersed with her memories of her life as a field hand, particularly her love for Kaine. The section provides Dessa's background and the circumstances that led to the slave revolt, her imprisonment, and her second escape, which leads her to Rufel's home, where the next section of the novel begins. Just as the title of the first section, "The Darky," is the epithet Nehemiah uses for Dessa, the second section's title, "The Wench," is how Rufel thinks of the sickly escaped slave who is recuperating in her bed. Nehemiah and Rufel rarely use Dessa's name, for they think of her as property. The second section provides Rufel's background, showing how she has come to live as the only white person on a rundown plantation inhabited by escaped slaves. It also reveals the lessons Rufel has learned about what to expect from her life, including her relationships with slaves. As Rufel contemplates her past, she also slowly comes to realize that she no longer has anyone— not parents, husband, or "Mammy"—to guide her and that she will have to start making decisions about the management of the plantation herself.

Williams has created a plot that dispenses with Rufel's husband and community, two impediments to Dessa and Rufel's relationship that would have reinforced Rufel's stereotypical beliefs about both slaves and herself. Rufel's husband Bertie is on an extended trip. As the novel progresses, it becomes increasingly clear that he has abandoned her, though Rufel is apparently the last person on the plantation to realize she has married a gambler who will not return. Williams has created in Rufel the stereotypical Southern belle, a dreamy girl who married young and has no real capabilities or knowledge of the world. Her naïveté demonstrates that if her husband were present, she would submit to his will and never choose to help the escaped slaves living on their property. Bertie is portrayed as having been a careless master who treated his slaves only as property. Rufel wants to believe that he stopped beating the slaves because of her protests, yet she has heard and chosen to ignore the rumor that he merely moved the beatings farther away from the house so she could not hear the slaves scream (148). Rufel worries about Bertie's reaction to her allowing escaped slaves to reside on their property, knowing he would not approve, but when she thinks of his response, "she resolutely closed her mind against the thought of her husband. She had done what she could do. He would see that when he came" (92–93). Williams also sets Sutton's Glen, Bertie and Rufel's supposed up-and-coming plantation, far from any other dwellings or main roads; indeed, you can barely see the house from the road (109). Bertie has alienated his neighbors through previous dealings, as well as through the pretentiousness of his extensive farming of cotton, a crop no farmer has raised successfully in that part of Alabama, so Rufel has no visitors (108). Williams thus removes the dominant structures upon which the propagation of slavery depends: the patriarch and slave-holding society.

With Bertie's prolonged absence, Rufel loses not only a dominant spouse but also her protector and the person who bore the responsibility (not very well, as it turns out) of running the plantation. The day-to-day operations of the field and house work are taken over by Mammy and the runaway slaves, who are happy to have found a safe haven in the Deep South of Alabama. Rufel is easily swayed into agreeing with Mammy and the other slaves' decisions about the crops and remains ignorant of much of the plantation management. Mammy protects Rufel from the awareness that her husband is a gambling rogue as well as from the knowledge of how the plantation is being run, including how many people are doing the work and living in the slave quarters. In this way, Mammy simultaneously protects the runaways' safety. Rather than focus on practical matters, Rufel increasingly fantasizes about her life in Charleston before her marriage. Trying to justify her decision to marry Bertie and defend her husband against her family's accusations, she finds herself aping Bertie's thoughts: "unconsciously, Rufel quoted Bertie, and shrugged, impatient with herself" (97). Her impatience reveals her growing awareness that she has never thought for herself.

Whereas Mammy fulfills the role of Rufel's comforter and allows the white woman to maintain her illusions about her life, Ada, one of the escaped slaves living and working on Rufel's property, voices a critical perspective of Rufel's position and ignorance. Ada works harmoniously with Mammy but maintains an antagonistic relationship with Rufel, whom she calls "Miz Ruint" (91). Rufel responds to Ada out of her whiteness; she distrusts the escaped slave and refuses to believe that Ada's master raped her, producing her daughter Annabelle. Ada escaped when she saw that the master was planning to rape her daughter as well. Rufel responds to Ada's story not with sympathy but with disbelief, for "she could see nothing attractive in the rawboned, brown-skinned woman or her lanky, half-witted daughter" (93). Mammy prevents Rufel from accusing Ada of lying, but when Rufel expresses her doubts about Ada's story to Mammy, the older woman tells her "men can do things a lady can't even guess at." When Rufel counters by saying, "Everyone know men like em half white and whiter," thereby admitting that white men might be attracted to black women but still denying Ada's claim, Mammy tells her, "Lawd know it must be some way for high yeller to git like that!" (94). In Rufel's rejection of Ada's story, Williams evokes the sexual jealousy white mistresses often experienced when their husbands had sex with their slaves. Rufel's jealousy is mirrored later in the novel by Dessa's angry response to Nathan and Rufel's affair; Dessa cannot accept that Nathan, whom she loves as a brother, would choose to have sex with a white woman. Jealousy thus connects the two women thematically. The two characters' jealousies also relate the resentment some African American women express when African American men and white women date each other to the historical sexual jealousy between black and white women.

Rufel's resentment of Ada stems only partly from the sexual jealousy aroused by Ada's story. Rufel also projects onto Ada the anger at her husband she is unable to express more directly:

> Often, misery washed over her. She would struggle against the familiar tide, feeding her indignation at Ada's story. At least Uncle Joel and Dante, the darkies Bertie had brough back from that last trip, had stayed, she would remind herself then. And, forgetting her angry, and silent, exasperation at Bertie's conviction that he had somehow gotten the best of a deal that netted him an old darky and a crippled one, took some satisfaction in their loyalty to the place. Mammy said they had been some help at harvest, but the real work was done by the darkies Ada knew. (93–94)

Unable to admit her husband's weaknesses and failures, Rufel turns her anger at him toward Ada, who has brought the help that is maintaining the plantation and is in effect providing for Rufel in Bertie's stead. Rufel thereby rejects the lesson she should learn about the dangers of slave women's lives, choosing instead to believe the racist lie of black women's voracious sexual appetites: "Both of them [Ada and Annabelle] probably run off by the mistress for making up to the master," she concludes (95). Rufel even resists Mammy's words: "Mammy had probably not believed Ada's story herself, Rufel thought now, but had not wanted to antagonize Ada" (95). Rufel's reaction to Ada's story shows that her loyalty is to her whiteness and the dominance it affords; she chooses to believe the scripted tale of the masters rather than the truth in front of her, even when that truth is presented to her by the "mammy" she claims to love.

Williams's novel exposes the machinations and faulty logic of white superiority; it also reverses the metaphorical moral meanings attributed to whiteness and blackness in the dominant white culture.[2] The color white terrifies Dessa, and she feels trapped by it when she awakens in Rufel's bedroom: "The raftered ceiling had been whitewashed and recently, the walls, too, and where the sunlight struck them, they gave off a sharp light that hurt her eyes. She closed them, but even behind her lowered lids, she could still see the light striking the white walls and it filled her with terror" (82). Coming to consciousness, she fears "the white woman would kill her kill her [*sic*] and . . . the baby," so she lashes out, hits Rufel, and must be restrained by Ada, whom she does not yet know but whose hands she sees are "Black" (83, ellipsis in original). That the word "black" stands alone as a sentence shows the importance of the racial marker to Dessa and emphasizes its comfort to her. She hopes that the hands are Harker's, but the presence of another black person is enough to assuage her fear, and she again slips into unconsciousness. When she next awakens, she pretends still to be asleep so that she can watch the "white woman *white* [who] stared at her from the shadows of some room" (83). Dessa slips in and out of consciousness, amazed, terrified, and confused by the white woman. At one point, reality becomes mixed with her dream world, and she tries to figure out what her dreaming of a white woman signifies. Her first thought is her mammy's statement that "To dream of death is a sign of marriage" (84). For Dessa, particularly after her beloved Kaine has been killed by their master, whiteness symbolizes death, so to dream of a white woman is to dream of death. As a field hand, Dessa has had few interactions with white people, whose presence has typically indicated danger. Following the uprising in which she tried to kill her master, her time on the coffle, and her imprisonment, she can imagine white people only as dangerous and violent. When she is awake, she focuses on Rufel's mouth, which she compares to "a bloody gash" (88) and "an open wound" (90).

Rufel's distrust of Ada extends to Dessa, though she is disturbed by Dessa's youth: "Thirteen, even fourteen was young to have a baby, even for a darky. Well . . . fifteen. But no older and Ada talked about her as if she were a grown woman" (92). Rufel is torn between her sympathy for Dessa's weakened condition and her fear of the wild behavior of Dessa's few conscious moments. Rufel is also wary because her son has told her that Dessa's nickname is "debil woman" (96).

But her grief over Mammy's recent death makes her curious about Dessa and more open to her than she had ever been to Ada. In fact, as she considers Dessa, her thoughts mix with her memories of Mammy, indicating her longing and need for another woman to take Mammy's place.

> What could there be to fear in this one little sickly, colored gal? Oh, she was wild enough to have some kind of devil in her, Rufel would think, smiling, remembering the way the girl's eyes had bucked the first time she awakened in the bedroom, just the way Mammy's used to when something frightened her. Mammy, Mammy's hands in her hair— Sudden longing pierced Rufel. Mammy's voice: "Aw, Miz 'Fel"; that was special, extra loving, extra. (96)

Rufel recognizes that Dessa must have panicked upon waking in a bed, but the same whiteness that terrifies Dessa comforts Rufel: "Even the open-beam ceiling, so long an ugly reminder of that good-for-nothing darky's unfinished work, seemed, since Mammy had hit upon the idea of painting the rough wood white, almost elegant" (96). At this point in the story, Rufel cannot imagine that another person's reaction could differ from her own. By placing Rufel in an unfinished house, Williams has effectively forced Rufel and Dessa to share the most intimate room of the home at the beginning of their relationship. Further, the whiteness of the room and the sheets emphasizes the white power structure of the slave household. The fact that the house is unfinished and the patriarch absent opens the possibility for the remaining characters to change the story.

When Harker first brings Dessa to the Glen, Rufel's sympathy for another new mother's weak state overcomes her initial urge to prevent him. He rides up on horses Rufel assumes he has stolen and whose owners she expects to come looking for them: "There was something in the ashen skin, like used charcoal, the aimless turning of the head that had kept Rufel silent. The baby had started to cry, a thin wail muffled by layers of covering. The girl's eyes had fluttered open and seemed to look imploringly at Rufel before rolling senselessly back into her head" (97). Rufel's recognizing Dessa as a mother and resulting identification with her as such disrupts her habituated response to slaves. Rufel's memory of the arrival of Harker, Dessa, and the other escaped slaves interrupts a reverie in which she had been comparing her home at the Glen with other, grander plantations she had known. She is torn between thinking of the "darkies" as property, as she has been trained to do, and recognizing their humanity; it is the former and not the latter that feels natural, not to mention proper, to her.

Despite her negative feelings about the adult African Americans, however, Rufel instinctively reaches out to Dessa's infant, who is not so much younger than her own baby.

Williams inverts women's historical racialized roles by making Rufel the wet nurse to Dessa's baby. For Rufel, nursing the baby was initially a natural impulse, but she later worries about what people think of her nursing a black child. She admonishes herself, both for taking Dessa in and for nursing the baby:

> She shouldn't have done it; Rufel had been over that countless times, also. If anybody ever found out. If they [Harker, Dessa, and the other escaped slaves] had been followed. But nothing of that had entered her head as she picked her way carefully up the steep back steps, the baby hugged close to her body. The girl's desolate face, the baby's thin crying—as though it had given up all hope—had grated at her; she was a little crazy, she supposed. But she could do something about this, about the baby who continued to cry while she waited in the dim area back of the stairs for the darkies to bring the girl in. Something about the girl, her face— And: She—Rufel—could do something. That was as close as she came to explaining anything to herself. The baby was hungry and she fed him. (98)

Feeling useful and capable—two things for which her upbringing has not prepared Rufel—is an even stronger lure to action than sympathy. Having been abandoned by her husband in an isolated spot and then losing Mammy, her one connection to all her preparation for her prescribed role in society as wife and mother, Rufel had passively and aimlessly grieved and waited. Dessa and her baby's arrival and need provide Rufel with an immediate sense of purpose, and she begins to act decisively. Nevertheless, her independent thinking discomfits Rufel, so she rationalizes her behavior by filtering it through her husband's attitude (and most likely lies): "Though it would serve the neighbors right, she thought, resentful now, if the darky did belong to someone around here. Many times as Bertie had gone looking for a darky and been met with grins and lies. Truly, it would not surprise her to learn that some jealous neighbor had been tampering with their slaves, just as Bertie had always said, urging them to run away" (98). By mimicking Bertie's rationalizations, Rufel minimizes the radical nature of her actions.

Later, as Rufel nurses Dessa's child, she again remembers the first time she nursed the baby. She does not question the morality of her action but minimizes her accountability.

> Rufel had taken the baby to her bosom almost without thought, to quiet his wailing while Ada and the other darkies settled the girl in the

bedroom. More of that craziness, she knew; but then it had seemed to her as natural as tuneless crooning or baby talk. The sight of him so tiny and bloodied had pained her with an almost physical hurt and she had set about cleaning and clothing him with a single-minded intensity. And only when his cries were stilled and she looked down upon the sleek black head, the nut-brown face flattened against the pearly paleness of her breast, had she become conscious of what she was doing. A wave of embarrassment had swept over her and she had looked guiltily around the parlor. . . . No one would ever know, she had assured herself, and, feeling the feeble tug at her nipple, he's hungry and only a baby. (105)

Only when Rufel is caught by Ada and Harker does she actively claim her choice; their shock lends her courage, leaving her "feeling somehow vindicated in her actions by their very confusion. She had confounded them—rendered Ada speechless" (105). Although she remains ambivalent about others' knowing that she is the baby's wet nurse, it serves as her first act of rebellion against her culture and all she has been taught concerning how she should interact with black people. The fact that her actions noticeably shock her nemesis Ada but no doubt also impress the slave woman who dismissively calls her "Miz Ruint" further satisfies Rufel and colors her action as bold and decisive rather than accidental.

If Bertie and Mammy's absence frees Rufel to act independently, it also increases her suspicion of the blacks, most of whom she does not know. Her seven-year-old son Timmy becomes her source of information, for

the darkies talked before him as they would not with her; it was through him that Rufel kept some kind of track of the comings and goings in the Quarters. She was not entirely convinced that some of those darkies were not Bertie's nigras taking his continued absence as an opportunity to slip back and live free. Neither she nor Timmy would ever recognize them. Mammy had been the one who knew them all. (100)

Rufel is torn between her sympathies for Dessa and her suspicions and fears of the stranger. Her grief for Mammy nurtures her sympathy; Rufel's own need for a sympathetic presence leads her to see similarities between Dessa and Mammy. Rufel's racism causes her to view the sleeping Dessa as "a sooty blur against the whiteness of the pillow," but she reflects that Dessa's eyes "when open . . . looked like Mammy's, a soft brown-black set under sleepy, long-lashed lids" (100). The way Dessa looks at her, however, incites her fear and anger.

Rufel fears that Dessa may recognize her from Charleston, even though she knows that is unlikely. It is Dessa's own anger and fear that upset Rufel: "never, never had Rufel done anything to anyone to deserve such a look. But to see eyes so like Mammy's, staring such hatred at her. It had given Rufel quite a turn. She wanted the girl to wake up, wanted to see that look banished from her face" (101). Rufel does not consider that Dessa's look may stem from how she has been treated by other white people, and she wants absolution from the accusation implied by that look.

At this point, Dessa, still very weak, has learned from Ada that her baby is healthy and that she need not fear the white woman. Waking one night to discover Rufel sleeping in the bed with her—and Rufel's hair covering her face—increases her confusion about her situation: "Once she woke in arms, her face tangled in a skein of fine webbing that seemed alive, it clung and itched her skin so bad. She almost suffocated in terror for she knew the white woman held her and they were together in the big feather bed." Although Dessa is terrified by Rufel, she is also comforted by her, for "really, it was the white woman's breathing that saved her, brought her to her senses; its calm regularity imposing order on her own wildly beating heart" (120). Dessa's conflicted emotions are characteristic of her relationship with Rufel until the very end of the novel. Her precarious existence as an escaped slave renders her safety dependent not only on the sustained kindness but also on the intelligence of Rufel. If at any time, by whim, intent, or accident, Rufel were to betray the black men and women living on her land, they would lose their freedom, and in Dessa's case her life. As Ada points out, their freedom is provisional: "I wouldn't exactly call it free," Ada tells Dessa, "she let us stay here; she need the he'p. Man gone; slaves runned off" (122). Their vulnerability explains Ada's penchant for calling Rufel "Miz Ruint" to dispel her power. That, and the sharing of the bed, lead Dessa to question Rufel's sanity. Dessa is further confused by Rufel's caring for her child, but, like Rufel, she is reluctant to question her beliefs about the other race: "Dessa knew the white woman nursed her baby; she had seen her do it. It went against everything she had been taught to think about white women but to inspect that fact too closely was almost to deny her own existence" (123).

One parallel between Dessa's and Rufel's lives is that they both draw strength from their memories of women named "Mammy," a coincidence that leads them to fight with each other early in Dessa's recovery. As Dessa awakens, she often finds Rufel in the room talking to her, and when she first hears Rufel mention "Mammy," she thinks of the woman from her own slave past and wonders, "what could this white woman know of mammy; or mammy of 'dropped waists' and 'Dutch sleeves'—unless they were cows?" (120). As Rufel tells stories and talks about Mammy, Dessa, still in her sickbed, begins to be confused, as she tries to reconcile her memories of the woman she remembers as "Mammy" with what the white woman is saying. Rufel's talk upsets Dessa because it makes her doubt her memories of her past, her sinecure against the uncertainty of her present. She tells herself that Rufel is "crazy, making up this whole thing," until she can no longer maintain her silence: " 'Wasn't no "mammy" to it.' The words burst from Dessa. She knew even as she said it what the white woman meant" (124). Even as her exclamation appears to return her to full consciousness and the practical realization that they are thinking of two different women, she maintains her denial of Rufel's experience because she is offended by the white woman's appropriation of a slave's affection, which Dessa wants to believe could be given, at least genuinely, only to other slaves. Both women rely on their memories of the love and guidance they received from the woman they knew as "Mammy" for their own sense of self and strength. The memories nurture them, and each woman needs to believe that the relationship she remembers was unique and special. Rufel is stunned by Dessa's refutations, which fuels Dessa's urge to continue, thinking "anybody could make this white woman's wits go gathering" (125). Mary Kemp Davis argues that "Williams uses the word 'Mammy' rather than Dessa's own name or nickname to evoke autobiographical memories because Dessa's amnesia threatens to erase not merely her own past, but her family's past and, therefore, an important segment of the racial past." For Davis, the sickbed is Dessa's place of rebirth, where "she realizes that she, alone, is an authoritative witness to what she has seen and suffered; she, alone, is the bearer of her family's names, its tragic history" (554). In this middle section of the novel, both women begin to come to terms with their pasts and to form the identities they need to carry them into their futures.

Rufel also immediately assumes that they are speaking of different women, emphasizing "*My* mammy," but is interrupted by Dessa, who refuses to believe that slave women who were caretakers for white children could feel genuine affection for those children: "No *white* girl could ever have taken *her* place in mammy's bosom; no one." She finally confounds Rufel by asserting " 'Mammy' ain't nobody name, not they real one," even though she herself remembers the beloved woman from her own past by that name. Dessa compounds the insult by informing Rufel, "Mammy have a name, have children." But Rufel, who needs to be unique, answers, "She just had me! I was like her child" (125). Dessa continues her taunt with a litany of her mammy's children's names, and Rufel must confront for the first time the possibility that Mammy had a life she knew nothing about, which may have included her own family and children.[3] Rufel both feared and "half-hoped" (128) that Dessa might know her Mammy because she longs for a connection to her former existence. Even Dessa's listening had held that promise: "Rufel had not talked of Charleston with the raw yearning that Mammy had come to hate and fear, but as simple proof that that life had existed; the darky's credulous, if drowsy, attention had seemed somehow to confirm that existence" (129). By blaming her own lapse of judgment, for having "fallen into reminiscing with a strange darky" and "gossiping like common trash," Rufel consoles herself in the sense of superiority she takes from her whiteness and the class status of her upbringing, but she also acknowledges "that she was lonely, that the silence since Mammy's death sometimes came near to crushing her. And to be invited to speak—Resentment flared in her" (129). Her need for someone to listen to her—so much like Temple's need for Nancy to listen in Faulkner's *Requiem for a Nun*—makes her vulnerable and causes her to react in anger when Dessa rejects the story she never in fact "invited."

In her isolation, Rufel leaves the house to get away from Ada and Dessa. On her walk she encounters Nathan, whom she recognizes as one of Dessa's visitors. At this point, the narrative begins to veer away from a realistic plot. The first section of the novel, "The Darky," portrayed a reasonably credible account of a white historian's interviewing an imprisoned slave, reminiscent of Nat Turner's story and a commentary on William Styron's 1967 *The Confessions of Nat Turner*, which Williams references in her author's note, though not by name.[4] The second section, "The Wench," which concerns Dessa and Rufel's burgeoning relationship, certainly requires the suspension of disbelief but remains at least plausible. The final section of the novel, however, entitled "The Negress," becomes an adventure tale that although it is set in the nineteenth century, has the sensibilities of the twentieth.[5] The strain on belief begins at the end of the middle section when Rufel first meets Nathan. He approaches her and, crying for Mammy, she embraces him. Her need for Mammy becomes her need for Nathan. She is so caught up in her thoughts of the woman whose name she finally remembers was Dorcas that she is startled to find herself being held by a black man. His physical proximity causes her actually to look at a black man as though for the first time, and she sees not the stereotype she expects but a human face: "She turned to the darky aghast, and caught her breath. Never had she seen such blackness. She blinked, expecting to see the bulbous lips and bulging eyes of a burnt-cork minstrel. Instead she looked into a pair of rather shadowy eyes and strongly defined features that were—handsome! she thought shocked, almost outraged" (132).

The fight with Dessa causes Rufel to reconsider her relationship with Dorcas and finally to recognize her role in the woman's enslavement: "wanting desperately to believe that Mammy had loved her not only fully, but freely as well. Almost she felt personally responsible for Mammy's pain, personally connected to it, not as the soother of hurt as Mammy had always been for her, but as the source of that pain" (147).[6] Rufel also begins to reevaluate the other men and women on the plantation not as property but as human beings with stories. Her relationship with Nathan begins with her seeking him out and asking him about his, Dessa's, and the others' stories, particularly their escape.

Williams avoids an easy alliance between Rufel and Dessa following the white woman's burgeoning awareness. Nathan and Rufel's relationship moves quickly from her relying on him for information to their becoming lovers, a move that escalates Dessa's anger and allows Williams to address the resentment many African American women feel when African American men date white women.[7] The second section of the novel culminates in Dessa's discovering the new lovers in bed together. In her shock, she calls Rufel "Miz Ruint," and the final words of the chapter are Rufel's realization: "Ruined, that was what the wench had said. Ruined. That was what she meant" (172). Her affair with Nathan has exacerbated the tension between her and Dessa. More important, in being seen, Rufel realizes she has relinquished any tie to the white womanhood she claims in all her fantasies about her Charleston youth. If nursing a black infant spurred anxieties about her ability to maintain that privileged identity, violating the miscegenation taboo unmistakably bars her from inhabiting the role of white lady.

The third section of the novel, "The Negress," begins with Dessa feeling that Nathan has betrayed her by choosing a white woman: "I never thought one of them could be so ignorant to something that hurt me so bad. White woman was everything I feared and hated, and it hurt me that one of them [Nathan, Harker, and Cully] would want to love with her" (182). Dessa's memory evokes the violent end interracial relationships—even supposed ones—had for black men; she recalls, "The remembrance of them in that bed kept stabbing at my eyes, my heart—black white red. I knowed that red was her hair, but it looked like blood to me" (176–177). Dessa moves out of the house to the quarters where the other blacks live. When Ada reports Nathan and Rufel's liaison to the group, Harker and Cully rejoice, the latter exclaiming, "Miz Lady bound to come in on the deal now" (179). The three men—Harker, Nathan, and Cully–have developed a plan based on a scam run by Harker's old master to enable the whole group to move West, where they can be free and own land. They need Rufel to travel with them and sell a few of them as slaves. Those who were sold would then escape, rejoin the group, and move to the next place. Dessa does not trust Rufel, whose naïveté she fears will endanger them. But Rufel agrees to participate only if Dessa apologizes for calling her "Miz Ruint" and travels with them playing the role of Rufel's maid. Eventually, at Harker's urging, Dessa "apologize[s] for being rude" (207).

A group of six blacks and Rufel set out to work their plan, leaving the others behind to tend the crops. Once they acquire sufficient money to finance their move West, they will return for the others. The first night of their trip, they find shelter at the home of Mr. Oscar, whose family is away. As a former field worker, Dessa has much to learn about being a lady's maid, and she resents being treated as a slave by Rufel in front of strangers. When Rufel returns to their room after dining with Mr. Oscar and is tipsy, Dessa is particularly annoyed and feels her suspicions have been confirmed: "I hurried her out that dress and into bed, uneasy at having her like this—what if she'd slipped in front of that white man? . . . She wasn't acting no better than what I'd said and I had a earful I was going give [*sic*] Harker that next morning" (218).

Dessa's attitude changes after she is woken by the sounds of Mr. Oscar in Rufel's bed. At first, she believes his presence is welcome, as his flirtations had been earlier that day, but she soon realizes Rufel is fighting him. Together, the two women force the drunken man from the room. Their shared victory and fear overcome some of the tension that has remained between them, and when Rufel silently asks Dessa to sleep with her in the bed, Dessa agrees. The incident is revelatory to Dessa, whose recognition of white women's vulnerability keeps her awake:

> The white woman was subject to the same ravishment as me. I hadn't knowed white mens could use a white woman like that, just take her by force same as they could with us. Harker, neither Nathan could help us there in that House, any House. I knew they would kill a black man for loving with a white woman; would they kill a black man for keeping a white man off a white woman? I didn't know; and didn't want to find out.

> I slept with her after that, both of us wrapped around Clara [Rufel's baby daughter]. And I wasn't so cold with her no more. I wasn't zactly warm with her, understand; I didn't know how to be warm with no white woman. But now it was like we had a secret between us, not just that bad Oscar—though we kept that quiet. I couldn't bring myself to tell Harker, neither Nathan, about that night. Seemed like it would've been almost like telling on myself, if you know what I mean. I was posed to be keeping an eye on her and something had almost got by me. Sides, I told myself, that bad Oscar had paid Miz Lady back twice over for coming on so hankty with me. But really, what kept me quiet was knowing white mens wanted the same thing, would take the same thing from a white woman as they would from a black woman. Cause they could. I never will forget the fear that come on me when Miz Lady called me on Mr. Oscar, that knowing that she was as helpless in this as I was, that our only protection was ourselfs and each others. (220)

Dessa feels allied with Rufel in their shared vulnerability, as well as the shared shame that results from it, as neither woman initially tells the men.

Their experiences as they travel reconcile Dessa to both Nathan and Rufel. At the next stop, when Dessa becomes upset seeing her friends auctioned as property to the highest bidder, Nathan comforts her. After a tender moment, he asks, "why can't I like you and her [Rufel] too?" (224). They emerge from their exchange closer, but Dessa fears their relationship will never be the same. She becomes more comfortable being with Nathan and Rufel because their behavior does not betray their intimacy; rather, they focus on their purpose and on maintaining their cover story. Dessa admits to growing closer to Rufel, stating, "You can't do something like this with someone and not develop some closeness, some trust" (225). Dessa also comes to admire Rufel's negotiating skills and appreciate how the white woman's charms enhance their project:

> And Miz Lady was good; she could hold and pacify Clara and bargain over a slave at the same time, matter a fact, she liked to do that to throw peoples off guard; they'd be up there playing with Clara and she had closed the sale. She bat her eyes and the sheriff want to put up handbills for her. She smile and a planter raise his price fifty dollars, just to be what she called "gallant." All that bat the eye and giggle was just so much put-on now, and it give me a kick to see how she used these to get her way with the peoples we met. (226)

The exposure to other white people, which Dessa never had previously, also helps her appreciate Rufel's former expectations for her life and that she had never treated the escaped slaves living on her property as badly as many whites treated black people.

Despite the shared experiences, the disparity in their social status limits their developing closeness, as do their very different perspectives on slavery. As Dessa explains, "See, Miz Lady didn't believe most white folks was mean. She thought that if white folks knew slaves as she knew us, wouldn't be no slavery. She thought that was what'd ruined her husband—seeing how much money you could make if you owned other peoples" (231–232). Dessa perceives both Rufel's sincerity and her naïveté: "If they [whites] just knew, she kept saying. Well, I believed this of *her*, but I couldn't understand how she could watch white folks buying up our peoples right and left and say this" (232). Rufel has come to care for the people she is working with and has come to recognize some of the evils of slavery, but she still does not discern the horrors of the institution, the depravity of slave owners, or the danger their current project poses to the men and woman they are selling.

Toward the end of the journey, they sell Nathan as well as the others, leaving Dessa and Rufel alone with the baby. The two women get along well until Rufel suggests that she might move West with the others. She wants to dissociate herself from the "white peoples [who] act so hateful" as well as from slavery (238). The suggestion shocks Dessa, who, thinking again of Rufel's relationship with Nathan, responds, "I think it scandalous, white woman chasing all around the country after some red-eyed negro." Dessa immediately regrets her words, but her efforts at an apology, saying "something about it not being [her] place to speak" anger Rufel as much as, if not more than, the initial outburst. Rufel responds to the hypocrisy of the phrase, repeating it and acknowledging that it is used as a way of "mocking" whites. As Dessa leaves their room, Rufel yells at her, "I'm talking friends" (239). For Dessa, the suggestion that she and a white woman could be friends is initially as disconcerting as a white woman and black man's being lovers, although, as she calms down, she realizes she also wants to believe friendship is possible:

> This was the damnedest white woman. White as a sheet and about that much sense—sleeping with negroes, hiding runaways, wanting to be my friend. Who wanted to be her friend anyway? . . . It was like her to take for granted that I'd want to be her friend, that *we*-all would want her to come West with us, that she could have what she want for the asking. . . . And she want to be my friend. . . . This was something I hadn't thought of in her. And I wanted to believe it. I don't think I wronged her at first, but the white woman I'd opened my eyes to at

the start of the summer wasn't the one I partnered with on that
journey; I admitted this to myself that afternoon. . . . I wanted to
believe I'd heard the white woman ask me to friend with her. I wouldn't
put no dependence on her holding to it, I told myself, not tarrying
now, wanting to see how this would end. "Friend" to her might be like
"promise" to white folks. Something to break if it would do them some
good. But I wouldn't draw back from her neither. (240–241)

Dessa remains wary but is clearly excited about the possibility of
friendship. No sooner does she realize her interest, however, than she
is stopped by Nehemiah, or Nemi, the white man who interrogated
her in the first section of the novel.

Forgetting Rufel's current alias, Dessa calls out that she "belongs
to Mistress Sutton." After Nehemiah takes her to the sheriff, Dessa
corrects her mistake, telling him she belongs to "Miz Carlisle" (242).
The sheriff is wary of Nemi, who has brought other black women to
him claiming they are the escaped slave he is looking for. The would-
be scholar and slave catcher argues that she can be identified because
she is "branded . . . R on the thigh, whipscarred about the hips"
(244). The sheriff sends men to find Miss Carlisle at the hotel and
puts Dessa in a jail cell. Dessa despairs, believing her scars will give her
away. Nemi has clearly become crazed in his search for Dessa, and
he taunts her in her cell. When Rufel arrives, she tries to convince the
sheriff that Nemi is mistaken. Nemi proceeds to recount Dessa's
crimes, real and imagined. Dessa fears that his argument will remind
Rufel of all her initial suspicions when the so-called devil woman
arrived on her plantation. The prison serves as proving ground of
Rufel's feelings and trustworthiness. When Nemi will not be satisfied,
the sheriff sends for a black woman, Aunt Chole, to inspect Dessa for the
scars. Dessa gives the woman a quarter, and Chole assures the men she
has found no scars.

After they leave the prison, an excited Dessa begins to speak to Rufel,
calling her "Mis'ess" and "Miz." Rufel responds to the appellation
angrily, stating, "My name Ruth . . . Ruth. I ain't your mistress" (255).
Dessa answers, "Well, if it come to that . . . my name Dessa, Dessa
Rose. Ain't no O to it." The two women finally call each other by
name, not title or slur. They have come to respect one another and
have achieved an equality, if only temporarily. As Dessa states,
"We couldn't hug each other, not on the streets . . . we both had
sense enough to know that . . . but that night we walked the board-
walk together and we didn't hide our grins" (256). Despite the many
limitations of their relationship, they walk side by side. Williams has

shown the enormous difficulty of a white woman and a black woman overcoming their differences to forge an alliance. Although the novel is set in the antebellum South, many of the racial anxieties it evokes resonate with contemporary times. For all its hopefulness, ultimately the text acknowledges that nineteenth-century society posed insurmountable barriers to interracial friendship. As Dessa states in the epilogue, "We come West and Ruth went East . . . some city didn't allow no slaves. . . . Miss her in and out of trouble. . . . Negro can't live in peace under protection of law, got to have some white person to stand protection for us. And who can you friend with, love with like that?" (259).

"A Girl from a Whole Other Race": Toni Morrison's "Recitatif," *Beloved*, and *Paradise*

Whereas Gibbons and Cox explore the possibilities of interracial friendship and examine its effect on white characters' conceptions of racial identity, Toni Morrison uses interracial relationships in her fiction to challenge readers' conceptions of racial identity. Like Williams, she returns to the historical roots of those relationships in slavery in the United States. In her 1983 short story "Recitatif," as in her 1987 novel *Beloved*, Morrison emphasizes the intersections of race and economic class. Morrison never identifies which character is black and which is white in "Recitatif," although much of the story concerns the impact of the women's racial difference on their relationship. The racial ambiguity in the story creates a mystery that forces readers to confront their racialized assumptions about characters. In *Beloved*, Morrison explores how the historical construction of women's interracial relationships situates the interplay of race, class, and bodies through the white girl Amy Denver's acting as midwife to Sethe at Denver's birth. And the provocative opening sentences of her 1998 novel *Paradise*—"They shoot the white girl first. With the rest they can take their time" (3)—plays with readers' assumptions about the meanings of racial identity and difference by making a racial distinction that ends up not being meaningful because the novel never explicitly identifies which of the Convent women is white. By setting the reader on a fruitless quest, Morrison thus comments on the central regrettable irony of race in the United States—a trait that is in itself meaningless has been overloaded with meanings. Furthermore, although the hostility of the men of Ruby has its root in racial exclusion, the hatred they unleash on the women of the Convent is not based on the women's race. All three works thus force readers to confront their own racialized expectations for characters. And in all three, Morrison uses marginalized cultural spaces as settings that allow for women's interracial friendships, suggesting that these relationships are not merely difficult but virtually prohibited by typical social structures and by Americans' assumptions about what race means.

Engaging readers' conceptions of race is a practice closely aligned to some of the projects Morrison outlines in her critical works that examine the role of race in American literature. In her 1989 essay "Unspeakable Things Unspoken: The Afro-American Presence in American Literature," she addresses the arguments over revising the literary canon and argues that African American literature needs to be conceived of as a body of work that has contributed to and influenced the development of the nation's literature, not just as an additional and marginalized subcategory of American literature, an entity that "according to conventional wisdom, is certainly not Chicano literature, or Afro-American literature, or Asian-American, or Native American, or . . ." (1, ellipsis in original). Morrison's purpose is "to address ways in which the presence of Afro-American literature and the awareness of its culture both resuscitate the study of literature in the United States and raise that study's standards" (3–4). Similarly, in *Playing in the Dark: Whiteness and the Literary Imagination* (1992), Morrison explores the ways whiteness has been developed in contrast to what she calls an "Africanist" presence in canonical American literature. She argues that the concept of racial difference is central to American literature and culture, even though that centrality has been denied. Morrison asks

> whether the major and championed characteristics of our national literature—individualism, masculinity, social engagement versus historical isolation; acute and ambiguous moral problematics; the thematics of innocence coupled with an obsession with figurations of death and hell—are not in fact responses to a dark, abiding, signing Africanist presence. It has occurred to me that the very manner by which American literature distinguishes itself as a coherent entity exists because of this unsettled and unsettling population. Just as the formation of the nation necessitated coded language and purposeful restriction to deal with the racial disingenuousness and moral frailty at its heart, so too did the literature, whose founding characteristics extend into the twentieth century, reproduce the necessity for codes and restriction. (5–6)[1]

Her criticism thus places racial difference at the center of American literature and identity.

"Recitatif"

In *Playing in the Dark*, Morrison explicitly connects "Recitatif" to her attempt "to maneuver ways to free up the language from its sometimes sinister, frequently lazy, almost always predictable employment of racially informed and determined chains." She states, "The only short story I have ever written, 'Recitatif,' was an experiment in the removal of all racial codes from a narrative about two characters of different races for whom racial identity is crucial" (xi). Without identifying the race of either character, the story chronicles the friendship of a black woman and a white woman from their initial meeting in a shelter for girls through their coincidental meetings over two decades. By carefully manipulating economic markers and bodily descriptions, Morrison creates a matrix of class, race, and bodies that highlights our tendency to read race *as* class and to attribute meanings to physical bodies. The racial ambiguity about the main characters, coupled with the centrality of race to the story, creates in the reader a desire to solve the mystery of racial identity, but the only clues to racial identity are economic, cultural, and bodily. By compelling readers to read economic and bodily descriptions as racial clues, Morrison's story reveals people's tendencies to make economic and even moral assumptions about others based on the visual cue of their race. These problematics of interpretation indicate the anxieties aroused by racial ambiguity.

Morrison establishes the girls' racial difference by presenting it as an obstacle to their relationship at the beginning of the story. As Twyla narrates her arrival at the shelter, she says,

> The minute I walked in . . . I got sick to my stomach. It was one thing to be taken out of your own bed early in the morning—it was something else to be stuck in a strange place with a girl from a whole other race. And Mary, that's my mother, she was right. Every now and then she would stop dancing long enough to tell me something important and one of the things she said was that they never washed their hair and they smelled funny. (243)

Twyla's assertion reveals the reciprocal nature of racial stereotypes, which adapt to fit whatever race is being referred to. Early in the story, however, the girls' racial difference is more easily overcome by them than the story's racial ambiguity is by the readers. When Twyla tells Roberta that her mother "just likes to dance all night," she is reassured because Roberta knows not to ask further questions: "I liked the way she understood things so fast. So for the moment it didn't matter that we looked like salt and pepper standing there and that's what the other kids called us sometimes" (244). The racial difference foreshadows the characters' later conflicts; more important, it establishes narrative tensions for readers, who are left wondering which girl is which race.

Elizabeth Abel has speculated, based on her own informal survey, that readers tend to identify the race of Twyla, the first-person narrator, as their own: white readers believe that Twyla is white and Roberta black, whereas black readers assume Twyla is black and Roberta white. I find, probably like many readers, that I can read either girl as either race, and I often switch the characters' racial identities as I read the story. What I cannot do is read the story without assigning race to the characters. My interpretation of the characters depends on my conceptualization of their race, suggesting that race may be conceived of as primary to American identity—or at least that we have been conditioned to believe it is so.

The plot of "Recitatif," however, focuses primarily on how women's relationships with other women—mothers, friends, and even apparently casual acquaintances—constitute identity. Race arises as a significant constituent of identity because of the connections and separations of those relationships. Whereas racial difference, once established, is delayed as a subject, relationships are construed through sameness and difference from the beginning. Marked by difference at the shelter because they are not "real orphans with beautiful dead parents in the sky" (244), Twyla and Roberta share a sameness that unites them, but their differences from one another, the first of which is the troubling spectacle of their racial difference in their initial meeting, threaten and test that unity. Overall, their experience in the shelter is one of togetherness and sameness, but their subsequent meetings are dominated by their differences, which are cultural and economic and only secondarily connected to race. The dynamic of their needing and resisting their identifications with one another marks the conflicts of their meetings over the years in a Howard Johnson's, an upscale market, a school picket line, and an after-hours cafe. Twyla and Roberta's shared experiences of being in the shelter and having mothers who could not adequately care for them create a shared knowledge of one another. These ties are the source of their mixed sense of connection and disconnection, comfort and discomfort with one another. Whereas the racial ambiguity may create anxiety in the story's readers, Twyla and Roberta's anxieties stem from their mothers' ambiguities.

From the beginning of the story, the girls' relationship is construed through their mothers' differences—from one another and from those mothers who are able to take care of their children. The terms used to describe their mothers—"dancing" and "sick"—are themselves paradoxical to the expectations for normative motherhood. The girls seem to think that the mothers' meeting each other would have a recuperative effect, as Twyla says: "I thought if my dancing mother met her sick mother it might be good for her. And Roberta thought her sick mother would get a big bang out of a dancing one" (246). The mothers' difference from other mothers constitutes the girls' "sameness," but their solidarity is also necessitated because the older girls, whose "lipstick and eyebrow pencil" help make them appear "tough . . . and mean" (244) and whom they "called gar girls— Roberta's misheard word for the evil stone faces described in civics class" (253), like to torment them. They are also exiled from the other children their own age: "nobody else wanted to play with us because we weren't real orphans with beautiful dead parents in the sky. We were dumped. Even the New York City Puerto Ricans and the upstate Indians ignored us. All kinds of kids were in there, black ones, white ones, even two Koreans" (244). Thus, despite Twyla's initial offense at having to share a room with "a girl from a whole other race," it is clear that a range of races occupy the shelter and that the meaningful difference in this context is less race than it is the status of one's parents: because their mothers are visible, embodied, and flawed, they cannot be imagined as idealized parents.

When the girls' mothers visit, their difference from each other is portrayed through their bodies and clothes, which make them seem practically a symbolic juxtaposition of sexuality and religion. Twyla's mother Mary, the "dancing mother," is inappropriately dressed for chapel in "green slacks that made her behind stick out" and a fur jacket with torn pocket linings. Twyla is ashamed of the improper dress but enraptured by her mother's effusive greeting, beautiful face, and the smell of her "Lady Esther dusting powder" (247). Twyla's mother's inviting body contrasts starkly with Roberta's mother's foreboding one. Roberta's mother, the "sick mother," overwhelms Twyla with her size: "She was big. Bigger than any man and on her chest was the biggest cross I'd ever seen. I swear it was six inches long each way. And in the crook of her arm was the biggest Bible ever made" (247). Roberta's mother (who is never given a name) refuses to shake Mary's hand, glancing at her disdainfully before pulling her daughter away.

How do we read these bodies when we are trying to determine the race of the characters? For Abel, this scene and the next, the girls' first post-shelter meeting eight years later at a Howard Johnson's where Twyla is a waitress, are crucial to her reading of Twyla as white. Roberta's mother's large body, the morally authoritative position of her expressed contempt for Mary, and Roberta's own position as the perceptive one combine with Roberta's sexualized dress at the Howard Johnson's—she sports a halter top, hoop earrings, big hair, and heavy makeup—to construct Roberta as black. Twyla's waitress outfit and her cultural ignorance (she does not know who Jimi Hendrix is) contrast starkly with both Roberta's sexuality and her authority. As Abel puts it, "the power of metonymy generates a contrast between the amplitude of the sexualized body [Roberta's] and the skimpiness and pallor of the socially harnessed body [Twyla's]" ("Black Writing, White Reading" 473). The signs functioning in this metonymy are confoundingly slippery, however; for instance, Twyla's mother Mary wears the sexualized dress at the shelter, but Roberta sports the sexy clothing in the Howard Johnson's. As for the daughters, is not Roberta's halter-and-shorts outfit, accessorized by big earrings and hair, just as "socially harnessing" as Twyla's waitress uniform?

Abel herself acknowledges the inadequacy of her interpretation: "Pivoting not on skin color, but on size, sexuality, and the imagined capacity to nurture and be nurtured, on the construction of embodiedness itself as a symptom and source of cultural authority, my reading installs the (racialized) body at the center of a text that deliberately withholds conventional racial iconography" (474). She admits that her interpretation reveals her "white woman's fantasy . . . about black women's potency" that "persist[s] in the face of contrary evidence" (474). Abel contrasts her reading with that of a black friend who believes Twyla is black and Roberta white on the basis of the characters' economic status and politics. Abel's article delineates many of the possible readings of economic, psychological, political, and cultural details as racial clues, and in so doing shows how unconscious stereotypes affect both interpretation and the relationships of certain white and black feminisms. Perhaps the point of all the story's descriptions, particularly the bodily ones, is that despite the bifurcation of conceptions of women along racial lines, stereotypes of both black and white women are used against them in very similar ways. Women's bodies, regardless of race, are always excessive—too big, too sexy, too inappropriate, too awkward. If women's bodies are excessive, mothers are always inadequate. Feeling rebuffed by Roberta at the Howard Johnson's, Twyla ends the conversation by asking her the forbidden question:

> "How's your mother?" I asked. Her grin cracked her whole face. She swallowed. "Fine," she said. "How's yours?"
> "Pretty as a picture," I said and turned away. The backs of my knees were damp. (250)

The question works as a rebuke because *having* an inadequate mother evokes the daughters' guilt.

Although race and motherhood are central themes of the story, they are also largely unspoken anxieties. Throughout the story, Twyla and Roberta remain reticent about their mothers, and once their racial difference is established, it is rarely mentioned again, even though their other differences tempt racialized readings. What holds the story together structurally is the racially ambiguous Maggie, who at first appears incidental, a character brought up only because Twyla cannot figure out the prominence of the shelter's apple orchard in her dreams:

> I don't know why I dreamt about that orchard so much. Nothing really happened there. Nothing all that important, I mean. Just the big girls dancing and playing the radio. Roberta and me watching. Maggie fell down there once. The kitchen woman with legs like parentheses. And the big girls laughed at her. We should have helped her up, I know, but we were scared of those girls with lipstick and eyebrow pencil. Maggie couldn't talk. The kids said she had her tongue cut out, but I think she was just born that way: mute. She was old and sandy-colored and she worked in the kitchen. I don't know if she was nice or not. I just remember her legs like parentheses and how she rocked when she walked. . . . She wore this really stupid little hat—a kid's hat with ear flaps—and she wasn't much taller than we were. A really awful little hat. Even for a mute it was dumb—dressing like a kid and never saying anything at all. (245)

The illogic of Twyla's criticism—blaming a mute person for not talking—reveals her anxieties about Maggie. The cause of those anxieties is apparently resolved by her guilt at having called Maggie "Dummy" and "Bow legs," purportedly to find out whether she could hear: "And it shames me even now to think there was somebody in there after all who heard us call her those names and couldn't tell on us" (245). The memories of Maggie that Twyla tries to piece together structure the narrative, providing reference points and transitions and creating a mystery for Twyla that compels the narrative. Maggie also becomes a point of contention between Twyla and Roberta, the figure that fosters their discussion of their racial difference and conflicts.

In the figure of Maggie, the mysteries of race and motherhood coalesce. Twyla even references their mothers' visit to the shelter by Maggie: "I think it was the day before Maggie fell down that we found out our mothers were coming to visit us on the same Sunday. We had been at the shelter twenty-eight days (Roberta twenty-eight and a half) and this was their first visit with us" (246). Maggie thus becomes somehow primary to Twyla's story, which is inextricably intertwined with Roberta's. She is the ambiguous figure at the margin of their childhood world, one who resides in their adulthood at the edge of their consciousness, the symbol for all they cannot figure out about their mothers, race, their identities, and the relationships among all of these.

Just as Twyla and Roberta cannot bring themselves to speak about their mothers except in cursory terms, they have difficulty telling Maggie's story. Their attempts at articulation unify their final meetings, as their interaction inevitably leads to the question "Whatever happened to Maggie?" When they finally resolve that question and acknowledge their identifications with Maggie as a figure who represents both the ineptitude of their mothers and their own powerlessness, the story ends. She is the touchstone that both connects and divides them. Her image and what happened to her haunts them, taps all their secret fears from their past.

Maggie's story also provides the connection between the first sections of the story, in which bodily markers summon readings of race, and Twyla and Roberta's adult interactions, in which class markers become the prominent distinctions. Twyla, guiltily shopping in a new upscale market, is approached by a woman she does not recognize as Roberta, at least partially because of her affluent dress: "the woman leaning toward me was dressed to kill. Diamonds on her hand, a smart white summer dress" (251). Both women are married: Twyla to a fireman, Roberta to an IBM executive. The blue-collar/white-collar distinction of their husbands' jobs is another ambiguous racial marker. Morrison herself has pointed out that IBM actively recruited black executives, whereas the firemen's union in upstate New York resisted integration (Abel, "Black Writing, White Reading" 476). This meeting is friendlier than their previous one, and they share stories and laugh until Twyla brings up Maggie's fall in the orchard and Roberta corrects her. Roberta's revelation—that the older girls pushed Maggie down and ripped her clothes—disturbs Twyla, who keeps saying that she does not remember those events. But Roberta is adamant. Twyla is disturbed and becomes aggravated with Roberta. It is interesting that in her aggravation she returns not just to the incident at the Howard Johnson's but specifically to the change in Roberta's appearance: "My ears were itching and I wanted to go home suddenly. This was all very well but she couldn't just comb her hair, wash her face and pretend everything was hunky-dory. After the Howard Johnson's snub. And no apology. Nothing" (254–255).

Twyla asks Roberta about her attitude that day, and her response—
"Oh, Twyla, you know how it was in those days: black—white. You
know how everything was"—brings up another difference, this time
in their experience of a cultural moment. For Twyla's memories of the
civil rights movement of the 1960s tends toward the peace-loving
version: "I thought it was just the opposite. Busloads of blacks and
whites came into Howard Johnson's together. They roamed together
then: students, musicians, lovers, protesters. You got to see everything
at Howard Johnson's and blacks were very friendly with whites in
those days" (255). This difference, at least partly, amounts to
insider/outsider status: Roberta, dressed as a hippie, on her way to
her friend's audition with Jimi Hendrix, sees the conflicts from the
inside; Twyla observes the changes in race relations from her position
as a waitress in a road-stop restaurant. When the women part, speaking
of their mothers again gives their conversation closure. Roberta tells
Twyla to call her, but Twyla does not plan to because "Roberta had
messed up my past somehow with that business about Maggie" (255).

The women next meet when Twyla spots Roberta on a picket line
protesting busing to integrate public schools. Twyla does not even
know what she thinks about the busing until she hears Roberta's
opposition. Their disagreement over this issue shatters their alignment, and each woman says to the other, "I wonder what made me
think you were different" (256). The implication, of course, is
"different from others of your race." Again their disagreement turns
into comments about their physical bodies. Roberta tries to quell their
argument by reminding Twyla, "I used to curl your hair." Twyla vin-
dictively responds, "I hated your hands in my hair" (257). (The comment recalls Twyla's mother's admonition that "they never wash their
hair.") When the women from the picket line begin to rock Twyla's
car, however, she automatically reaches her arm out to Roberta for
help, "like the old days in the orchard when they [the older girls] saw
us watching them and we had to get out of there, and if one of us fell
the other pulled her up and if one of us was caught the other stayed to
kick and scratch, and neither would leave the other behind" (257).
Twyla's almost instinctive reach for Roberta indicates the primacy of
their emotional tie, which persists despite their anger and sense of
betrayal. Roberta just looks at her, and after the police make the pick-
eters desist, she lashes out, saying, "Maybe I am different now, Twyla.
But you're not. You're the same little state kid who kicked a poor old
black lady and you have the nerve to call me a bigot" (257). At this
point Maggie's racial ambiguity becomes a source of tension between
Twyla and Roberta. Twyla is stunned, and answers, "She wasn't

black." "Like hell she wasn't," Roberta retorts, "and you kicked her. We both did. You kicked a black lady who couldn't even scream" (258). The story comes full circle, and the racial difference that in the beginning of the story alarmed Twyla but was so easily overcome by the girls' similar positions now becomes the focus of an argument that arises out of the women's different economic and political alignments.

The opposing picket lines become the setting for Twyla and Roberta's conversation with each other, which they carry out through coded picket signs about motherhood. The next day, to answer Roberta's "MOTHERS HAVE RIGHTS TOO!" sign, Twyla paints a sign that says "AND SO DO CHILDREN****." She returns to the school to find that another picket line has formed in opposition to the first, and she joins it. Twyla realizes in retrospect that her "sign didn't make sense without Roberta's," though at the time she thought it was "obvious" (258). Likewise, Twyla seems to need Roberta to confirm her own identity. Twyla positions herself in the line so that her movements mirror Roberta's and they face each other when they reach the turn. When Roberta fails to acknowledge her presence, Twyla creates a new sign that answers Roberta's "MOTHERS HAVE RIGHTS TOO!" with the question "HOW WOULD YOU KNOW?," alluding to the fact that Roberta's children are stepchildren. Twyla states, "I had gotten addicted now. My signs got crazier each day, and the women on my side decided that I was a kook. They couldn't make heads or tails out of my brilliant screaming posters" (258). Only Roberta's reaction matters to Twyla; the fact that the other women think she's crazy does not disturb her sense of self. Twyla's final sign asks "IS YOUR MOTHER WELL?," in response to which Roberta leaves and does not return, and neither does Twyla. The political issue has become for them personal; the intensity of their relationship both drives their protest and extinguishes it. Twyla appears to need to work out her relationship with Roberta to have a stable sense of her past and her identity.

Maggie's racial ambiguity is what haunts Twyla. She does not believe she participated in the kicking, and Roberta later confirms that they did not. But Twyla needs to know Maggie's race. She muses, "When I thought about it I actually couldn't be certain." Twyla remembers physical characteristics other than skin color: "the kiddie hat, and the semicircle legs." The realization she comes to is not about race:

> I tried to reassure myself about the race thing for a long time until it dawned on me that the truth was already there, and Roberta knew it. I didn't kick her; I didn't join in with the gar girls and kick that lady, but I sure did want to. We watched and never tried to help her and

never called for help. Maggie was my dancing mother. Deaf, I thought, and dumb. Nobody inside. Nobody who would hear you if you cried in the night. Nobody who could tell you anything important you could use. Rocking, dancing, swaying as she walked. And when the gar girls pushed her down, and started roughhousing, I knew she wouldn't scream, couldn't—just like me—and I was glad about that. (259–260)

Twyla identifies Maggie not only with her mother but with herself, and watching the older girls attack the woman allows her to experience viscerally a violent expression of her anger at her mother's neglect and her own powerlessness.

Twyla and Roberta's final meeting in a coffee shop around Christmastime reveals that the incident with Maggie is emotionally resonant for Roberta as well and that she too identified Maggie with her mother. Roberta approaches Twyla to tell her the truth about Maggie:

Listen to me. I really did think she was black. I didn't make that up. I really thought so. But now I can't be sure. I just remember her as old, so old. And because she couldn't talk—well, you know, I thought she was crazy. She'd been brought up in an institution like my mother was and like I thought I would be too. And you were right. We didn't kick her. It was the gar girls. Only them. But, well, I wanted to. I really wanted them to hurt her. I said we did it, too. You and me, but that's not true. And I don't want you to carry that around. It was just that I wanted to do it so bad that day—wanting to is doing it. (261)[2]

The women reconcile by confirming their mothers' fates: " 'Did I tell you? My mother, she never did stop dancing.' 'Yes. You told me. And mine, she never got well.' " The story ends with Roberta's plaintive question, through her tears: "Oh shit, Twyla. Shit, shit, shit. What the hell happened to Maggie?" (261). This final question reflects the women's longing for an explanation of "what happened" to their mothers that made them unable to care for their daughters. As their confusion about Maggie's race mirrors the reader's confusion over the characters' racial identity, perhaps the question translates into "What happened to make race mean so much?"

BELOVED

That "What happened?" is partially answered by the setting of *Beloved*, in which Morrison explores how the historical context of women's interracial relationships situates the interplay of race, class, and bodies. Sethe's and Denver's brief relationships with white women, particularly the story of Sethe's encounter with the whitegirl Amy Denver, a recently freed indentured servant, both evoke and interrogate the traditional structures of women's interracial relationships. Mrs. Garner and Mrs. Bodwin represent two typically portrayed privileged white women in nineteenth-century America, the Southern slave mistress and the Northern reformer; Amy Denver represents not only those white women without class privilege but also the potential of political coalition between black and white women.[3] Through Amy's relationship with Sethe, Morrison attempts to relocate politics in physicality and thereby connect political to bodily experience.

Primarily the story of an escaped slave's recovery of her sense of self, *Beloved* is also very much a story of mothers and daughters. Sethe's surviving daughter Denver is born before Sethe reaches Ohio and freedom; although this event (like so much of the drama) precedes the narrative time of the novel, it is narrated several times by Sethe and, later, Denver.[4] The first, brief mention of the events of this birth comes when Sethe is telling Paul D, who has just arrived, of her and her baby's survival; Sethe "lowered her head and thought, as he did, how unlikely it was that she had made it. And if it hadn't been for that girl looking for velvet, she never would have." Paul D is "proud that she had done it, annoyed that she had not needed Halle or him in the doing." When Sethe tells him "a whitegirl helped me," he responds, "then she helped herself too" (8). Narratively, through Paul D's aggravation at Sethe's independence from male help and his acknowledgment that Amy "helped herself too," Morrison establishes at the beginning of the novel the interconnectedness of black and white women's history in America. Trudier Harris addresses the improbability of Amy and Sethe's interaction:

> Sethe's story violates the rules of interracial interaction with which her fellow blacks are familiar. The more logical expectation would have been for Amy to turn Sethe in. This seeming discrepancy, combined with Sethe actually escaping in her condition, leads some of the locals to speculate that there is something unnatural about her even before she kills Beloved and pridefully shuns them all. The tale, then, already has components of legend, myth, and outright lying before it begins to get reshaped in the minds and memories of Sethe, Denver, and their neighbors. (*Fiction and Folklore* 165)

The first account of Denver's birth comes from Denver herself. Arriving home from her secret spot in the bower, she sees the ghost that has inhabited their home for the first time, kneeling beside her mother, who is praying: "The dress and her mother together looked like two friendly grown-up women—one (the dress) helping out the other. And the magic of her birth, its miracle in fact, testified to that friendliness as did her own name" (29). Denver's perception of this scene testifies to her faith, amidst her pervasive loneliness, in the sustenance of women's friendship. That faith, which will enable her eventually to reach out to the larger community, is rooted in the story of her birth.

The story is also predicated on Denver's agency. Sethe tells Paul D that Denver is a "charmed child" who, when Sethe thought they both were going to die, "pulled a whitegirl out of the hill. The last thing you'd expect to help" (41, 42). In the story Denver remembers, she figures as "the little antelope [that] rammed her [Sethe] with horns and plowed the ground of her womb with impatient hooves" when Sethe was still (30). Sethe's choice of the image of an antelope comes from the dance she saw the adults, including her mother, do when she was a child: "They shifted shapes and became something other. Some unchained, demanding other whose feet knew her pulse better than she did. Just like this one in her stomach" (31). Both the dance and the as-yet-unborn Denver promise a future freedom and strength, symbolized by the antelope. Sethe had given up and believed she was going to die when she heard what she took to be a white boy and pre-pared to attack him, but what turns up instead is a white girl, "the raggediest-looking trash you ever saw" (31–32). Amy Denver is searching for food; finding none, she turns to leave, but Sethe asks her questions to get her to stay.

Amy was born into a condition of servitude, just as Sethe's Denver would have been born into slavery had not her mother run away. Because Amy's mother died after giving birth, Amy was forced to work off the cost of her mother's passage. Amy's status as an inden-tured servant shows that the institutions of servitude created class divisions that are often construed as solely racial divisions. This cir-cumstance gives Amy and Sethe an atypically similar economic class alignment, despite Amy's racial privilege. The women's marginalized status—they are both literally and figuratively on the outskirts of society—opens a space for their interaction. As Marianne Hirsch argues, Sethe and Amy's interaction represents

> the collaboration of a white woman and a black woman, united by their gender, their poverty, their subordinate social status, and by their stories of cruel masters, absent mothers, unknown fathers—yet forever sepa-rated by the absolute reality of slavery. In a privileged moment of con-nection around a work they share, privileged because they are allowed to

> have a space separate from any social framework . . . Sethe and Amy can
> talk for a few brief hours, Amy can rub Sethe's feet and wrap Sethe's baby
> in her undergarment. Significantly, as well, she takes the place not only of
> the other black women who would have acted as midwives in such a birth
> but also of the black father whose power to name the child she occupies
> by "giving" the baby the name Denver. (100)

Fleeing the roles in which society has placed them has at least partially
freed them from both the demand and the habit of ritualized social
engagement between black and white women. Amy helps Sethe not
out of obligation or guilt but out of a sense of shared circumstances
and suffering. She repeatedly states that she cannot risk being caught
with a runaway slave, and her first concerns are her hunger and her
need to get to Boston, where she intends to find carmine velvet.
Nevertheless, she leads Sethe to a lean-to and bandages the wounds
on her back as best she can. She tells Sethe as she massages her feet,
" 'It's gonna hurt, now.' . . . Anything dead coming back to life
hurts,' " a statement that Denver thinks is "a truth for all times" (35).

The next time Denver narrates the story of her own birth, it is to
Beloved's eager ears. Although Denver acknowledges that her mother
"never told [her] all of it" (76),

> she anticipated [Beloved's] questions by giving blood to the scraps her
> mother and grandmother had told her—and a heartbeat. The mono-
> logue became, in fact, a duet as they lay down together, Denver nurs-
> ing Beloved's interest like a lover whose pleasure was to overfeed the
> loved. . . . Denver spoke, Beloved listened, and the two did the best
> they could to create what really happened, how it really was, something
> only Sethe knew because she alone had the mind for it and the time
> afterward to shape it: the quality of Amy's voice, her breath like burn-
> ing wood. . . . How recklessly she behaved with this whitegirl—a reck-
> lessness born of desperation and encouraged by Amy's fugitive eyes and
> her tenderhearted mouth. (78)

Beloved's audience enables Denver to experience the story anew, "to
see what she was saying and not just to hear it" (77). She narrates
the story of how Amy Denver helped her mother give birth to her,
"the part of the story she loved . . . because it was all about herself;
but she hated it too because it made her feel like a bill was owing
somewhere and she, Denver, had to pay it. But who she owed or what
to pay it with eluded her" (77). That debt turns out to be the responsibility to restore her mother to the larger community, by telling their
need to the women in the African American community, accepting

their food, and gaining employment, through Janey's intercession, from the Bodwins.

Amy's role as caretaker of and midwife to Sethe reverses the conventional role of black women's tending to white women's bodies. By giving Amy a past of indentured servitude, Morrison diffuses the power dynamic underlying the historical paradigm of white and black women's relationships. Morrison then rewrites the history of women's interracial touch through Amy's bringing Sethe back to feeling by rubbing her feet and tending to her back. That history is represented by "the sycophancy of white identity" that Morrison finds in Willa Cather's *Sapphira and the Slave Girl*, in which the white woman Sapphira perversely and vicariously reroutes aspects of her own identity through her "absolute power over the body of another woman [Nancy, her slave]" (*Playing in the Dark* 19, 23). Morrison describes Sapphira's sycophancy:

> She escapes the necessity of inhabiting her own body by dwelling on the young, healthy, and sexually appetizing Nancy. She has transferred its care into the hands of others. In this way she escapes her illness, decay, confinement, anonymity, and physical powerlessness. . . . The surrogate black bodies become her hands and feet, her fantasies of sexual ravish and intimacy with her husband, and, not inconsiderably, her sole source of love. (*Playing in the Dark* 26)

Amy's care for Sethe, in contrast, heals her not only physically but mentally. She convinces Sethe that she can physically endure, and she also helps Sethe reimagine her past by narrating the scars on her body as a beautiful image. As Amy bandages the wounds on Sethe's back, she describes the scars as a chokecherry tree, an act of imagination she no doubt developed as a survival skill for her own situation. She tells Sethe (who has said her name is Lu):

> It's a tree, Lu. A chokecherry tree. See, here's the trunk—it's red and split wide open, full of sap, and this here's the parting for the branches. You got a mightly lot of branches. Leaves, too, look like, and dern if these ain't blossoms. Tiny little cherry blossoms, just as white. Your back got a whole tree on it. In bloom. What God have in mind, I wonder. I had me some whippings, but I don't remember nothing like this. Mr. Buddy had a right evil hand too. Whip you for looking at him straight. Sure would. I looked right at him one time and he hauled off and threw the poker at me. Guess he knew what I was a-thinking. (79)[5]

Amy's caretaking of Sethe's body both reverses the paradigm of women's interracial relationships and emphasizes the two women's political alignment.

Morrison's own portrayal of the slave mistress is more sympathetic than her description of Cather's. Mrs. Garner works alongside first Baby Suggs and later Sethe: "What she [Baby Suggs] did was stand beside the humming Lillian Garner while the two of them cooked, preserved, washed, ironed, made candles, clothes, soap and cider; fed chickens, pigs, dogs and geese; milked cows, churned butter, rendered fat, laid fires . . . Nothing to it" (139–140, Morrison's ellipsis). Mr. and Mrs. Garner also show genuine, if limited, concern for their slaves' well-being. After Halle purchases his mother's freedom, Mr. Garner takes her north and helps her find a home and work. When Mrs. Garner notices Sethe, who had been disappointed to learn that her marriage to Halle would receive no ceremony or acknowledgement, trying to piece together a wedding dress and some sense of occasion, she gives Sethe a pair of crystal earrings as a gift, saying, "I want you to have them and I want you and Halle to be happy" (60). Sethe responds with devotion; in fact, Sethe's memories of Mrs. Garner's illness mix with her memories of her own mother's death. Sethe says she

> tended her like I would have tended my own mother if she needed me. If they had let her out the rice field, because I was the one she didn't throw away. I couldn't have done more for that woman than I would my own ma'am if she was to take sick and need me and I'd have stayed with her till she got well or died. And I would have stayed after that except Nan snatched me back. Before I could check for the sign [her mother's brand]. (200–201)

Mr. and Mrs. Garner represent the most benevolent slave owners imaginable and therefore serve as the ultimate indictment of slavery as an institution that deprives people of their very selves, no matter how well they may be treated. The Garners' kindness marks them as the exception as slave owners. Baby Suggs is relieved to find that at Sweet Home, "nobody, but nobody, knocked her down." Nevertheless, she is not recognized as a fully individualized person, as signified by the Garners' not knowing her name: "Lillian Garner called her Jenny for some reason but she never pushed, hit or called her mean names. Even when she slipped in cow dung and broke every egg in her apron, nobody said you-black-bitch-what's-the-matter-with-you and nobody knocked her down" (139). Sethe's memories are similar to Baby Suggs's and likewise emphasize both the physical labor done by female house slaves and their mistresses on a plantation and the impersonal nature of Mrs. Garner's attachment to her slaves:

> A strong woman, used to be. And when she talked off her head, she'd say it. "I used to be strong as a mule, Jenny." Called me "Jenny" when

> she was babbling, and I can bear witness to that. Tall and strong. The
> two of us on a cord of wood was as good as two men. Hurt her like the
> devil not to be able to raise her head off the pillow. Still can't figure why
> she thought she needed schoolteacher, though. (201)

However sympathetic Mrs. Garner may be, to her Sethe is a replacement for Baby Suggs; slaves are interchangeable commodities.
Mrs. Garner is also ineffectual beyond the narrow confines of her
household, and the loss of her husband renders her completely powerless. By the time Sethe tells her that Schoolteacher's nephews
restrained and nursed her, Mrs. Garner is literally voiceless because of
the tumor on her throat, though "her eyes rolled out tears" (17).

The abolitionist Miss Bodwin, by contrast, seems to have more
independence. Abolition and then the Civil War have given her life
purpose as well as work. Reminiscing about the Christmas gifts the
woman brought, Denver remembers of Miss Bodwin that "talking of
a war full of dead people, she looked happy" (28). Like Mrs. Garner's,
Miss Bodwin's power stems from her alignment with a man, though her
brother rather than husband. The Bodwins are an ambivalent pair. Their
devotion to abolition makes them powerful allies for the members of the
black community, yet Morrison shows that their political commitment
does not necessitate a personal one; they "gave Stamp Paid, Ella and
John clothes, goods and gear for runaways because they hated slavery
worse than they hated slaves" (137), yet Sethe remembers Miss Bodwin
as "the whitewoman who loved" Baby Suggs (46). Despite the
Bodwins' helpful works, the members of the black community recognize
the white siblings' limitations. In the late nineteenth century, friendly
whites remain a puzzle. As Janey says to Denver when she suggests that
the Bodwins need extra help, "Don't ask me what whitefolks need at
night" (255). Barbara Christian points out that "Denver—whose name
is specifically American and related to a white woman—is the one who
encounters, in the home of the liberal abolitionist Bodwin, a portent of
the future" in the form of a black figurine with his head thrown back and
his mouth open unnaturally wide to hold money, with the words "At Yo
Service" (*Beloved* 255) painted on the bottom ("Beloved, She's Ours"
46). Denver's role as the one who reconnects her family to the community thus signifies an ambivalent future of both hope and prejudice.

The Bodwins' politics have made their relationships with the white
community similarly problematic, as the description of Edward
Bodwin on his way to 124 to pick up Denver indicates:

> The horse trotted along and Edward Bodwin cooled his beautiful mus-
> tache with his breath. . . . Dark, velvety, its beauty was enhanced by his

strong clean-shaven chin. But his hair was white, like his sister's—and had been since he was a young man. It made him the most visible and memorable person at every gathering, and cartoonists had fastened onto the theatricality of his white hair and big black mustache whenever they depicted local political antagonism. Twenty years ago when the Society was at its height in opposing slavery, it was as though his coloring was itself the heart of the matter. The "bleached nigger" was what his enemies called him, and on a trip to Arkansas, some Mississippi rivermen, enraged by the Negro boatmen they competed with, had caught him and shoe-blackened his face and his hair. Those heady days were gone now; what remained was the sludge of ill will; dashed hopes and difficulties beyond repair. A tranquil Republic? Well, not in his lifetime. (259–260)

When he approaches 124, Sethe, seeing him, is thrown back to the day she saw Schoolteacher coming with the slave catcher and runs toward Mr. Bodwin with the ice pick she is holding. This time the women of the community are there to stop her, and Denver is the first to reach her. Stamp Paid recounts these events to Paul D, who believes that Mr. Bodwin must have realized that Sethe tried to attack him. Stamp replies, "If he did think it, I reckon he decided not to. That be just like him, too. He's somebody never turned us down. Steady as a rock. I tell you something, if she had got to him, it'd be the worst think in the world for us. You know, don't you, he's the main one kept Sethe from the gallows in the first place" (265). His comment acknowledges both the black community's debt to Bodwin and the precariousness of their political alignment—had Sethe reached him or had he himself chosen to respond differently, the outcome could have been tragic.

The Bodwins' helpfulness distinguishes them from the pervasive threat that white people pose to blacks. The paradoxical necessity and fruitlessness of making distinctions among whites is a pervasive challenge for the characters in the novel. All the central characters of the novel struggle with the temptation to hate all white people. Baby Suggs finally succumbs and takes to her bed, saying, "Those white things have taken all I had or dreamed . . . and broke my heartstrings too. There is no bad luck in the world but whitefolks" (89). Sethe comes to believe Baby Suggs's final pronouncement, though she remembers trusting the Garners and the "Earrings that made her believe she could discriminate among them. That for every schoolteacher there would be an Amy; that for every pupil there was a Garner, or Bodwin, or even a sheriff, whose touch at her elbow was gentle and who looked away when she nursed" (188). She also remembers, however, that when she told her husband Halle that she found the Garners different from other white people she had known, his reply was "It don't matter, Sethe. What they say is the same. Loud or soft" (195). As she points out their good qualities, he reminds her that they have total power over their lives and that ultimately the Garners are the ones who benefit from the kindness they show their slaves. Finally, the danger posed by white people is what Sethe feels she must make Beloved understand is worse than her own act of infanticide: "That anybody white could take your whole self for anything that came to mind. Not just work, kill, or maim you, but dirty you. Dirty you so bad you couldn't like yourself anymore. Dirty you so bad you forgot who you were and couldn't think it up. And though she and others lived through and got over it, she could never let it happen to her own" (251).

But it is Stamp Paid's analysis of white people's racism that recognizes the pervasive damage it does to the racists themselves:

> Whitepeople believed that whatever the manners, under every dark skin was a jungle. Swift unnavigable waters, swinging screaming baboons, sleeping snakes, red gums ready for their sweet white blood. In a way, he thought, they were right. The more coloredpeople spent their strength trying to convince them how gentle they were, how clever and loving, how human, the more they used themselves up to persuade whites of something Negroes believed could not be questioned, the deeper and more tangled the jungle grew inside. But it wasn't the jungle blacks brought with them to this place from the other (livable) place. It was the jungle whitefolks planted in them. And it grew. It spread. In, through and after life, it spread, until it invaded the whites who had made it. Touched them every one. Changed and altered them. Made them bloody, silly, worse than even they wanted to be, so scared were they of the jungle they had made. The screaming baboon lived under their own white skin; the red gums were their own. (198–199)

Stamp articulates the postcolonial analysis of the detrimental effects of the colonists' fears and fantasies on the colonists themselves.

As Denver prepares to leave 124 to seek help, the memories of all she has learned about white people immobilize her: "What was more—much more—out there were whitepeople and how could you tell about them? Sethe said the mouth and sometimes the hands. Grandma Baby said there was no defense—they could prowl at will, change from one mind to another, and even when they thought they were behaving, it was a far cry from what real humans did" (244). Denver remembers a conversation between her mother and Baby

Suggs in which Sethe defended the actions of some white people, but it is her hearing her grandmother's laugh and injunction to "Know it [that there is no defense], and go on out the yard" that propels her forward (244). The stories of helpful whites, and particularly the role of Amy Denver in the story of her birth, counter the fearful stories of hurtful white people and help give Denver the hope to brave the danger posed by the world outside of 124.

The ambivalence about race and race relations is embodied by Lady Jones, the biracial teacher whose classes Denver attends until Nelson Lord's question about her mother keeps her away. That Denver followed the other children and watched the classes through Lady Jones's window until the woman invited her in was a source of pride for her, because she had gone out into the world on her own. She will have to repeat that going forth to save herself and her mother—and she returns to Lady Jones for that purpose—but on her second journey she is aware of the price she must pay as well as the wonder of learning she experienced.[6] Lady Jones received her own education in part because of her light skin. That privilege and the negative responses to her light skin from other blacks have given her her mission to teach black children, but the white heritage her skin color signifies has also burdened her with self-hatred:

> Lady Jones was mixed. Gray eyes and yellow woolly hair, every strand of which she hated—though whether it was the color or the texture even she didn't know. She had married the blackest man she could find,[7] had five rainbow-colored children and sent them all to Wilberforce, after teaching them all she knew right along with the others who sat in her parlor. Her light skin got her picked for a colored-girls' normal school in Pennsylvania and she paid it back by teaching the unpicked. . . . She believed in her heart that, except for her husband, the whole world (including her children) despised her and her hair. She had been listening to "all that yellow gone to waste" and "white nigger" since she was a girl in a houseful of silt-black children, so she disliked everybody a little bit because she believed they hated her hair as much as she did. With that education pat and firmly set, she dispensed with rancor, was indiscriminately polite, saving her real affection for the unpicked children of Cincinnati. (247)

If Lady Jones and the Bodwins represent the ambivalence felt by African Americans about trusting white people enough to forge political alignments with them, the plot of the novel also shows the necessity of such interracial coalitions in a country where almost all the political and economic power is wielded by white people. *Beloved*, then, presents the complex and multivalent potential of interracial engagement. The novel also provides the historical patterns that underlie the more contemporary interracial relationships in "Recitatif" and *Paradise*.

PARADISE

As in "Recitatif," in *Paradise* Morrison withholds information about race—in this case, which of the Convent women is white—to compel readers to confront the meanings they ascribe to race. The novel opens with a slaughter, as nine representative men of Ruby, Oklahoma, break into the building on the outskirts of town known as the Convent to kill the women who live there. The men are fueled by righteous anger; they have convinced themselves that the women are evil and have caused the generational, gender, and religious divisions that threaten to ruin the town. To the men who break into the Convent, these women are "detritus: throwaway people that sometimes blow back into the room after being swept out the door" (4). The men's sense of justification also stems from their belief that their actions enact the townspeople's wishes, although later chapters will show that some town members try to prevent the attack.

The novel's first sentence—"They shoot the white girl first"—sets up the racial mystery, which may or may not be solvable. Various critics have identified different characters as the white woman, including Mavis, Seneca, and Pallas. Such identifications miss Morrison's point, however, which is not that the character's race matters but that we have been taught by our culture to believe that it does. She repeatedly emphasizes that knowing someone's race provides no real information, stating:

> It was important to me to demonstrate that [concept] in *Paradise*, by withholding racial markers from a group of black women, among whom was one white woman, so that the reader knew everything, or almost everything, about the characters, their interior lives, their past, their faults, their strengths, except that one small piece of information which was their race. And [for the reader] to either care about that, like the characters, dislike them, or dismiss the characters based on the important information which was what they were really like. And if I could enforce that response in literature, it was a way of saying that race is the least important piece of information we have about another person. Forcing people to react racially to another person is to miss the whole point of humanity. ("Timehost Chat")

What interests Morrison is people's investment in illusory racial meanings and their tendency toward exclusivity, or, as she puts it, "why paradise necessitates exclusion" (Mulrine). She points out:

> The isolation, the separateness, is always a part of any utopia. And it [the novel] was my meditation . . . and interrogation of the whole idea of paradise, the safe place, the place full of bounty, where no one can harm you. But, in addition to that, it's based on the notion of exclusivity. All paradises, all utopias are designed by who is not there, by the people who are not allowed in. (Farnsworth)

What provokes the men more than anything else is the Convent women's deviant (to the men, as they imagine it) sexuality. The men try to purge that sexuality from their town, just as at an earlier date the nuns, when they took possession of the mansion originally built by an embezzler, had tried to eradicate its sensual decor. In this emphasis on the efforts to suppress what is perceived as women's transgressive or excessive sexuality, *Paradise* echoes Faulkner's *Requiem for a Nun*. The women's frank and blatant sexuality not only scandalizes the men but stirs their imaginations. The youngest of the group, K. D., experiences the attack as if it were a dream sequence, and the colors he sees remind him of "the clothes of an easily had woman" (4). Another man wonders how women's "plain brains [could] think up such things: revolting sex, deceit and the sly torture of children" (8), even though he has no reasonable evidence for his conclusions. Changes in their town have created rumors, fear, and their desire for a scapegoat. The very men who hunt these women paradoxically pride themselves on having founded a town where women are safe because "nothing for ninety miles around thought [they] were prey" (8). The repetition of that sentiment throughout the first chapter reveals the men's protective attitude toward the women of Ruby and emphasizes that those women must conform to the men's idea of virtue in order to be valued.

The novel indicates that the strict regulation of women's sexuality is not part of the town's heritage. Steward Morgan who along with his twin brother Deacon is one of the most prominent men of the town, remembers the story of his older brother Elder, who represents for his younger sibling the exacting moral standards the Morgan men had. Elder never forgot the fight he got into upon his return to the United States after the First World War. Seeing two white men arguing with a black woman whom Elder assumes is a prostitute because of the way she is dressed, he initially identifies with the men. When they beat her, however, he finds himself physically defending her. Arriving home, he chooses to keep his uniform in its tattered condition and asks to be buried in it when he dies. His attitude toward the woman is greatly changed: "Whatever he felt about her trade, he thought about her, prayed for her till the end of his life" (94–95). He cannot forgive himself for fleeing after the fight rather than staying to help her. Steward is proud of his brother's strict personal moral code but does not relate to Elder's charitable attitude toward the woman: "it unnerved him [Steward] to know [the story] was based on the defense of and prayers for a whore. He did not sympathize with the whitemen, but he could see their point, could even feel the adrenaline, imagining the fist was his own" (95). Steward's judgmental tendency and his aversion to women's sexuality ultimately lead him to abandon his own moral code.

Although the men react primarily to the Convent women's sexuality, the divisiveness the townspeople of Ruby are experiencing is also racial. Ruby was founded by a group of families after the all-black town established by their ancestors, Haven, failed. Haven had been founded in 1889 in Oklahoma Territory by a group of freedmen who refused to become tenant farmers or settle for the other limited opportunities available to them in the South. Initially successful, Haven had been severely weakened by economic hardship by 1934 and was barely surviving by 1948. Following the Second World War, some of the grandsons of Haven's founders decided to move to a new location and try again.

When the original settlers of Haven first traveled west to find a home, they were rejected by the blacks of Fairly, Oklahoma. Some suspected that they were turned away not because they lacked the funds to support themselves but because of their dark skin color. The fact that the Fairly residents offered them food, blankets, and money deepened the insult. The rejection comes to be known in Haven mythology as "The Disallowing." The alleged prejudice of Fairly's inhabitants represents an internalized racism that values lighter skin tones as well as a practical realization that those with lighter skin were more likely to be able to deal profitably with whites. This shared history—the attempt to escape racial oppression by moving away from white people, only to be shunned by other blacks—unites the townspeople but also reinforces their belief that all threats to the town come from outside it.

The fact that many of the residents maintain their suspicion of white people is shown by an incident in Anna's store. She and Richard Misner are helping a lost white couple with an ill baby. The white woman will not enter the store, no doubt because they are in an all-black town. Steward's reaction reveals the extent of his animosity toward white people, whom he describes as "born lost. Take over the world and still lost." When he seeks agreement from Richard, however, Misner reminds him that "God has one people." Undaunted, Steward rejects this guidance from his minister, declaring, "Richard . . . I've heard you say things *out* of ignorance, but this is the first time I heard you say something *based* on ignorance" (123). Steward's suspicion of outsiders and contempt for whites dominate his thoughts, overshadowing all other lessons he has learned from the history of the town he knows so well. The fact that the lost couple fail to heed the warnings about the oncoming blizzard suggests that their own sense of racial superiority undermines their judgment, and later their dead bodies are discovered.

Steward's and Deacon's wives Dovey and Soane, who are also sisters, are more sympathetic toward and less judgmental of the Convent women. They also recognize their husbands' limitations and the changes in their community but, like their husbands, believe that any significant threat to their peaceful existence is external. They cannot understand why the young people act as if the town's problem is an internal one. Thus, Dovey cannot identify the source of their anger because "there were no whites (moral or malevolent) around to agitate or incense them" (102). Yet she resents their acting as if their realizations about white people are new and unique, and she finds the connection the young people feel to Africa even more mysterious.

Soane hears in the young people's speech an "accusation" against all the founders of Ruby (and by implication, Haven) for the choice to move away from white people to evade their racism. The young people seek direct confrontation and act "as though there was a new and more manly way to deal with whites . . . some African-type thing full of new words, new color combinations and new haircuts. Suggesting that outsmarting whites was craven. That they had to be told, rejected, confronted. Because the old way was slow, limited to just a few, and weak" (104). The generational conflict in Ruby is representative of that experienced throughout the United States in response to the civil rights and Black Power movements of the 1960s. The novel shows that Ruby's isolation cannot make its inhabitants immune to the changes in the country; separatism does not provide protection.

The Disallowing has also left the town with a reversed skin-color bias.[8] To Pat, a teacher who is compiling a town history, the most significant feature of the original founding families and their descendants is the racial purity signified by their dark black skin, a quality she labels "eight-rock," for a low level in coal mines. Pat suspects that this quality makes them feel superior, a feeling resulting from the discrimination they suffered during Reconstruction as they realized that light skin was prized even among African Americans:

> For ten generations they had believed the division they fought to close was free against slave and rich against poor. Usually, but not always, white against black. Now they saw a new separation: light-skinned against black. Oh, they knew there was a difference in the minds of whites, but it had not struck them before that it was of consequence, serious consequence, to Negroes themselves. (194)

On the basis of this theory, Pat believes the words on the Oven read "Beware the Furrow of His Brow," which she interprets as a reference to the Disallowing, a warning to the light-skinned people of Fairly who turned the Haven settlers away. This concept of racial purity, based on physical features and the line of descent from ancestors in the Louisiana Territory, is illusory. Although Pat believes there is a miscegenation taboo in the town, her descriptions of the very straight hair of the Blackhorse family, as well as the surname itself, indicate that an unacknowledged Native American ancestry exists.

The Second World War disrupted Haven's separatism when grand-sons of the town's founders became soldiers. Pat feels that the disre-spect shown to those men in their own country when they returned intensified their commitment to separatism and to protecting their eight-rock purity. Many of them disapproved of her father Roger Best's marriage to a woman with skin light enough that she could pass as white, none louder than Steward, who said, "He's bringing along the dung we leaving behind" (201). Pat believes that her parents' marriage is the source of her father's unpopularity, not the fact that he prepared his wife Delia for burial. Delia died in childbirth, while Roger was away at mortuary school. Many Ruby women, including Dovey Morgan, begged the men to go to the Convent to summon help from the nuns, who ran a boarding school there at the time, but the men refused and the women could not drive. Although her father does not agree, Pat suspects that the men would not go for help because they did not want to seek it from white people and because they resented Delia's light skin. By making skin-color bias one of the elements that divides the townspeople and connecting the town's divisiveness to the slaughter that begins the novel, Morrison further emphasizes how attributing meaning to racial identity contributes to violence.

All three of Morrison's fictional works discussed here, then, show that the tendency to interpret race as if it were primary to identity causes interracial relationships to be fraught with tension. Using ambiguously raced characters, overturning readers' racialized expectations, and emphasizing the divisiveness caused by racial identification, Morrison interrogates the operation of racial meanings in American literature and culture.

Getting Past White Women's Fantasies: *Living Out Loud*

For a particular plotline to be satirized successfully in a popular film, it needs to have been repeated often enough that a general audience can be expected to laugh. When the plot involves race, such satire can indicate an emerging awareness of the racism underlying stereotypical depictions. The fact that the 1998 movie *Living Out Loud* critiques portrayals of interracial relationships in which the role of the African American character is to facilitate the white character's growth suggests that such plotlines are beginning to seem reductive and out-of-date, at least to some audiences.[1]

Living Out Loud tells a familiar feminist tale. Judith Moore, played by Holly Hunter, is a wealthy white woman whose doctor husband leaves her for a younger woman. For Judith, putting together a new life for herself involves remembering and discovering who she is, apart from her identity and social status as Bob Moore's wife. Energized by her newfound freedom, she seeks out new people and experiences and eventually returns to medical school, the path she abandoned to marry. The movie reveals her thoughts through stream-of-consciousness voice-over narration as well as by playing out what she imagines will happen in certain situations before showing what actually occurs. These techniques emphasize that the central focus of the film is how Judith Moore's perceptions of herself and her world change.

Judith's imagined identification with the jazz singer Liz Bailey, played by Queen Latifah, is established at the beginning of the film. In the opening scene, Judith and Bob discuss his being seen having lunch with another woman, which he claims was simply a meal with a colleague. The film then cuts to the opening credits, which are displayed first over the New York skyline and then beside Latifah, dressed in a red satin gown against a black background, singing "life is lonely again," a line of the song "Lush Life." Mid-song, the film cuts to

Judith lip-syncing in her apartment to Bailey's CD, which features the singer in the red gown on its cover.

A few scenes later, Judith is listening to Bailey sing at a club. When the singer approaches the bar near her seat, Judith imagines initiating the following exchange.

> "You were great."
> "Well, thank you. Look a little sad tonight. You alone?"
> "I don't know anybody on the Upper West Side."
> "Oh. Where are you from?"
> "Upper East Side. My husband left me. Our friends were his friends. I haven't really spoken to anyone. I mean, really spoken to anyone. I feel so invisible, sometimes I forget I'm here."
> "I was married. My husband cheated on me left and right, and it made me feel like I was crazy all the time. One day he tells me it was *my* fault he was seeing other women. So I picked up a knife and told him it was *his* fault I was stabbing him. I did a little jail time; it was worth it. Now I'm free, and he is scared shitless of me."
> "That's great. I wish I would have stabbed my husband. I used to be dangerous. I don't know what happened. I've got so scared. I mean, what's so important about living longer and feeling safe?"

Judith creates for Bailey a stereotypical biography for an African American woman—left by a no-good man, she retaliates by trying to kill him—that allows her to vicariously imagine vengeance against her own cheating husband. The imagined exchange also shows that Judith is looking to a black woman she does not know, but whose songs stir her emotions, to play the same role Temple Drake needed Nancy to play in Faulkner's *Requiem for a Nun*: empathetic listener and confessor. Identifying with the black woman enables Judith to feel braver and freer. On some level, she associates her conventional life choices with her whiteness and assumes the black jazz singer has a more exciting past. (Although Judith says she "used to be danger-ous," the only indication of that former self is her later memory of herself as a tattooed adolescent kissing a young man. This flashback occurs as she receives an erotic massage, and the scene represents her sexual reawakening.) What actually happens when Bailey approaches the bar is that she does not hear—or chooses to ignore—Judith's say-ing, "You were great." The more realistic plot contrasts with Judith's stereotypical desire.

The two women do become friends. On the club's amateur night, Judith drunkenly heckles one of the performers, and Liz and another woman physically pull her away from her table and into the ladies' restroom. Judith tells Liz, "You know, I once heard you sing, and I complimented you and you completely ignored me." Liz replies, "I'm sorry. That was rude." The conversation that ensues between the two women complicates the racial awareness signified by their earlier exchange. Judith admits to Liz that she abandoned the friends she had before her marriage because their husbands were not as wealthy as hers, that she had accepted her husband's affairs for years because being married to him made her feel safe, and that she now feels lost. She thus makes Liz the confidante she had wanted her to be. Although one drunken woman revealing secrets to another woman in the ladies' room is a plausible plot, the film could also be said to have gone out of its way to create that plausibility. Moreover, the fact that the two women do become friends and that on another night Liz gives Judith ecstasy and takes her to an after-hours all-women dance club called "The Confessional" where Judith is able to "let loose"—another emancipatory experience in her awakening—suggests that the earlier scene functions as an excuse for the film to use the black character to facilitate the white character's development.

Nevertheless, the film does avoid some of the pitfalls of the standard plot's use of interracial relationships. Liz is not the only character Judith forms a relationship with—she also befriends her building's elevator operator, Pat, played by Danny DeVito. In addition, Liz and Judith's friendship is not completely one-sided; Liz also shares her romantic troubles with Judith. Furthermore, Judith relinquishes her Fifth Avenue apartment and moves to a more modest apartment both for financial reasons and because she is renouncing the privileged identity that feels inauthentic. As a result, she no longer feels like an imposter in the jazz club. At the end of the film, Liz does not disappear; she and Judith are still friends. Finally, the film returns to its initial critique of white women's fantasies about black women. Liz is shown trapped in a conversation with a particularly insipid white woman who tells her, "You make me cry. . . . Because when you sing, it's not about just you. It's not about now. It's the whole black experience. You know what I'm saying? Because you see, black people—African American people—when they sing sentimental songs, they're not sentimental—not sentimental, right? You know why? Because of the pain. Because they have the pain to back it up." Liz just agrees with her and smiles, and when the woman, as she leaves, tells her, "You keep on singing. You keep on singing now," Liz replies, "I've got plenty of bad times to sing about. Don't you worry." She then turns to Judith and admonishes, "This is your fault . . . because you said I was rude. Ever since you said I was rude, it's like I've got to talk to every psycho that comes in the place just so I don't feel bad." By the end of the film, the friendship has come to appear authentic, and Judith appears to have renounced her fantasies of black womanhood along with her privileged lifestyle.

Notes

Chapter 1   Introduction

1. Jeff Abernathy addresses this pattern in *To Hell and Back: Race and Betrayal in the Southern Novel.*
2. Nancy Porter's 1991 article "Women's Interracial Friendships and Visions of Community in *Meridian*, *The Salt Eaters, Civil Wars*, and *Dessa Rose*" essentially continues Schultz's. Porter interprets the novels by Alice Walker, Toni Cade Bambara, Rosellen Brown, and Sherley Anne Williams listed in the article's title, asserting that Schultz's methodology needs to be supplemented with a psychoanalytic perspective on women's friendships. She maintains that the novels she has chosen supply "the necessary political connection" of women's friendship "by contextualizing relationships between black and white women in historical movements for social change" (252). Porter, however, fails to provide the psychoanalytic analysis she claims is essential, and her conclusions do not differ much from Schultz's: either the interracial friendships are overly idealized and the black character is a one-dimensional positive stereotype or the relationships do not last.
3. See also Diane Roberts's *The Myth of Aunt Jemima: Representations of Race and Region* (1994) and Sharon Monteith's *Advancing Sisterhood? Interracial Friendships in Contemporary Southern Fiction* (2000), both of which analyze white women's writings about race. Primarily devoted to nineteenth-century U.S. writers, Roberts's work also includes a chapter on twentieth-century writers and one on British women's writings about slavery in the United States. Monteith's book focuses on novels written by white Southern women in which interracial friendship figure prominently.
4. Barbara Welter originated the term in her 1966 essay "The Cult of True Womanhood." Much didactic literature aimed at white women in the early nineteenth century urged them to aspire to True Womanhood, a state that demanded rigorous morality and domesticity.
5. In the afterword to her influential 1980 essay "Compulsory Heterosexuality and Lesbian Existence," Adrienne Rich addresses problems that may arise with use of her term "lesbian continuum":

> My own problem with the phrase is that it can be, is, used by women who have not yet begun to examine the privileges and solipsisms of

heterosexuality, as a safe way to describe their felt connections with women, without having to share in the risks and threats of lesbian existence. . . . *Lesbian continuum*—the phrase—came from a desire to allow for the greatest possible variation of female-identified experience, while paying a different kind of respect to *lesbian existence*—the traces and knowledge of women who have made their primary erotic and emotional choices for women. (73–74)

See also Rich's note following "It Is the Lesbian in Us . . . ," which discusses problems with the word "lesbian" and describes one response to her reading of that paper at the 1976 Modern Language Association convention: "One lesbian asserted that if 'the lesbian in us' was to become a figurative term, she, as a woman who had been oppressed for physically expressing her love for women, wanted another name for who she was" (202). Margaret Homans addresses a similar debate over the meaning of blackness in " 'Racial Composition': Metaphor and the Body in the Writing of Race" (1997). Homans analyzes the debate between those theorists who treat race as metaphorical and those who treat it as bodily, as well as the more specific "question: does the term *black feminist criticism* refer literally to writing produced only by black women, or can the term be metaphoric, referring to criticism by anyone so long as it bears a certain orientation and subject matter?" (83).

6. Nell Irvin Painter contends, in *Sojourner Truth: A Life, a Symbol*, that Truth functions less as a historical figure than as a symbol for strong black women. Painter convincingly argues that Gage's version, written twelve years after the convention, is not an accurate transcription and that Gage invented the phrase "Ar'n't I a Woman?"

7. Ann duCille discusses their conversation, and Jane Gallop's work in particular, at length in "The Occult of True Black Womanhood."

8. Frye further discusses whiteness (or "whiteliness" as she terms it in her later essay) in "White Woman Feminist: 1983–1992," an essay in her book *Willful Virgin* (1992). Another early influential essay is Peggy McIntosh's "White Privilege: Unpacking the Invisible Knapsack," (1988) in which she lists many of the unspoken and usually unrecognized privileges of having white skin.

9. Noel Ignatier and John Garvey, the editors of the journal *Race Traitor*, in the collection of the same name, contend that abolishing whiteness is necessary to ending racism and take as their slogan "treason to whiteness is loyalty to humanity." They distinguish their position from antiracist positions that try to change attitudes and behavior: "The abolitionists maintain, on the contrary, that people were not favored socially because they were white; rather they were defined as 'white' because they were favored. Race itself is a product of social discrimination; so long as the white race exists, all movements against racism are doomed to fail" (10).

CHAPTER 2   "SISTERS IN SIN"

1. For an analytical overview of feminist narrative theory, see Homans, "Feminist Fictions and Feminist Theories of Narrative" (1994). Faulkner described the genesis of the novel using the following questions: "I began to think what would be the future of that girl? and then I thought, What could a marriage come to which was founded on the vanity of a weak man?" (Gwynn and Blotner 96).

2. In Gavin Stevens (Temple's uncle and Nancy's lawyer) and the governor, Faulkner gives these cultural forces voice and name. As Noel Polk suggests, one of *Requiem*'s subjects is "the culture's concerted efforts to bring her [Temple] to judgment for her sexual history. The culture is personified in the ruthless figure of Gavin Stevens, who is . . . a surrogate . . . for the culture itself" (*Children of the Dark House* 158). See also Polk's comprehensive 1981 study of the novel, in which he convincingly argues that Gavin's motives are perverse. Gavin's motivation has been the source of much critical debate. Following Olga Vickery's interpretation, many critics confirm Gavin's stated purpose, saving Temple, and recent critics, including Jay Watson and Karl F. Zender, have continued to use a therapeutic model for Gavin and Temple's exchanges. Judith Wittenberg, on the other hand, in her Lacanian reading of Temple's speech in both *Sanctuary* and *Requiem for a Nun*, shows that Gavin's ineptitude as an analyst contributes to the decline of Temple's verbal sophistication and psychological awareness, thereby reversing the intended process of therapy.

3. To some extent, the difference in their strategies is analogous to the contrast between French and American feminisms Margaret Homans describes (with Nancy's strategy fitting the French model and Temple's the American):

> The French writers who accept the premise that language and experience are coextensive also understand language to be a male construct whose operation depends on women's silence and absence. . . . In contrast, most recent feminist criticism in this country has pragmatically assumed that experience is separable from language and thus that women are or can be in control of language rather than controlled by it. ("Her Very Own Howl" 186)

Although Homans acknowledges that this characterization is a simplification that does not do justice to the diversity of French and American feminist thought, it provides a useful paradigm. Her point is that the two views are not necessarily mutually exclusive, and combining the two approaches provides more productive possibilities.

4. Janet Wondra uses M. M. Bakhtin's theories to discuss the "linguistic disruptions" with which "Temple's marginalized voice protrudes through a capitalizing language" and points out that "it is specifically these two proper names Temple avoids inhabiting when she chooses to

speak of herself in the third person, as if speaking about a character playing a role" (48–49).

5. See pages 530–532 for similar exchanges. Although Stevens recognizes the bifurcation of Temple's identity, his recognition is problematic: the Temple Drake he sees is different from the Temple Drake that Temple sees (and neither is particularly accurate). This leads to further fragmentation and multiplication of identities. As Temple says to the governor, "I'm trying to tell you about one Temple Drake, and our Uncle Gavin is showing you another one. So already you've got two different people begging for the same clemency; if everybody concerned keeps splitting up into two people, you wont even know who to pardon, will you?" (578).

6. The importance of naming has been established in the history of the town, which is named Jefferson after the mailman, Pettigrew, who has threatened to turn the townsmen in for charging the replacement of the stolen lock to the U.S. government. After they name the town for him, Pettigrew tells them they can call the lock axle grease on the ledger and no one will ever find it; hence they can change what it is—its identity—by renaming it (492).

7. Appropriate here is Foucault's conception of the soul as

> the present correlative of a certain technology of power over the body. . . . It is produced permanently around, on, within the body by the functioning of a power that is exercised on those punished. . . . This is the historical reality of this soul, which, unlike the soul represented by Christian theology, is not born in sin and subject to punishment, but is born rather out of methods of punishment, supervision and constraint. . . . It is the element in which are articulated the effects of a certain type of power and the reference of a certain type of knowledge, the machinery by which the power relations give rise to a possible corpus of knowledge, and knowledge extends and reinforces the effects of this power. (*Discipline and Punish* 29)

8. Richard C. Moreland states that

> The emotional achievement of her [Temple's] analysis is much less the salvaging of her marriage with Gowan than her mourning of her daughter and her reunion with Nancy and her surviving child, even though a move in Gowan's direction is made in the last lines and gestures of the play. I am tempted to read this last-minute feint toward a more conventionally romantic, heterosexual ending . . . as a betrayal of the emotional center of the work in the two women characters' developing relationship with each other. . . . Temple . . . is in some ways being reintegrated with her alienated selves in Nancy and in "their" surviving child. (215, n.20)

This provocative suggestion appears to me, like much of the criticism that addresses Temple and Nancy's relationship, to idealize their sameness at the cost of neglecting their differences. I hope to show that their differences are important not only as a cause of their physical and emotional separation but also as a source of the potential power of that relationship.

9. For Foucault's explication of normalization, see *Discipline and Punish*, esp. 170–184; for his discussion of the containment of difference, see *The History of Sexuality*, esp. 95–96. Gowan's identity is likewise normalized, as he forcefully states: "call it simple over training. You know? Gowan Stevens, trained at Virginia to drink like a gentleman, gets drunk as ten gentlemen, takes a country college girl, a maiden: who knows? maybe even a virgin, cross country by car to another country college ball game . . ."; and "Marrying her was purest Old Virginia. That was indeed the hundred and sixty gentlemen" (520–521).

10. Lynda E. Boose notes that whereas

> we seldom find sons locked inside their father's castles, because retention and separation are not the defining stress lines of the father-son narrative, . . . the daughter's struggle with her father is one of separation, not displacement. Its psychological dynamics thus locate the conflict inside inner family space. . . . Within the spatial image, the daughter—the liminal or "threshold" person in family space—symbolically stands at the boundary/door, blocked from departure by the figure of the father (and/or the son or other male heir to the father's position). For the narrative to progress—for the daughter to leave the father's enclosure—the outside rival male must arrive and create a magnetic pull on the daughter, who otherwise remains within, in psychological bondage to her filial bonds. (32–33)

11. Moreland suggests that Cecelia, as "the writer of '*écriture féminine*,' " exerts an "indirect influence" on Nancy and Temple (196). He discusses Nancy and Temple as sorceress and hysteric, respectively. Cecelia's signature (especially considering the stranger's rereading of it, which I discuss later in this chapter) could be considered as one of the moments when the feminine erupts in Faulkner's texts. For an elucidating exploration of such moments, see Minrose Gwin's *The Feminine and Faulkner*, in which she employs what she calls "bisexual reading" to interpret the bisexuality (the interaction of masculine and feminine) in Faulkner's works.

12. The text seems to anticipate some of the major theories of late twentieth-century feminism, particularly women's relationship to writing, sexuality, and each other. I will counterpoise Cixous's arguments in "Laugh of the Medusa" and Irigaray's in *This Sex Which Is Not One* with portions of *Requiem* to elucidate my interpretation of Faulkner's text as well as to show how those theories work out in practical terms in that text. Cixous's and Irigaray's theories help reveal the leaks in the culture's containment of resistance—both the places

Temple and Nancy attempt to take advantage of and the potential sites for resistance they fail to realize.

13. Faulkner, explaining his use of the word "nun" to refer to Nancy, characterized the murder as follows: "she [Nancy] was capable within her poor dim lights and reasons of an act which whether it was right or wrong was of complete almost religious abnegation of the world for the sake of an innocent child [presumably Bucky]" (Gwynn and Blotner 196). Polk suggests that Nancy may be seeking revenge (*Faulkner's "Requiem"* 201). Faulkner's own first daughter, nine-day-old Alabama, died in 1931. For a brief account of infant deaths and the ensuing grief and suffering in Faulkner's work, as well as a condolence letter he wrote to Frances and James Warsaw "Sonny" Bell Jr., see Fowler and McCool, "On Suffering."

14. See Gwin's *Black and White Women of the Old South*, Trudier Harris's *From Mammies to Militants*, and Elizabeth Fox-Genovese's *Within the Plantation Household*.

15. This scene is typically read not for underlying motives but at face value: Temple and Gavin's turning to Nancy for answers, which she gives forthrightly. As such, it represents the tendency, which Toni Morrison discusses in *Playing in the Dark*, for white characters to need black characters in order to forge identities. Temple's dependence on her connection to Nancy throughout is likewise crucial to her identity formation.

16. Diane Roberts suggests that Nancy and Temple's relationship reveals Faulkner's awareness "that the South was confronting a social revolution, at the center of which were women and blacks" (*Fowlkner and Southern Womanhood* 219). Although she suggests the potential revolutionary power of their relationship, her interpretation remains fairly conventional: she reads Nancy as supporting the social order and Temple as succumbing to the moral demands of motherhood, according Temple far less intelligence and awareness of her situation than I do.

17. By making women considered "whores" central, *Requiem* to some extent answers *For Whom the Bell Tolls*—to which Temple refers: "somebody—Hemingway, wasn't it?—wrote a book about how it [rape] had never actually happened to a g—woman, if she just refused to accept it, no matter who remembered, bragged" (576–577). In Hemingway's book, Maria, the victim of a gang rape, is repeatedly referred to as a "whore." Temple's revision as she speaks—when she starts to say "girl," she corrects it to "woman"—is significant: Hemingway writes a character whom rape has paradoxically and perversely made innocent and girl-like; Faulkner writes about a woman facing the social and personal consequences of having been raped.

18. Moreland notes that with this decision "Temple acts out in an exaggerated (symptomatic) form the rejection of the mother in herself and the particular (vs. commodified) woman and lover in herself—as if

that rejection is required in order for her to enter into that same system of exchange" (225, n.23).

19. Similarly, isolated from all the other women, Temple could talk only to the "Negro maid" in the Memphis whorehouse (568).

20. Elizabeth Spelman's excellent study *Inessential Woman* shows how theoretical premises can erase race and class differences and undermine feminists' attempts to create inclusive theories.

21. An interesting example of this is Stevens's portrayal of Popeye: Stevens sets up a reading allegory, comparing Popeye's voyeurism to "princely despots to whom the ability even to read was vulgar and plebian" and who thus had slaves read to them and then killed the slaves at the end of the story so they would be the only ones who had had the experience (571). The allegory, which puts reading in the place of Popeye's sexual voyeurism, in which the woman is the text being "read," contrasts with the empowerment women's acts of writing provide in the novel.

22. Moreland posits:

> The lingering promise of such an unassimilated subject's and moment's articulate resistance to the "one boom" of modernity's vast skein, after the modernist experience with the reductive dialectics of enlightenment, civilization, signification, and other systematizations, is fraught with all the anxious ambiguity of the rest of the promises of postmodernity and "women's writing." Along with the possibility that she would found somewhere a resistant "matriarchy" of farmers, . . . is the more paranoid possibility that has occurred to the outlander-reader . . . : the possibility that this articulated, legible trace of a maternal anthropophagic order is an engulfing, devouring, castrating threat. (232)

CHAPTER 3   "THE IMAGE OF YOU"

1. Although much of my discussion focuses on the continued impact of cultural stereotypes of black women on Hellman's portrayal, responses to her memoirs indicate that those portrayals were progressive for their time. A letter from Jeanne Noble, then vice president of the National Council of Negro Women, to the editors of *The Atlantic* in response to an excerpt from *An Unfinished Woman*, for instance, praises Hellman's portrayals of Sophronia and Helen. "We blacks usually 'turn off' the very second whites speak of 'loving their domestics,'" Noble writes, but adds that "Miss Hellman comes off as warm, but knows well the pitfalls of deluding oneself about honest affection between blacks and whites." (Lillian Hellman Collection, Harry Ransom Center at the University of Texas at Austin. Quoted with permission of the Lantz Office.)

2. Pamela S. Bromberg argues that *An Unfinished Woman* "reveals Hellman's central, continuing conflict (both as subject and biographer) about her identity and achievement as a woman in a man's world without fully recognizing that conflict as a problem requiring analysis" (115).

3. I will refer to Sophronia Mason by her first name throughout, following Hellman's practice in her memoirs, which rarely mention Sophronia's surname.

4. Adrienne Rich has also written of the cultural demand that white children raised in part by black caretakers, when grown, deny their feelings for those women. In *Of Woman Born*, she describes

> the confusion of discovering that a woman one has loved and been cherished by is somehow "unworthy" of such love after a certain age. That sense of betrayal, of the violation of a relationship, was for years a nameless thing, for no one yet spoke of racism, and even the concept of "prejudice" had not filtered into my childhood world. It was simply "the way things were," and we tried to repress the confusion and the shame. (254)

> Ten years later, for the 1986 anniversary edition of that work, Rich added a note stating that she feels her discussion "overpersonalizes" and does not adequately account for the material realities of the black domestic worker's position. Rich quotes Trudier Harris's 1982 *From Mammies to Militants*, which emphasizes the demands and control of white women employers, as a commentary on her own unbalanced perspective. Ann duCille's "The Occult of True Black Womanhood: Critical Demeanor and Black Feminist Studies" (1994) provides an extended critique of this part of Rich's work and argues that Rich's objectification of her "Black mother" is particularly insulting, given *Of Woman Born*'s intent to illuminate and thereby eradicate the cultural myths of mothering.

5. In their Lacanian reading of *An Unfinished Woman*, Marcus K. Billson and Sidonie A. Smith attribute this sense of loss to Hellman's need for a stronger mother figure:

> Sophronia becomes the locus of a sense of loss and of unfulfilled desire. This earliest embodiment of the self-sufficient female, the desired "other," remains beyond Hellman's grasp. All through her life, then, she will seek out, admire, and look for guidance from those women she identifies as self-sufficient: Sophronia, Bethe, Julia, Helen. Hellman's search for surrogate mothers involves a desire for identification with a female model who contains the inner conviction and calm Hellman knows she lacks herself. The search also insures the experience of unfulfilled desire. Sophronia and Helen choose to maintain a reserve with Hellman, a psychological distance prompted by their difference of race. Bethe and Julia die. (167)

6. Richard Poirer connects what Sophronia teaches Hellman in this episode to Hellman's statement before the House Un-American Activities Committee (HUAC), in which she stated that while she would answer for herself, she would not discuss the actions of others. He finds the similarity between the two reactions evidence of the profound influence of Sophronia on Hellman's moral development (Introduction to *Three* x).

7. Patricia Meyer Spacks, writing about *An Unfinished Woman*, states, "Miss Hellman dreams of living successfully by masculine standards: honor, courage, aggression" (297). She further argues that in the work Hellman's

> central effort has been to create, for her own benefit as well as for others, a character to meet masculine standards. This is not a mere "image": her life substantiates it. The life of constant action (in this case "masculine" rather than "feminine" accomplishment) rests on a foundation of intense self-concentration. Lillian Hellman's work has been to make a self, rejecting in the process many traditional concomitants of femininity. (298–299)

The last sentence implies that some aspects of traditional femininity have to be cast off to create a self and thereby undercuts the force of Spacks's criticism. Bromberg offers a more sympathetic interpretation, stating that "Hellman in this first memoir is establishing for herself a public image that fits comfortably into the literary culture and mythology of her own era" (117). As Sidonie Smith argues in *A Poetics of Women's Autobiography* (1987), women writers of autobiography have had to negotiate the male-defined history of the genre as a narrative of public rather than private events as well as their audience's resulting expectations for the genre.

8. Billson and Smith state of Hellman's claim to be related to Sophronia that "the adolescent symbolically kills off the father" (166). But they also add that "the recourse to the black neighborhood and the identification with Sophronia suggest the degree to which Hellman fears an inevitable identification with white womanhood embodied in her own passive mother" (167).

9. In the last three chapters of *An Unfinished Woman*, Hellman changes to the form she will continue in *Pentimento*, creating portraits of people important in her life. For an analysis of Hellman's narrative structures in her four autobiographies, see Linda Wagner-Martin's "Lillian Hellman: Autobiography and Truth" (1983). Although a number of critics have chastised Hellman's autobiographies for factual inaccuracies and have proceeded therefore to broadly condemn Hellman as a liar, Wagner-Martin argues that in her retelling of events, "clearly, Hellman is using the process of autobiography both to explore her memories and to challenge the notion that recollection is a means to truth" (128).

10. "Sophronia's Grandson Goes to Washington" appeared in the December 1963 edition of *Ladies' Home Journal*. In the article, Hellman repeats an account given to her by some young people from Gadsden, Alabama, of the use of cow prods on protesters there—particularly on women's breasts and men's genitals. The lawyer for the sheriff of Etowah County sent a letter to the magazine that demanded a retraction and quoted the sections they wanted retracted in full. The editors printed a retraction in the March 1964 issue but also printed the entire letter, thereby giving the story a second run in the magazine. Hellman also wrote a statement in which she apologized for wrongly identifying the sheriff and his deputies as the ones who used the cow prods, but also stated that her "article, in all important matters, tells the truth and I wish to disassociate myself from the above retraction. What is true should not be obscured by the fear of lawsuits" (82). The sheriff proceeded to file a 3 million dollar libel suit against Hellman and *Ladies' Home Journal*. The magazine's retraction inspired an unpublished letter from Lorraine Hansberry in support of Hellman's article; many other responses, particularly those from the South, however, were far more critical.

CHAPTER 4   "THE VERY HOUSE OF DIFFERENCE"

1. Toni Morrison uses a similar strategy of not identifying characters' racial identities in her short story "Recitatif," which I discuss in chapter 7.
2. Brenda Carr discusses Lorde's use of identity markers and the problem of the essentialism such terms seem to imply. Carr asserts that "Lorde's insistence on multiple self-naming implicitly problematizes the politically necessary invocation of the seemingly essentialist descriptors 'woman,' 'Black,' and 'lesbian' " (143).
3. Jennifer Browdy De Hernandez interprets Lorde's focus on physical and sexual experience in *Zami* as moments of the "lesbian sublime," which is "characterized by a return to pre-oedipal bonding with the mother" (246).
4. See also Lorde's essay "The Uses of Anger: Women Responding to Racism," which describes many antagonistic reactions of white women to the topic of racism.
5. Valerie Smith, duCille, and others have since pointed out that white women's use, for their own growth or ends, of African American cultural symbols and traditions can be problematic.
6. One of Lorde's early jobs, which she describes in *Zami*, was with an electronics factory and required working with X-ray machines and hazardous materials. Most of the employees were black or Puerto Rican. Lorde states, "nobody mentioned that carbon tet destroys the liver and causes cancer of the kidneys. Nobody mentioned that the X-ray machines,

when used unshielded, delivered doses of constant low radiation far in excess of what was considered safe even in those days" (126).

7. For a discussion of the impact of the strong black woman stereotype and its literary incarnations, see Trudier Harris's essay "This Disease Called Strength" (1991).

8. Lorde here asks questions about language similar to those of Irigaray and Cixous that I discuss in chapter 2. Barbara Christian argues in her essay "The Race for Theory" (1989) that theoretical ideas in works by writers of color often are not valued—or even recognized—as "theory" because they are not in theoretical language: "For people of color have always theorized—but in forms quite different from the Western form of abstract logic" (226). See also Michael Awkward's response, "Appropriative Gestures: Theory and Afro-American Literary Criticism" (1989). Deborah McDowell's "Transferences: Black Feminist Discourse: The 'Practice' of 'Theory' " (1995) discusses Linda Kauffman's collection *Gender and Theory*, in which both of these essays appear, and provides a detailed comparison of black feminist criticism and post-structuralist theory.

9. Lorde describes her second experience of cancer—this time liver cancer, which eventually was fatal—and her pursuit of alternative treatments in the essay "A Burst of Light," which appears in the volume of the same name.

10. For a historical account of the 1950s lesbian bar scene in New York, see Elizabeth Lapovsky Kennedy and Madeline D. Davis's *Boots of Leather, Slippers of Gold* (1993).

CHAPTER 5   "JUST THIS SIDE OF COLORED"

1. Indeed, even the concept of a "self" has been considered a fiction. Sidonie Smith, applying Judith Butler's theory of gender performativity to the autobiographical act, has argued that "the interiority or self that is said to be prior to the autobiographical expression or reflection is an *effect* of autobiographical storytelling" ("Performativity" 18, her emphasis). Thus, autobiography can be said to be a performance, one that responds to, and sometimes revises, the cultural demands on identity, and the distinction between autobiography and fiction all but disappears.

2. As Giavanna Munafo says of Gibbons's novel, "Ellen must endeavor to reconstitute her own lived experience of white female racial identity, engendering, as much as possible, a white female self capable of interrupting complicity in white supremacy" (40).

3. Ellen senses that she and Starletta are growing apart, mostly because of Starletta's increasing interest in boys. Although they remain friends, the suggestion that their friendship is ending gestures to the pattern in white American literature that Elizabeth Schultz discusses: that

characters of color are written out of the story once they have served the purpose of white characters' growth. Sharon Monteith reads this ending, in part, as a result of the monologic nature of the novel, in which Starletta is never given a voice, and states, "Finally, individualism overrides the friendship plot in *Ellen Foster*" (72). Monteith acknowledges "that the history of segregation restricts representations of a childhood friendship that seek to incorporate realism in their form or credibility in their content" (73). Cox's novel serves as an example of the exception to that rule, in that it remains realistic and believable because it acknowledges the difficulties of the girls' continuing their relationship into adulthood.

4. The concept of degrees of whiteness also has economic as well as moral connotations. Dyer points out that historically in Western representation, "whites may . . . be hue differentiated according to class. Working-class and peasant whites are darker than middle-class and aristocratic whites" (57).

5. Monteith relates Ellen's preoccupation with cleanliness to her chaotic family life as well as her internalized racism:

> disorder has ruled Ellen's life . . . so Ellen concerns herself with order and cleanliness and fixes Starletta as her opposite in order to judge what those characteristics might be. Starletta is inextricably linked into the dialectic of order and cleanliness versus disorder and dirt that preoccupies Ellen. Her first comment upon seeing Starletta in the church at her mother's funeral focuses in on this most precisely: "I see Starletta and she looks clean" is immediately followed by the statement "Starletta and her mama both eat dirt." Her observations bespeak a social conditioning, according to southern design, whereby poor white people learned to differentiate themselves at any and every level from poor black people. (55)

Although I agree with Monteith that Ellen's observations reveal her racialized social conditioning, I think the desire implicit in Ellen's description that follows of Starletta and her mother's eating dirt shows that Ellen identifies with Starletta even as she differentiates her own whiteness from Starletta's blackness.

6. As Gibbons has said, Ellen "can't be a child but Starletta can be a child and she does. She acts out. So Ellen Foster looks at that and longs to be that way, but she can't be that way because she's too busy trying to make sure her own needs are met. She's a perfect child of an alcoholic but because . . . Starletta's parents look after her she can do things that a ten-year-old is supposed to do" (*Broken Silences* 69).

7. Veronica Makowsky makes a similar point about this scene: she states that "Ellen is expressing contradictory desires: to return to the womb's safety where she was fed and to take over the life-sustaining role of the mother's heartbeat and nourishing bloodstream" (104).

8. Grosz describes her project as an attempt to show "that all the effects of subjectivity . . . can be as adequately explained using the subject's corporeality as a framework as it would be using consciousness or the unconscious. All the effects of depth and interiority can be explained in terms of the inscriptions and transformations of the subject's corporeal surface. Bodies have all the explanatory power of minds" (vii). Here I am relying on her thesis that what happens to the body creates consciousness; her earlier chapters argue a related but different point: that consciousness develops in response to the social meanings of the characteristics of the body: "the subject's psychical interior can be understood as an introjection, a form of internalization of (the meaning and significance of) the body and its parts, and conversely, how the body is constituted through projection as the boundary, limit, edge, or border of subjectivity, that which divides the subject in the first instance from other subjects" (115). These latter points apply to the effect of Ellen's whiteness on her consciousness: the social meanings of her white skin establish her racial identity, which consists of both her conception of herself as white and her conception of herself as not black (hence creating for her the category of the "other").

9. Told that they are the "foster family," Ellen mistakes "Foster" for their surname and later adopts it as her own. Munafo points out that Ellen's mistake "underscores Gibbons's persistent antagonism toward naturalized conceptions of 'family' " (40).

CHAPTER 6   "WHO CAN YOU FRIEND WITH, LOVE WITH LIKE THAT?"

1. Mae G. Henderson notes that "the name of Williams's character, Adam Nehemiah, reverses the name of Nehemiah Adams, a Boston minister who wrote a proslavery account of his experiences in the South, *A South-side View of Slavery* (1854), and who, in an earlier tract, warned women not to speak out in public against slavery—a stance that set him in opposition to both women's rights and abolition" ("The Stories of O(Dessa)" 304).

2. On the relationship between the moral and racial meanings of black and white, see Richard Dyer's *White*, pp. 58–70. See also Dyer's final chapter, pp. 207–223, in which he considers the association of whiteness with death.

3. This is similar to Hellman's own too-late realization that Helen had a life and family Hellman knew virtually nothing about.

4. Williams writes, "I admit also to being outraged by a certain, critically acclaimed novel of the early seventies that travestied the as-told-to memoir of slave revolt leader Nat Turner. Afro-Americans, having survived by

word of mouth—and made of that process a high art—remain at the mercy of literature and writing; often, these have betrayed us" (ix).

5. Henderson points out similarities between the periods of the novel's setting and publication:

> Significantly both the mid-1840s (the historical period of the novel's enactment) and the mid-1980s (the contemporary period of the novel's production) represent eras of retrenchment on the racial question. Just as the abolitionist movement of the 1840s was undermined by the internal divisions of political pragmatism versus moral suasion, so the civil rights and Black Power movements were undermined by internal strife in the 1970s and 1980s. Moreover, just as the issue of women's participation in abolition provided the background for the subsequent emergence of the women's rights movement in the 1840s, civil rights and Black Power movements set the stage for feminism's challenge to the priority of race as a privileged locus of dissent. Further, just as the abolitionist movement generated a counterresponse from the proslavery faction of southern ideologues, so the politics of civil rights generated a counterresponse from an empowered religious right, a reconstituted conservative Supreme Court, and a polarizing presidential politics of Reaganomics in the 1980s. Finally, the decade of the 1980s also saw emergence of a new academic discourse—the feminist critique, as a counterpart and counterpoint to the racial critique. Like the 1980s, then, the 1840s had been a period of racial turbulence as well as progressive agitation for women's rights. ("The Stories of O(Dessa)" 289)

6. For an extensive discussion of Dorcas's role in the novel, particularly Rufel's use of her story, see Ashraf H. A. Rushdy's "Reading Mammy: The Subject of Relation in Sherley Anne Williams' *Dessa Rose.*" Rushdy examines how characters communicate and "read" one another and argues that these readings "can lead either to dialogue and community or to dissonance and chaos" (365). He explores how Rufel's relationships with Dessa and Nathan lead her to stop controlling Dorcas's story and to reconceptualize Dorcas as a woman with agency.

7. Henderson reads the sexual scenes in *Dessa Rose* as intertextual references to William Styron's *Confessions of Nat Turner* and Pauline Réage's *Story of O*:

> In Réage's novel, psychosexual subordination is the condition of (white) woman's subjectivity; in Styron's novel, psychosexual repression is the condition of black (male) subjectivity. *Dessa Rose* seeks to deconstruct these antecedent constructions and, at the same time, open up a space for the black female, marginalized in Styron's text and subsumed under the categories of "slave" and "woman" in Réage's text. ("The Stories of O(Dessa)" 296)

CHAPTER 7 "A GIRL FROM A WHOLE OTHER RACE"

1. Michael Nowlin argues that these critical pieces, along with the novels *Beloved* and *Jazz*, reflect Morrison's "expanding vision that transfigures her usual subject matter, the complex world of black Americans, into a synecdoche for America" and that "one of the clearest signs of Morrison's debt to American modernism is her commitment to a notion of cultural pluralism grounded in racial difference" (151, 152).
2. The girls' watching the attack on Maggie is very similar to Nel and Sula's watching Chicken Little drown in *Sula*. Abel notes the similarity of the plots: "By tracing the course of a friendship from girlhood through adulthood, 'Recitatif' filters the narrative of *Sula* (1973) through the lens of race, replacing the novel's sexual triangulation with the tensions of racial difference" ("Black Writing, White Reading" 475, n. 7).
3. See Ann Firor Scott's *The Southern Lady: From Pedestal to Politics, 1830–1930* for an account of the limitations of the stereotype of the Southern lady and what white Southern women's lives were actually like, including their political engagements.
4. Trudier Harris argues that the multiple narration of this story is evidence of the ways in which Morrison "shares with her characters the creation of her novel" (*Fiction and Folklore* 164). Shlomith Rimmon-Kenan connects the multiple narration to Sethe's statement in the novel that "freeing yourself was one thing; claiming ownership of that freed self was another" (95). Rimmon-Kenan contends that "the layering of focalization and narration is necessary because it is through memory and storytelling that the mere fact of birth is transformed into a claiming of ownership and a birth into self" (113). Ashraf H. A. Rushdy makes a related argument about Denver's function in the novel: "What, finally, Denver is to *Beloved* is the space for hearing the tale of infanticide with a degree of understanding—both as sister of the murdered baby and as the living daughter of the loving mother. Denver, that is, is a site of participation" ("Daughters Signifyin(g) History" 586).
5. Mae G. Henderson argues that Amy's interpretation of Sethe's scars reveals the persistence of power relations: "It is the white man who inscribes; the white woman, the black man, and the black woman may variously read, but not write. Because it is her back . . . that is marked, Sethe has only been able to read herself through the gaze of others. . . . Sethe's dilemma is that as a female slave without the benefit of literacy, she finds herself the written object of a white male discourse and the spoken subject of a black male and white female discourse" ("Toni Morrison's *Beloved*" 69). Although Amy's whiteness certainly grants her privilege and social power unavailable to Sethe, I do not see an oppressive power operating in this moment.

6. Later in the novel, Miss Bodwin becomes Denver's teacher; Denver tells Paul D that Miss Bodwin "says I might go to Oberlin. She's experimenting on me." Paul D keeps to himself his thought that there is "nothing in the world more dangerous than a white schoolteacher" (266).

7. In *Paradise*, the light-skinned Pat Best similarly marries the dark-skinned Billy Cato because the townspeople have shamed her and her light-enough-to-pass mother.

8. Ana María Fraile-Marcos argues that "the adoption of the Puritan foundational paradigms on the part of Ruby seems to corroborate Homi Bhabha's view of mimicry as a site of resistance . . . since the citizens of Ruby are able to reverse the racist discriminatory practices they suffer by appropriating the ideas which oppressed and excluded them from mainstream America" (4).

Coda

1. The film was written and directed by Richard LaGravanese, who, it is interesting to note, was also among the screenwriters credited for the movie *Beloved*.

WORKS CITED

Abel, Elizabeth. "(E)Merging Identities: The Dynamics of Female Friendship in Contemporary Fiction by Women." *Signs* 6 (1981): 413–435.

———. "Black Writing, White Reading: Race and the Politics of Feminist Interpretation." *Critical Inquiry* 19 (1993): 470–498.

Abel, Elizabeth, Barbara Christian, and Helene Moglen, eds. *Female Subjects in Black and White: Race, Psychoanalysis, Feminism.* Berkeley: U California P, 1997.

Abernathy, Jeff. *To Hell and Back: Race and Betrayal in the Southern Novel.* Athens: U Georgia P, 2003.

Alexander, Elizabeth. " 'Coming Out Blackened and Whole': Fragmentation and Reintegration in Audre Lorde's *Zami* and *The Cancer Journals.*" *American Literary History* 6 (1994): 695–715.

Awkward, Michael. "Appropriative Gestures: Theory and Afro-American Literary Criticism." *Gender and Theory: Dialogues on Feminist Criticism.* Ed. Linda Kauffman. New York: Basil Blackwell, 1989. 238–246.

Billson, Marcus K., and Sidonie A. Smith. "Lillian Hellman and the Strategy of the 'Other.' " *Women's Autobiography: Essays in Criticism.* Ed. Estelle C. Jelinek. Bloomington: Indiana UP, 1980. 163–179.

Boose, Lynda E. "The Father's House and the Daughter in It: The Structures of Western Culture's Daughter-Father Relationship." *Daughters and Fathers.* Ed. Lynda E. Boose and Betty S. Flowers. Baltimore: Johns Hopkins UP, 1989. 19–74.

Bromberg, Pamela S. "Establishing the Woman and Constructing a Narrative in Lillian Hellman's Memoirs." *Critical Essays on Lillian Hellman.* Ed. Mark W. Estrin. Boston: G. K. Hall, 1989. 115–128.

Bryer, Jackson R., ed. *Conversations with Lillian Hellman.* Jackson: UP of Mississippi, 1986.

Carr, Brenda. " 'A Woman Speaks . . . I Am Woman and Not White': Politics of Voice, Tactical Essentialism, and Cultural Intervention in Audre Lorde's Activist Poetics and Practice." *College Literature* 20.2 (1993): 133–153.

Christian, Barbara. "Response to 'Black Women's Texts.' " *NWSA Journal* 1 (1988): 32–36.

———. "The Race for Theory." *Gender and Theory: Dialogues on Feminist Criticism.* Ed. Linda Kauffman. New York: Basil Blackwell, 1989. 225–237.

———. "Beloved, She's Ours." *Narrative* 5 (1997): 36–49.

Cixous, Hélène. "The Laugh of the Medusa." *Signs* 1 (1976): 875–893.

Cox, Elizabeth. *Night Talk*. St. Paul, MN: Graywolf, 1997.

———. Interview with Kelly Reames. *Mississippi Quarterly* 52 (1999): 307–321.

Curtis Publishing Company. Retraction. *Ladies' Home Journal*. March 1964: 82.

Daly, Mary. *Gyn/Ecology: The Metaethics of Radical Feminism*. Boston: Beacon, 1978.

Davis, Angela Y. *Women, Race, and Class*. 1981. Rept. Paperback Ed. New York: Vintage, 1983.

Davis, Mary Kemp. "Everybody Knows Her Name: The Recovery of the Past in Sherley Anne Williams's *Dessa Rose*." *Callaloo* 12 (1989): 544–558.

De Hernandez, Jennifer Browdy. "Mothering the Self: Writing through the Lesbian Sublime in Audre Lorde's *Zami* and Gloria Anzaldúa's *Borderlands/La Frontera*." *Other Sisterhoods: Literary Theory and U.S. Women of Color*. Ed. Sandra Kumamoto Stanley. Urbana: U Illinois P, 1998. 244–264.

duCille, Ann. "The Occult of True Black Womanhood: Critical Demeanor and Black Feminist Studies." *Signs* 19 (1994): 591–629. Rpt. in *Skin Trade*. Cambridge, MA: Harvard UP, 1996. 81–119.

Dyer, Richard. *White*. London: Routledge, 1997.

Erickson, Peter. "Seeing White." *Transition* 5.3 (1995): 166–185.

Farnsworth, Elizabeth. "Conversation: Toni Morrison." *Online NewsHour with Jim Lehrer Transcript*. 9 March 1998. PBS. 14 March 2001 <http://www.pbs.org/newshour/bb/entertainment/jan-june98/morrison_3-9.html>.

Faulkner, William. *Requiem for a Nun* (1951). *Novels 1942–1954*. New York: The Library of America, 1994.

Foucault, Michel. *The History of Sexuality*. Vol. 1: *An Introduction*. 1976. Transl. Robert Hurley. New York: Vintage, 1990.

———. *Discipline and Punish: The Birth of the Prison*. 1975. Transl. Alan Sheridan. 2nd edn. New York: Vintage, 1995.

Fowler, Doreen, and Campbell McCool. "On Suffering: A Letter from William Faulkner." *American Literature* 57 (1985): 650–652.

Fox-Genovese, Elizabeth. *Within the Plantation Household: Black and White Women of the Old South*. Chapel Hill: U North Carolina P, 1988.

Fraile-Marcos, Ana María. "Hybridizing the 'City upon a Hill' in Toni Morrison's *Paradise*." *MELUS* 28.4 (2003): 3–33.

Frye, Marilyn. "On Being White: Thinking Toward a Feminist Understanding of Race and Race Supremacy." *The Politics of Reality: Essays in Feminist Theory*. Freedom, CA: Crossing, 1983. 110–127.

———. "White Woman Feminist: 1983–1992." *Willful Virgin: Essays in Feminism, 1976–1992*. Freedom, CA: Crossing, 1992. 147–169.

Gallop, Jane, Marianne Hirsch, and Nancy K. Miller. "Criticizing Feminist Criticism." *Conflicts in Feminism*. Ed. Marianne Hirsch and Evelyn Fox Keller. New York: Routledge, 1990. 349–369.

Gardiner, Judith Kegan. "The (US)es of (I)dentity: A Response to Abel on '(E)Merging Identities.' " *Signs* 6 (1981): 436–442.

Gibbons, Kaye. *Ellen Foster.* New York: Vintage, 1987.

———. Interview. *Broken Silences: Interviews with Black and White Women Writers.* Ed. Shirley M. Jordan. New Brunswick, NJ: Rutgers UP, 1993. 65–82.

———. Interview. *The Oprah Winfrey Show.* 7 December 1997. ABC. WTVD, Chapel Hill.

Gilman, Sander L. "Black Bodies, White Bodies: Toward an Iconography of Female Sexuality in Late Nineteenth-Century Art, Medicine, and Literature." *"Race," Writing, and Difference.* Ed. Henry Louis Gates Jr. Chicago: U Chicago P, 1986. 223–261.

Grosz, Elizabeth. *Volatile Bodies: Toward a Corporeal Feminism.* Bloomington: Indiana UP, 1994.

Gubar, Susan. *Critical Condition: Feminism at the Turn of the Century.* New York: Columbia UP, 2000.

Gwin, Minrose C. *Black and White Women of the Old South: The Peculiar Sisterhood in American Literature.* Knoxville: U Tennessee P, 1985.

———. "A Theory of Black Women's Texts and White Women's Readings, or . . . The Necessity of Being Other." *NWSA Journal* 1 (1988): 21–31.

———. *The Feminine and Faulkner: Reading (beyond) Sexual Difference.* Knoxville: U Tennessee P, 1990.

Gwynn, Frederick L., and Joseph L. Blotner, eds. *Faulkner in the University.* Charlottesville: UP of Virginia, 1995.

Harris, Trudier. *From Mammies to Militants: Domestics in Black American Literature.* Philadelphia: Temple UP, 1982.

———. *Fiction and Folklore: The Novels of Toni Morrison.* Knoxville: U Tennessee P, 1991.

———. "This Disease Called Strength: Some Observations on the Compensating Construction of Black Female Character." *Literature and Medicine* 14 (1995): 109–126.

Heilbrun, Carolyn G. *Writing a Woman's Life.* New York: Ballantine, 1988.

Hellman, Lillian. "Sophronia's Grandson Goes to Washington." *Ladies' Home Journal* December 1963: 78–82.

———. *Three: An Unfinished Woman, Pentimento, Scoundrel Time.* Boston: Little, Brown, 1979.

Hemingway, Ernest. *For Whom the Bell Tolls.* New York: Macmillan, 1940.

Henderson, Mae G. "Toni Morrison's *Beloved*: Re-Membering the Body As Historical Text." *Comparative American Identities: Race, Sex, and Nationality in the Modern Text.* Ed. Hortense J. Spillers. New York: Routledge, 1991. 62–86.

———. "The Stories of O(Dessa): Stories of Complicity and Resistance." Abel, Christian, and Moglen, 285–306.

Hirsch, Marianne. "Maternity and Rememory: Toni Morrison's *Beloved*." *Representations of Motherhood.* Ed. Donna Bassin, Margaret Honey, and Meryle Mahrer Kaplan. New Haven: Yale UP, 1997. 92–110.

Holloway, Karla F. C. *Codes of Conduct: Race, Ethics, and the Color of Our Character.* New Brunswick, NJ: Rutgers UP, 1995.

Homans, Margaret. " 'Her Very Own Howl': The Ambiguities of Representation in Recent Women's Fiction." *Signs* 9 (1983): 186–205.

———. "Feminist Fictions and Feminist Theories of Narrative." *Narrative* 2 (1994): 3–16.

———. " 'Racial Composition': Metaphor and the Body in the Writing of Race." Abel, Christian, and Moglen, 77–101.

hooks, bell. *Ain't I a Woman: Black Women and Feminism*. Boston: South End, 1981.

———. "Where Is the Love: Political Bonding between Black and White Women." *Killing Rage: Ending Racism*. New York: Holt, 1995. 215–225.

Hull, Gloria T., Patricia Bell Scott, and Barbara Smith. *All the Women Are White, All the Blacks Are Men, but Some of Us Are Brave: Black Women's Studies*. New York: Feminist, 1982.

Ignatiev, Noel, and John Garvey, eds. *Race Traitor*. New York: Routledge, 1996.

Irigaray, Luce. *This Sex Which Is Not One*. 1977. Transl. Catherine Porter with Carolyn Burke. Ithaca, NY: Cornell UP, 1985.

Keating, AnaLouise. *Women Reading Women Writing: Self-Invention in Paula Gunn Allen, Gloria Anzaldúa, and Audre Lorde*. Philadelphia: Temple UP, 1996.

Kennedy, Elizabeth Lapovsky, and Madeline D. Davis. *Boots of Leather, Slippers of Gold: The History of a Lesbian Community*. New York: Routledge, 1993.

Living Out Loud. Dir. Richard LaGravanese. Perf. Holly Hunter, Danny DeVito, and Queen Latifah. Videocassette. New Line Video, 1998.

Lorde, Audre. *The Cancer Journals*. San Francisco: Aunt Lute, 1980.

———. "The American Cancer Society Or There Is More Than One Way To Skin a Coon." *Undersong: Chosen Poems Old and New*. 1982. Rev. edn. New York: Norton, 1992. 125–126.

———. *Zami: A New Spelling of My Name*. Freedom, CA: Crossing, 1982.

———. "An Open Letter to Mary Daly." *Sister Outsider: Essays and Speeches*. 66–71.

———. *Sister Outsider: Essays and Speeches*. The Crossing Press Feminist Series. Freedom, CA: Crossing, 1984.

———. "The Uses of Anger: Women Responding to Racism." *Sister Outsider: Essays and Speeches*. 124–133.

———. *A Burst of Light*. Ithaca, NY: Firebrand, 1988.

Makowsky, Veronica. " 'The Only Hard Part Was the Food': Recipes for Self-Nurture in Kaye Gibbons's Novels." *Southern Quarterly* 30 (1992): 103–112.

McDowell, Deborah E. "New Directions for Black Feminist Criticism." *The New Feminist Criticism: Essays on Women, Literature, and Theory*. Ed. Elaine Showalter. New York: Pantheon, 1985. 186–199.

———. "Transferences: Black Feminist Discourse: The 'Practice' of 'Theory.' " *Feminism beside Itself*. Ed. Diane Elam and Robyn Wiegman. New York: Routledge, 1995. 93–118.

McIntosh, Peggy. "White Privilege: Unpacking the Invisible Knapsack." *Race, Class, and Gender in the United States: An Integrated Study.* 4th edn. Ed. Paula S. Rothenberg. New York: St. Martin's, 1998. 165–169.

Michie, Helena. *Sororophobia: Differences among Women in Literature and Culture.* New York: Oxford UP, 1992.

Monteith, Sharon. *Advancing Sisterhood? Interracial Friendships in Contemporary Southern Fiction.* Athens: U Georgia P, 2000.

Moraga, Cherríe, and Gloria Anzaldúa. *This Bridge Called My Back: Writings by Radical Women of Color.* New York: Kitchen Table, 1981.

Moreland, Richard C. *Faulkner and Modernism: Rereading and Rewriting.* Madison: U Wisconsin P, 1990.

Morrison, Toni. "Recitatif." *Confirmation: An Anthology of African American Women.* Ed. Amiri Baraka (LeRoi Jones) and Amina Baraka. New York: William Morrow, 1983. 243–261.

———. *Beloved.* New York: Knopf, 1987.

———. "Unspeakable Things Unspoken: The Afro-American Presence in American Literature." *Michigan Quarterly Review* 38 (1989): 1–34.

———. *Playing in the Dark: Whiteness and the Literary Imagination.* New York: Vintage, 1993.

———. *Paradise.* New York: Knopf, 1998.

Mulrine, Anna. "This Side of *Paradise*: Toni Morrison Defends Herself from Criticism of Her New Novel." *U.S. News and World Report.* 19 January 1998. *U.S. News Online.* 8 March 2001 <http://www.usnews.com/usnews/issue/980119/19new.htm>.

Munafo, Giavanna. " 'Colored Biscuits': Reconstructing Whiteness and the Boundaries of 'Home' in Kaye Gibbons's *Ellen Foster.*" *Women, America, and Movement: Narratives of Relocation.* Ed. Susan L. Roberson. Columbia: U Missouri P, 1998. 38–61.

Naylor, Gloria. *Bailey's Cafe.* 1992. New York: Vintage, 1993.

Noble, Jeanne. Letter to the Editors of *The Atlantic.* 3 May 1969. Folder 16.1. Lillian Hellman Papers. Harry Ransom Humanities Research Center. U Texas at Austin.

Nowlin, Michael. "Toni Morrison's *Jazz* and the Racial Dreams of the American Writer." *American Literature* 71 (1999): 151–174.

Painter, Nell Irvin. *Sojourner Truth: a Life, a Symbol.* New York: Norton, 1996.

Palmer, Phyllis Marynick. "White Women/Black Women: The Dualism of Female Identity and Experience in the United States." *Feminist Studies* 9 (1983): 151–170.

Poirer, Richard. Introduction. *Three: An Unfinished Woman, Pentimento, Scoundrel Time.* By Lillian Hellman. Boston: Little, Brown, 1979. vii–xxv.

Polk, Noel. *Faulkner's "Requiem for a Nun": A Critical Study.* Bloomington: Indiana UP, 1981.

———. *Children of the Dark House: Text and Context in Faulkner.* Jackson: UP of Mississippi, 1996.

Porter, Nancy. "Women's Interracial Friendships and Visions of Community in *Meridian, The Salt Eaters, Civil Wars,* and *Dessa Rose.*" *Tradition and the Talents of Women*. Ed. Florence Howe. Urbana: U Illinois P, 1991. 251–267.

Rich, Adrienne. "Disloyal to Civilization: Feminism, Racism, and Gynephobia." *On Lies, Secrets, and Silence: Selected Prose, 1966–1978*. New York: Norton, 1979. 275–310.

———. "It Is the Lesbian in Us . . ." *On Lies, Secrets, and Silence: Selected Prose, 1966–1978*. New York: Norton, 1979. 199–202.

———. "Compulsory Heterosexuality and Lesbian Existence." *Blood, Bread, and Poetry: Selected Prose, 1979–1985*. New York: Norton, 1986. 23–74.

———. "Notes toward a Politics of Location." *Blood, Bread, and Poetry: Selected Prose, 1979–1985*. New York: Norton, 1986. 210–232.

———. *Of Woman Born: Motherhood as Experience and Institution*. 1976. 10th Anniversary edn. New York: Norton, 1986.

Rimmon-Kenan, Shlomith. "Narration, Doubt, Retrieval: Toni Morrison's *Beloved*." *Narrative* 4 (1996): 109–123.

Roberts, Diane. *Faulkner and Southern Womanhood*. Athens: U Georgia P, 1994.

———. *The Myth of Aunt Jemima: Representations of Race and Region*. London: Routledge, 1994.

Rushdy, Ashraf H. A. "Daughters Signifyin(g) History: The Example of Toni Morrison's *Beloved*." *American Literature* 64 (1992): 567–597.

———. "Reading Mammy: The Subject of Relation in Sherley Anne Williams' *Dessa Rose*." *African American Review* 27 (1993): 365–389.

Schultz, Elizabeth. "Out of the Woods and into the World: A Study of Interracial Friendships between Women in American Novels." *Conjuring: Black Women, Fiction, and Literary Tradition*. Ed. Marjorie Pryse and Hortense J. Spillers. Bloomington: Indiana UP, 1985. 67–85.

Scott, Ann Firor. *The Southern Lady: From Pedestal to Politics, 1830–1930*. Chicago: U Chicago P, 1970.

Sedgwick, Eve Kosofsky. *Epistemology of the Closet*. Berkeley: U California P, 1990.

Sensibar, Judith L. "Who Wears the Mask? Memory, Desire, and Race in *Go Down, Moses*." *New Essays on "Go Down, Moses"*. Ed. Linda Wagner-Martin. The American Novel Series. New York: Cambridge UP, 1996. 101–128.

Smith, Barbara. "Toward a Black Feminist Criticism." *The New Feminist Criticism: Essays on Women, Literature, and Theory*. Ed. Elaine Showalter. New York: Pantheon, 1985. 168–185.

Smith, Lillian. *Killers of the Dream*. 1949. New York: Norton, 1994.

Smith, Sidonie. *A Poetics of Women's Autobiography: Marginality and the Fictions of Self-Representation*. Bloomington: Indiana UP, 1987.

———. "Performativity, Autobiographical Practice, Resistance." a/b: *Auto/Biography Studies* 10 (1995): 17–33.

Smith, Valerie. "Black Feminist Theory and the Representation of the 'Other.' " *Changing Our Own Words: Essays on Criticism, Theory, and*

Writing by Black Women. Ed. Cheryl A. Wall. New Brunswick, NJ: Rutgers UP, 1989. 38–57.

Spacks, Patricia Meyer. *The Female Imagination.* New York: Knopf, 1975.

Spelman, Elizabeth V. *Inessential Woman: Problems of Exclusion in Feminist Thought.* Boston: Beacon, 1988.

"Timehost Chat: Toni Morrison." *Time.com.* 21 January 1998. 8 March 2001 <http://www.time.com/time/community/transcripts/chattr012198.html>.

Vickery, Olga. *The Novels of William Faulkner: A Critical Interpretation.* Rev. edn. Baton Rouge: Louisiana State UP, 1964.

Wagner-Martin, Linda. "Lillian Hellman: Autobiography and Truth." *Critical Essays on Lillian Hellman.* Ed. Mark W. Estrin. Boston: G. K. Hall, 1989. 128–139. Rpt. of Linda W. Wagner. "Lillian Hellman: Autobiography and Truth." *Southern Review* 19 (1983): 275–288.

———. *Telling Women's Lives: The New Biography.* New Brunswick, NJ: Rutgers UP, 1994.

Walker, Alice. *Meridian.* New York: Harcourt, 1976.

Watson, Jay. *Forensic Fictions: The Lawyer Figure in Faulkner.* Athens: U Georgia P, 1993.

Welter, Barbara. "The Cult of True Womanhood." *American Quarterly* 18 (1966): 151–174.

Wittenberg, Judith Bryant. "Temple Drake and *La parole pleine*." *Mississippi Quarterly* 48 (1995): 421–441.

Wondra, Janet. " 'Play' within a Play: Gaming with Language in *Requiem for a Nun*." *Faulkner Journal* 8 (1992): 43–59.

Wyatt, Jean. *Risking Difference: Identification, Race, and Community in Contemporary Fiction and Feminism.* Albany: SUNY P, 2004.

Zender, Karl F. "*Requiem for a Nun* and the Uses of the Imagination." *Faulkner and Race.* Ed. Doreen Fowler and Ann J. Abadie. Jackson: UP of Mississippi, 1987. 272–296.

Index